T0274730

Praise for *The Myth of the Silver Spoon*

"Wealth and inheritance are a challenge for a lucky minority, but their path in life is complex and challenging even with their privilege. This book is a refreshing journey for inheritors and their family about how to unravel, nurture and pursue one's life purpose when your choices are infinite. It offers some wonderful learning activities for heirs as they make life choices and build their family's non-financial "wealth" for a new generation."

—Dennis T. Jaffe, PhD
Early architect of the field of family enterprise consulting,
clinical psychologist, and author of *Borrowed from Your
Grandchildren: The Evolution of 100-Year Family Enterprises*

"As Webster advises the proper meaning of the word wealth is "well-being." Kristin's wonderful book takes the proper meaning of wealth and applies it, using the tools of positive psychology, to enable the journeys of the rising generation members of financially significant families to achieve their individual well beings . . . So they become truly wealthy.

—James (Jay) E. Hughes, Jr., Esq.
Innovator and thought leader in the field of intergenerational
family wealth, author of *Family Wealth: Keeping it in the Family*,
Family the Compact Among Generations, and co-author of *Complete Family
Wealth* (second edition), *The Cycle of the Gift*,
The Voice of the Rising Generation, and *Family Trusts*

"Kristin Keffeler has brilliantly addressed the fundamental issue that families with significant financial capital face: how might we integrate our resources to shape flourishing individuals, families, and communities? Anchored in stories, evidence-based research of positive psychology and chalked full of reflective questions and practical ideas, this clever book is a must read for rising gen, their families and advisors looking for a better way. More than ever before, we need to harness the potential of an engaged, generous and purpose driven rising gen to make the world a better place."

—Stacy Allred, MST
Family Wealth Consultant

"*The Myth of the Silver Spoon* is a true "how to" guide for rising generation family members to learn how to discover, pursue, and realize their own dreams and passions in the context of significant family success. As an advisor, I have long been searching for the answer to my clients' all too common question, "what resources are available to help my kids thrive in the context of significant wealth?" I now have the answer and it is *The Myth of the Silver Spoon*! I can't wait for my young adult daughters to read this gem—it provides the keys to unlock the secrets to flourishing as a rising gen wealth inheritor.

—Brandon Johnson
CEO Johnson Financial Group, rising gen, and
parent to rising gen

"It is finally here! A book written for rising gen (and the people that support them)! As a rising gen myself and now raising kids in wealth, this book is a much-needed trail map into hard topics and truths. This book breaks this complicated terrain it down into navigable steps using research-based guidance. It's a must read."

—Lacey Books
Non-profit founder and parent

"Keffeler reframes the misconceptions and critical challenges faced by those born into wealth, providing the tools and resources necessary for the rising gen to create a meaningful life. This practical hands-on book uses personal stories, including her own, to humanize the complex issues faced by many young adults, making the topics more accessible to family members and advisors thereby creating a clear pathway for the rising gen and those of us who support them to flourish and grow."

—Glen W. Johnson
President, Family Office Exchange (FOX)

"As an inheritor and parent of 2 rising gens, with 20 years of professional experience working with families of wealth, this book spoke to every aspect of who I am. It was so healing to see my own feelings compassionately reflected in the narratives. I appreciated that the book is grounded in positive psychology research, offering actionable steps towards mindset and behavior change. Finally, I applaud Kristin's call to action for advisors to "pivot from a fear-based approach to a strengths-&-capacity based approach" in working with families of wealth. No matter who you are, an inheritor, a parent or grandparent of one, or a trusted advisor, you will greatly benefit from reading this book."

—Jamie Traeger-Muney, PhD
Family wealth consultant, founder of
Wealth Legacy Group, and
second-generation family business owner

"The Myth of the Silver Spoon is the book we have been waiting for! It provides clear and, more importantly, actionable ideas and strategies for the rising generation regardless of age. This book belongs on the bookshelf of every advisor who is involved in family generational wealth planning."

—Timothy Belber, JD AEP
Family wealth consultant and author of
*The Middle Way: Using Balance to
Create Successful Generational Family Wealth Transition Plans*

"We found and retained Kristin after two years of research and countless books. As a G3 charged with helping to transition and prepare G4 for their roles in the world, I was acutely aware of the history of the number of families who were painfully unsuccessful in that transition. Wealth can be a tremendous tool that can be used for good – good of the family, good of the company(ies) and good of communities. But it can also, if not managed well, be an albatross that can ultimately ruin (referring to Samuel Taylor Coleridge's poem "The Rime of the Ancient Mariner," in which a sailor who shoots a friendly albatross is forced to wear its carcass around his neck as punishment—that metaphor can be quite apt in this instance). Through Kristin, we have learned that the process can indeed be managed well—helpful guardrails can be erected, thoughtful understanding of wealth and its responsibilities can be taught, and most important, the critical aspect of giving back can be demonstrated and modeled from a very early age. She taught us the "dimmer switch" philosophy—appropriate learnings and disclosures at specific ages so as not to overwhelm and impede, but to empower and engage. And we are so much the better for it. This book is an encapsulation of Kristin's work, a superb tool to begin a process (and make no mistake, it is a process) and most important, a manual to have the very necessary conversations that so many families of wealth shy away from. "To whom much is given, much will be required" (Luke 12:48) is not a punishment, but an opportunity that can span generations—and Kristin and this book is a first step on that journey."

—Cara Esposito, DPDD, JD, MPA
Executive Director of the
Leonetti-O'Connell Family Foundation

"The Myth of the Silver Spoon is a much-needed resource for rising generation family members who might be ready to claim their narrative and control their trajectory. Keffeler captures the complex reality facing inheritors and empowers them with practical and approachable tools for moving forward. *The Myth* will also serve parents and advisors who want to bring empathy and a plan to the rising gen they care about. Let's get this book into as many hands as we can."

—Jim Coutré
Family office and philanthropy professional

"Any inheritor navigating the journey toward the life they're meant to lead would benefit from having Kristin as a guide. Reading her book is like taking a road trip with your best friend - one who also happens to wisely understand the challenging road inheritors face as they work to integrate their identity and their wealth and has brought along not only the map to chart the route but also snacks to make the journey fun!"

—Coventry Edwards-Pitt, CFA, CFP®
Chief Creative Officer of Ballentine Partners and
author of *Raised Healthy, Wealthy & Wise*

"The Myth of the Silver Spoon offers a practical, seven-step method to think through money, identity, relationships, and work that is grounded in the science of positive psychology and in Kristin Keffeler's deep and personal understanding of the emotional complexities of wealth. It is a masterful contribution to anyone trying to build a life of meaning and purpose."

—Scott Peppet, JD
President, Chai Trust Company

THE
MYTH
OF THE
SILVER
SPOON

NAVIGATING
FAMILY WEALTH
& CREATING AN
IMPACTFUL LIFE

KRISTIN KEFFELER

FOREWORD BY SHARNA GOLDSEKER

WILEY

Copyright © 2023 by John Wiley & Sons, Inc. All rights reserved.

Published by John Wiley & Sons, Inc., Hoboken, New Jersey.
Published simultaneously in Canada.

No part of this publication may be reproduced, stored in a retrieval system, or transmitted in any form or by any means, electronic, mechanical, photocopying, recording, scanning, or otherwise, except as permitted under Section 107 or 108 of the 1976 United States Copyright Act, without either the prior written permission of the Publisher, or authorization through payment of the appropriate per-copy fee to the Copyright Clearance Center, Inc., 222 Rosewood Drive, Danvers, MA 01923, (978) 750-8400, fax (978) 750-4470, or on the web at www.copyright.com. Requests to the Publisher for permission should be addressed to the Permissions Department, John Wiley & Sons, Inc., 111 River Street, Hoboken, NJ 07030, (201) 748-6011, fax (201) 748-6008, or online at http://www.wiley.com/go/permission.

Trademarks: Wiley and the Wiley logo are trademarks or registered trademarks of John Wiley & Sons, Inc. and/or its affiliates in the United States and other countries and may not be used without written permission. All other trademarks are the property of their respective owners. John Wiley & Sons, Inc. is not associated with any product or vendor mentioned in this book.

Limit of Liability/Disclaimer of Warranty: While the publisher and author have used their best efforts in preparing this book, they make no representations or warranties with respect to the accuracy or completeness of the contents of this book and specifically disclaim any implied warranties of merchantability or fitness for a particular purpose. No warranty may be created or extended by sales representatives or written sales materials. The advice and strategies contained herein may not be suitable for your situation. You should consult with a professional where appropriate. Further, readers should be aware that websites listed in this work may have changed or disappeared between when this work was written and when it is read. Neither the publisher nor authors shall be liable for any loss of profit or any other commercial damages, including but not limited to special, incidental, consequential, or other damages.

For general information on our other products and services or for technical support, please contact our Customer Care Department within the United States at (800) 762-2974, outside the United States at (317) 572-3993 or fax (317) 572-4002.

Wiley also publishes its books in a variety of electronic formats. Some content that appears in print may not be available in electronic formats. For more information about Wiley products, visit our web site at www.wiley.com.

Library of Congress Cataloging-in-Publication Data is Available:

ISBN 9781119909705 (Hardback)
ISBN 9781119909729 (ePub)
ISBN 9781119909712 (ePDF)

Cover Design: Wiley
Cover Image: © -slav-/Getty Images

SKY10036310_093022

Contents

Foreword

It was 8:00 A.M., and I was in a room full of the leading wealth advisors from the last three decades in U.S. history. I had recently been nominated and accepted into the Collaboration for Family Flourishing, an illustrious professional association founded by Jay Hughes, the father of wealth advising—and I was clearly the youngest person in the room. As someone who had been on a journey to earn the right to my family legacy of philanthropic stewardship and to build my own career as a philanthropic advisor, I couldn't help but make two observations quite quickly: one, my determination to build identity capital in my 20s and early 30s had landed me in a room with scores of people who were a generation, or two, older than me; and two, I was being asked to participate in an ice breaker at 8:00 A.M. when all I wanted to do was have a cup of coffee and gain my sea legs.

As the gathering unfolded amid a Chicago snowstorm, I rediscovered that being myself allowed me to connect with others in the room regardless of generation, gender, or geography. And it led me to Kristin Keffeler, someone who would become a friend and fellow traveler in this field for more than two decades now. In Kristin I found not only a peer in age and stage of life, but also a fellow colleague, consultant, researcher, and writer. I also discovered someone who, like myself, wears two hats as a rising gen and entrepreneur, aligning ourselves with our roles, aspiring to make meaning in our lives as well as for our clients. In the subsequent years since we met, our paths have continued to intersect, as they have once again through *The Myth of the Silver Spoon*.

Since 2002, I have founded and grown a nonprofit practice—21/64, Inc.—to provide high-capacity-giving families with next gen education and multigenerational advising, and to train the professionals who serve them. Along with my colleagues, and through our work with thousands of individual donors and families across the United States (as well as in Canada, Australia, and the Middle East), we have witnessed how wealth creation and the largest wealth transfer in history poised Gen Xers and millennials to become the most significant donors in history. Yet, from training professional advisors, we could also see that few understood how to engage with them. This gap led to my research and eventual book, with my coauthor, Michael Moody, *Generation Impact: How Next Gen Donors Are Revolutionizing Giving* (Wiley 2017, 2021). Together, Michael and I conducted quantitative and qualitative research to capture—in their own voices—how these next gen donors aspire to revolutionize the field of philanthropy with an earnestness and steadfast commitment to making an impact on the challenges facing our communities today.

In *Generation Impact,* we pulled back the curtain on these donors from high-capacity-giving families to offer first-of-its-kind research on how these next gen major donors have the potential to make an outsized impact on the world—especially if we can hear how they want to focus on impact, give strategically, be innovative, work in multigenerational teams, and use all the tools in their toolbox. And, by elevating their own voices, we hoped the audiences of families, grantees, and advisors would hear how next gen donors honored where they came from even while cultivating their own identities as givers. The book became a bestseller in its category and is now in its second edition.

By writing *Generation Impact* and continuing to consult with individual donors and multigenerational family foundations, I can appreciate the significance of *The Myth of the Silver Spoon* to the field. Kristin brings an innate understanding that the challenges faced by many next gen within families of significant wealth are real, and too often ignored or trivialized, something I've witnessed over the years in society, and even in the wealth advisory field. Instead, Kristin brings genuineness and commitment to her clients, listens to what they're grappling with, carves out a temporal reality in which they can be vulnerable, and helps them to get unstuck and find their flow. To this work, she conveys a combination of intuition, integrity, experience, and knowledge, a valuable combination in a practitioner. And so, I was delighted to hear she was finally putting her insights and ideas—herself—down on paper.

Kristin's work addresses the next gen who aren't yet ready to utilize their resources. Those rising gen who are still *becoming* and getting ready to launch. Without dismantling what Kristin calls the "hidden tripwires" that come from having wealth and "clearing the inner and outer clutter" created by them, those next gen could struggle to thrive personally. They might remain "paralyzed by predecessor, privilege and possibility," when we need them to step into their own power, both for themselves and because of the resources many could bring to bear on a world in much need. *The Myth of the Silver Spoon*, for many readers, could be a precursor to *Generation Impact*—for those who want Kristin's help to reflect on the kind of person they want to become and in doing so consider the kind of impact they can have.

As someone with the same last name as the private foundation her great uncle established upon his demise, I'm familiar with how the weight of legacy and responsibility can feel. I've spent many years trying to earn the right to that legacy, travel my own journey to "clear out the money clutter" and build an identity that allows me to stand comfortably in my own shoes, grow a purpose-driven practice and family of my own, and ultimately join the board of directors of the foundation.

If we want Gen X, millennials, and emerging Gen Zers to face their family's resources and craft their own identities, so that they can become the healthy, thriving adults we hope them to be (and possibly one day also become the next gen donors the world needs them to be), we need to understand what they're up against and how we can provide them with practical support as their families, allies, and advisors.

Unfortunately, the field has offered little training on how to talk about the unseen issues of having wealth that are lurking "below the water line." Therefore, *The Myth of the Silver Spoon* is a gift to those rising gen who want to find their purpose, to those parents, grandparents, and guardians who want to see them thrive, and to those advisors who are looking for an immensely readable and pragmatic way to serve their clients.

—Sharna Goldseker, founder of 21/64 Inc.
and coauthor of *Generation Impact:
How Next Gen Donors Are Revolutionizing Giving*

Acknowledgements

Every author I've ever talked to has told me that moving their spark of an idea into a finished narrative on the printed page took the effort, skill, love, and support of a small (or large) tribe of people. This has been my experience as well. First and foremost, I want to thank the two people who were most impacted by the all-consuming effort that bringing this book to life took—Mike and Clara (and, of course, my ever-present office companion, Olive the mini-Aussie). You two have supported and believed in me, spent countless dinners listening to me debrief my "good" writing days and my "bad" ones. You let me off the hook for chores in the house and picked up the slack for everything I stopped doing. Most of all, you showed me you loved me by giving me the space to breathe life into this book. Thank you. To Taylor, Alex, Darby and Clarke—thank you for giving over so many family dinner conversations to talk of "the book." You made me feel seen and celebrated. (And a special thank you to Alex for the Clutter Clearing graphic.) To my family of origin—Dad, Mom, Skip, Rob, and Rick—this book doesn't exist without you and our family story. Dad and Mom, thank you for parenting me the way you did. It worked—I'm proud of who I've become. And to my brothers, being your little sister has been the most formative identity of my life. I love you guys, and I always have. If ever I needed more proof of what an incredible group of sibs we are, these last few years have removed any doubt. It's been a firestorm, and I wouldn't want to be in it with anyone but you three. To my colleagues, those who have walked this journey with me since the beginning, those special elders who have believed in me and invested in me along the way, and the many heartful and generous advisors I've met in my journey—you all impact me and my thinking and I'm happy to call so many of you both colleague and friend. To my Johnson Financial Group colleagues, you said you'd support me and this book from the beginning, and you never wavered in your words or your actions. I'm proud to be a member of our team. To my Penn MAPP friends, if you would have told me that I'd still be as connected to, and feel as supported, by all of you as I did when we were all together in Philadelphia, I am not sure I would have believed it. MAPP13 truly changed my life and I'm indebted to my classmates, my teachers, and the MAPP staff. And to the extra special handful of MAPPsters who have been at my side during this book process, I owe you an extra hug. To Stacey Stern, book coach and editor who helped me to take my big ideas and start to distill them into the narrative that would eventually become this book, thank you. I needed you to get my ideas ready for what was next, and I'm grateful for your gentle guidance. To Heidi Toboni, my editor, thinking partner, and awesome marketing mind, you're like a book magician. You think in 3-D and I don't know how you track every component of a manuscript (and its marketing) the way you do. Your expertise regarding what makes for a compelling, publishable book has been invaluable. Thank goodness I had a growth mindset from the very beginning and could take your feedback with the intent you gave it—you made my ideas and my writing better. We did well together. To the team at Wiley: Brian O'Neill, thank you for believing in this project and making it a joy to publish with you; Deborah Schindlar and Manikandan Kuppan, thank you for your editing guidance. I am grateful for the expertise each of your brought to support this book. To Sharna Goldseker, you have been a true friend through this process. Thank you for believing in me and in this book enough to make connections, share ideas, and give me the greatest gift of all—honest and direct feedback. Having you write the Foreword is an honor. Finally, to my clients—the rising gen and families I have had the joy of supporting—your honesty, courage, and willingness to really do "the work" gives me such hope. You are good people with big ideas and the ability to deliver on those ideas. Thank you for sharing your hearts with me and trusting me as a guide on your journeys.

Wait and see.
The temporary emptiness
Of not discovering
The answers of life
Cannot last,
For the Answer itself
Is blossoming
Petal by petal
For you.

—Chinmoy Kumar Ghose

About the Author

Kristin Keffeler, MSM, MAPP is a thought leader, speaker, and consultant at the forefront of a global shift in family wealth advising, known as Wealth 3.0. She guides affluent and enterprising families, rising gen, and the professionals who support them in embracing the positive power of wealth and doing the "inner work" of money.

As the founder of Illumination360 and the Chief Learning Officer for the Denver-based Johnson Financial Group, she specializes in human motivation and behavioral change, family dynamics, family governance, rising gen education and development, and intergenerational collaboration. Drawing upon her life experience as the daughter of wealth-creating parents and her years of research and private practice advising and coaching the rising generation in affluent and enterprising families, Kristin believes that members of the rising gen are uniquely positioned to create significant impact in the world, and uses a lens of strengths to help them to ignite their potential.

Keffeler brings a multi-dimensional approach to her work. She earned an undergraduate degree human biology and chemistry, with an emphasis on human peak performance. She also holds a Master of Science in Management with a concentration in Public Health from the University of Denver, and a Master of Applied Positive Psychology from the University of Pennsylvania. She lives in Boulder County, Colorado where she rides her bike, hugs her daughters, laughs with her husband, and works side-by-side with her dog, Olive.

Introduction

When I was growing up, I was mostly unaware of money, which of course is its own kind of privilege. I certainly never worried that we didn't have enough. But I also never considered that we maybe had more than we needed—which I now realize was part of the magic of my parents and their own approach to money and parenting. They were never showy or out to impress. To the contrary, my dad wore the same red down jacket that my mom made for him in the 1970s from a "sew-it yourself" kit until the coat fell apart in the early 2000s

Although I knew my father was a successful businessman and entrepreneur, I didn't think much about it until the end of my senior year in high school. That is when I had my first taste of how having money can make one feel different in ways that are alternately alluring and destabilizing.

My Shiny, Black Sports Car

When I got accepted to my first-choice, private college and was awarded a fairly significant academic scholarship, my father offered to buy me a car. Brand-new. After all, my father explained, my scholarship was saving them a lot of money. Surprised and delighted, I chose a shiny, black sports car—a significant upgrade from my decade-old, maroon Honda Civic hatchback. (Secretly, I think my father was also excited about the new car—being in my old Civic always annoyed him because the cheap, fuzzy, gray seat covers that I'd bought to hide the splitting faux-leather seats would shed on his black suits.)

I vividly remember the day we picked it up and the thrill that this fancy, fast, eye-catching little car was mine(!). I loved how I felt driving it home . . . the sunroof open . . . my music blasting on the stereo . . . and the power of the engine under the hood. But my feelings of joy and excitement dissipated as soon as I drove it to school.

My high school had two parking lots—one for students and one for teachers. When I pulled up to the school for the first time in my new car, I realized I didn't know where I should park. My car would stand out like a sore thumb in the student lot, but we were forbidden to park in the teachers' lot. To this day, I can still feel the twisting, internal discomfort as I realized that this shiny, new car of mine was going to draw the attention of both my peers and my teachers. And maybe not in the way I wanted attention. Although I'm a rule-follower by nature, I was suddenly so self-conscious and concerned about parking in the student lot that I broke the rules, drove into the teachers' lot, and parked there. I couldn't help noticing that my car stood out like a sore thumb in that parking area, too. I felt a pit in my stomach when I parked in a lot where I wasn't allowed and in a car that was nicer than most of the teachers' cars. I continued to park there for the last few weeks of school, slinking in from the staff lot before the first bell and feeling rotten about it every day.

It was an unsettling experience. But I never considered asking someone to help me sort it out. Who would I have talked to about it anyway? Not my parents. I didn't want them to think I was unappreciative of their generous gift. And not my friends, any one of whom would've happily traded cars with me. This was my first taste of the confusion of knowing I hadn't done anything wrong but was feeling guilty all the same. As it turns out, that was only the beginning of the internal "clutter" I began to experience as a result of what—from the outside—should have been nothing but a blessing: Wealth. Especially gifted wealth.

While every one of us interacts with money every day, the vast majority of us are unaware of our relationship with it at best and have an unhealthy relationship with it at worst. And trying to understand and engage with the abstract concept that is "wealth" is often even more fraught with confusion. How do you build a healthy relationship with something that few people—including your own family members—will talk openly about? How do you build a healthy relationship with something that generates as conflicted feelings within society as it does within you? Most people are both fascinated by wealth and quick to judge those who have it. Many people—particularly those who have not earned their affluence themselves—face a confusing, negative, and privately painful relationship with money.

My story is not atypical—this is a common problem of children of wealth in our society. Perhaps you've experienced confusing narratives too. Or someone you care about, influence, or advise has. You're not alone. Unfortunately, there aren't many outlets to address these problems openly when they begin to arise, so they tend to snowball. One example of this deficiency of resources is highlighted in the informal study that Jay Hughes, one of the preeminent thought leaders in the field of family wealth consulting, conducted with psychotherapists over the course of several years. Hughes asked more than 30 therapists how much training they received on dealing with issues of wealth and money—the majority said less than three hours in their entire graduate program—and how skilled they felt at dealing with issues of money and wealth with their clients—the majority said very unskilled.[1] In corroboration of Hughes' findings, most of my rising gen clients say they do not bring issues of wealth and money into their therapy conversations and that avoiding these topics limits what they can cover with their counselors. Furthermore, when preparing to write this book, I studied the competitive landscape and found that there were scarce few published resources that even broadly touched on this topic and no books that spoke directly to struggling next gens with a mindset approach and research-based solutions. While there are general parenting books in the marketplace that address money matters and wealth within families, there are none I know of that help the affluent get unstuck once problems arise. No wonder it feels like there are not many safe places to understand the tripwires that inherited wealth can create. There aren't.

Different and Isolated

While I was in college and deeply focused on all things Kristin, my father had started a new company. As was typical for my dad, he'd gone all in—re-mortgaging the house and putting all his chips on the table. My father's leadership team built a strong company, and with the economic winds at their backs, the business grew quickly. By the time my graduation neared, they were preparing an initial public offering. Enter wealth event number 1. Their second public offering was also successful, positioning them nicely on the NASDAQ. Within a few short years, the business became a very attractive purchase for a bigger company, and by the time I was in my mid-20s, the company was sold. Enter wealth event number 2.

After the company was bought out, my dad retired, followed soon by my mom, and they started doing things that people with a new financial windfall often do. They traveled a lot, built a beautiful home in the mountains, and filled a cellar with great wine.

While I loved learning to enjoy wine, taking special trips with my parents, and spending time with them in the Colorado mountains around their new home, I also started becoming distinctly aware of uneasy feelings emerging, emotions similar to those I had with my shiny, new, black sports car. One moment I might be enjoying these new treats and experiences, but back at grad school surrounded by my public health classmates, I was privately self-conscious about the ways in which my family's money made me feel different from my peers. Isolated. Even at times feeling like I was living a double life. The internal clutter piled up.

"No One Wants to Hear the Problems of a Rich Kid"

This presumption is why I wrote this book. Despite the common misconception that people who are born into wealth don't (or shouldn't) have problems, there is often a quiet suffering that these next generation family members experience. I call this misconception and struggle "the myth of silver spoon." Interviews with people who are raised in wealthy or well-known families often reveal themes of flagging self-identities, fear of failure, isolation, and lack of motivation. These experiences are so common I've dubbed them "the three paralyses": paralysis by predecessor, paralysis by privilege, and paralysis by possibility. Compounding the issue, the roadblocks on their path to a thriving life are often unseen and generally unacknowledged. As one of my consulting clients said to me, "No one wants to hear the problems of a rich kid. I know I'm really confused and totally stuck, but I feel like such an a-hole for not being able to figure it out. I mean, really, I've been given every advantage. Honestly, it just makes me feel even more flawed that I can't figure my life out when I've been given all that I have."

Just like with this client, ultimately, what can look like poor behavior—entitlement, disengagement, apathy, and a lack of motivation—is just camouflaging deeply felt confusion, self-doubt, fear, shame, and anxiety. That's *a lot* of internal clutter getting in the way of living a robust, authentic, and self-actualized life.

This book is about clearing that clutter—money clutter, self-identity clutter, relationship clutter, and the clutter surrounding our individual work and contribution–and then using the science of positive psychology and other tools to build a scaffolding to that thriving life that's waiting out there for us to claim.

Ask anyone the first thing that comes to their mind when they hear the words *rich, inheritor,* and *trust fund.* They'll likely reply with something derogatory—even if they personally are wealthy, have inherited money, or have trust funds(!). In fact, one of the few remaining prejudices still generally acceptable in American society today is to prejudge and have contempt for the very rich simply for being rich. Even more so if the person is an inheritor. But in my 15-plus years of private practice as a leadership coach to next generation family members and a human capital consultant to affluent families, I have seen more full-hearted, committed, and curious rising generation family members than I have seen anyone who fits the stereotype of an entitled, thoughtless heir. If you've picked this book up, I'm betting you're one of those full-hearted, committed, and curious rising gen—or someone who cares about and supports them.

It is important to name that this book is not a cry for sympathy for the "poor little rich girl (or boy)." In fact, the many earnest rising gen I interact with every day would cringe at that idea. Rather, this is a serious call for us to recognize inheritors' challenges as real and unimagined, for compassionate discourse around these challenges, and for the dissemination of practical and researched-based solutions to support them as well as their professional and familial support. Psychological well-being for every human—across the entire economic spectrum—is a goal that is autotelic. It is a valuable pursuit in and of itself. This applies to all humans, including the rising generation in affluent families. Their thriving also has instrumental value through its broader social implications—the scope of their potential influence being broader by virtue of the volume of their resources and their social networks. As the rising generation are supported to overcome the challenges to self-actualizing in a context of inherited wealth, they will be more able to focus their human capital— their gifts, talents, and expertise—outward, constructively impacting issues relevant to our communities and our world. For this to occur, we need to get beyond sympathy or blame to respect and problem solving.

To the rising gen, their parents, and their trusted advisors—welcome! This book is for you.

Claiming My Own Flame

I'm the daughter of a successful entrepreneur and of a mother who celebrated most of our family's daily messiness as "valuable creative expression." I'm the youngest of four and the only girl—my brothers nicknamed me "fast fist" growing up (being a little tough was the only way I'd be able to play with them!). As the youngest, I spent a lot of time watching family dynamics and other people's behavior. Observing the interplay between decisions and consequences within a family system—mine in this case—became an invaluable skill for my future career.

I believe this field chose me. After getting a combined graduate degree in public health and business, I spent my 20s on two parallel paths—working for organizations helping their employees make meaningful health-related behavior changes and trying to figure out how I could effectively fit into the landscape of my own family's unfolding money story, while still finding my own voice and calling in the shadow of a big-thinking wealth creator.

In 2005, I decided to connect these two parallel paths: I wanted to use my gifts in a career that helped individuals and families to thrive. In my consulting work today, I take a holistic, integrative approach to supporting the overall well-being of high-net-worth families and their individual members. I help my clients focus on the inner and outer work they can do to enhance their relationship with money, find their own vision and voice, and, ultimately, align that vision with the purposeful use of their inherited resources. As I discovered during my own journey of waking up to my relationship with money and uncovering my deeper values and goals, when there is clarity about what money is to you (and what it is not), it is much easier to make money-related and major life decisions based on what's important at your core.

Thankfully, I am not alone in my commitment to helping individuals and families to thrive. Though, as is captured in this recent conversation I had with a trustee, the path to providing true, integrated support to next generation family members remains difficult and confusing for many professionals. In our conversation, the trustee described a situation in which her 22-year-old beneficiary, a young woman who had recently lost her single mother to cancer, was floundering. Never a strong student, this beneficiary dropped out of college soon after her mother's death. She said she just wanted to ride horses and was happy working at the barn where her horse was stabled. The trustee said to me, "I've known this young woman since she was 1 year old. I know she is hurting, and I know she needs support in trying to understand what this money is supposed to be to her, but I don't even know where to start. I'm an accountant for crying out loud! I don't have the first clue about how to have a conversation with her that is beyond what she's getting and why. And that's not helpful right now. She needs someone to help her process her mother's death and *integrate* what her mother left to her into her own life."

In my work, I've encountered many cases like this concerned professional and her struggling client. I've seen how these issues—if left unspoken and unaddressed—can easily develop into confusing self-narratives, bad money habits, and roadblocks to growth where the noise of wealth inhibits focusing on the essential work of healthy self-development.

To support others in the journey of clearing the clutter from their lives and designing flourishing paths of impact, I bring to this work and book not only my personal and professional experiences, but also the wisdom of recent advancements in the field of positive psychology. While getting my masters in applied positive psychology at the University of Pennsylvania, I interviewed many successful, happy, rising generation family members of high-net-worth to learn the mindset and specific character traits and skills they had acquired to support their successes. Insights from that research inform these chapters, and we'll explore them together in ways that you can immediately act on in your life—whether you're a rising gen yourself or you care about and influence one.

How to Use This Book

The Myth of the Silver Spoon supports the well-meaning but struggling or stuck next generation of the highly affluent, and their families and the professionals who influence them, to face their wealth clutter, negative self-narratives, and problematic money-related behaviors head on—and to prevail. If you're reading this now, you are part of a group whose numbers—as we'll look at shortly—are larger than we might expect and whose challenges are deeper than society might want to admit.

This book is intended to be thought-provoking, perspective-shifting, and actionable. It contains many stories of rising gen, their family members, and trusted advisors—none of which are hypotheticals. They are real people in real situations whom I've encountered in my private practice or research (names, places, and some personal details have been changed to protect privacy). You'll see direct quotes from research participants. These quotes have been edited for clarity but are directly from the hearts and minds of rising gen just like you. The stories you'll encounter are either from my clients or the colleagues with whom I collaborate. In this book you'll also find lots of reflection questions as well as interactive tools and assessments that I hope you make yours. Mark it up and connect what you're learning to your own life. (If you're like me, there'll be lots of smiley faces, exclamation marks, highlighted key points, and folded page corners.) The book has four main parts, each examining either an aspect of the wealth inheritor's challenge or providing a roadmap for its solution:

- **Part I. Confronting the Myth of the Silver Spoon.** Whether we have a lot or a little, we all have a relationship with money. Part I will illustrate why so many next gens of affluent families experience a quiet pain—often feeling empty and inadequate—while everyone else thinks they "have it all." We'll learn about the common hidden "tripwires" that often catch the wealthy unaware and cause next gen family members to stumble. We'll conclude by highlighting what is lost to our greater society when the power of concentrated wealth to do good is dissipated by the masked suffering of the next generation.
- **Part II. Clearing the Clutter.** We all have clutter in our lives: disorganized, nonessential stuff that accumulates and takes up space, often in our private areas away from public view (think closets and desks, not foyers and front yards). Part II will explore the additional and distinct clutter—both in their inner and outer—that many next gens accumulate. This includes negative self-narratives and conflicting or unhealthy beliefs and behaviors. This clutter often smothers them or inhibits their ability to grow. Clearing out the clutter is inherently empowering. We'll explore each of these four types of clutter—money clutter, identity clutter, relationship clutter, and contribution clutter—and how to identify, reframe, and dispel these to create space so there's room for *you*.
- **Part III. The Big Logs for Your Fire: Human Thriving and Your Unique Spark.** Through interviews and stories, we'll discuss

the character traits and skills that are essential for aspiring rising generation family members to cultivate on their journey to thriving. Based on validated research from the field of positive psychology, and my own original findings studying rising generation family members, we'll review five specific psychological constructs that offer compelling counters to the challenges brought by unearned wealth. We'll conclude with a chapter that invites you (or the rising gen you care about) to begin uncovering your own "big idea" by connecting the flame within you to your innate skills and talents.

- **Part IV. Creating a Uniquely Impactful Life.** Here we put it all together with concrete, practical guidance and tools that support you to overcome the hidden tripwires of wealth and actively pursue (or help a rising gen pursue) a self-actualized life and, for those who are inclined, a life of impact. For the parents with newly acquired wealth who are curious how to support their children (the little ones or the big ones) to integrate wealth well, or the many rising gen who also want to heartfully parent their own children in ways that will help their kids avoid the pitfalls of wealth they had experienced, we will discuss how to parent in practical ways that encourage the essential character traits and skills for thriving as a high-net-worth inheritor. Similarly, we'll help trusted advisors to wealthy families and individuals see the important role they can play and offer perspective and tools that align with a significant shift that's taking place in advisory fields today.

By the end of this book, we will have cleared some clutter, created the space to ignite that spark that is waiting inside of you, and gathered the tools to not only light that fire, but to tend to it for the long haul. And if you're ready for it, you might just be inspired to consider how you can put your fingerprints on some of the greater community issues that matter most to you.

The Opportunity and My Hope

As the baby boomers—one of the largest generations alive—come to the end of their lives, tens of trillions of dollars will be transferred out of their estates and given to their families and their philanthropic causes. This is being termed the Great Wealth Transfer,[2] the largest known in history, and it has significant implications for the well-being of the next generation in affluent families as well as larger implications for society as a whole. Families with concentrated wealth are incredibly well positioned to affect massive positive changes in the world, but this privilege comes with its own pressures and burdens, especially for the inheriting generation. It is easy to dismiss the challenges of this affluent demographic as frivolous or trivial compared to the immense challenges faced by those without daily access to such things as food, shelter, and safety. The challenges are indeed different. But tragically, when family fortunes are squandered because of infighting, addiction, or lack of engagement and stewardship, family members (and society by extension) are robbed of the power to deploy their resources to better themselves, their communities, and the world at large.

By addressing the challenges faced by the rising generation and releasing the power of human capital contained within those individuals, it is possible that all boats will rise. As has been proven by the impact of the Giving Pledge—the pledge made by the world's wealthiest individuals to give the majority of their wealth away philanthropically (www.givingpledge.org)—when the attention of the rising generation can move off overcoming their own challenges of inherited wealth, it can instead focus on issues in the broader community most salient to them. It is not hard to imagine a world where the generation of inheritors combines their considerable wealth with a desire to make the world a better place. That is the larger opportunity here.

With this book, I hope you will embark on this fuller journey with me. Debunk the hindering myth of the silver spoon, explore the ways that wealth-related clutter can accumulate in our lives, learn how to clear it, discern what authentically matters to us as individuals, and put in place tools and a support structure for a thriving life for ourselves—as well as an impactful one for the world.

1

A Flickering Flame

Cassie is bright, conscientious, and engaged. She is an artist with a big imagination and compelling ideas. She has a broad smile and curious green eyes. She is unassuming and interested in others. She is also very stuck. Quietly, painfully, and totally undercover stuck.

Cassie is the granddaughter of a billionaire and, as the beneficiary of two different trusts—one from her grandfather and one from her parents—she hasn't had to worry about how to pay off any college or grad school debt or if she can afford an apartment in a nicer part of town. She is passionate about art and creative expression, and she has worked hard to find her place as an emerging artist. Her family is proud of her choice to pursue art as a career. From the outside it all looks pretty perfect. But from the inside, Cassie feels paralyzed. Small. Ineffective. And very lost.

Cassie's office drawer is stuffed with unopened quarterly statements from her trusts—her unconscious protest against engaging with the wealth that overwhelms and confuses her. While her art is being well received, she doesn't earn enough to support herself, and she struggles with whether she should get a job so she can be self-sufficient. But when she contemplates this, she quickly gets tied in knots—she has never tracked her cash flow and has no idea what her monthly expenses really are, so she doesn't even know what it would take to become self-sufficient. Plus, if she takes a job at the local café and she doesn't *need* the money, isn't she taking a job from someone who actually does need it? This is one of the many examples of how her good intentions get mired down in a maze of conflicting decisions.

Cassie loves the community of artist friends she has built in her adopted city. They are fun and funky, creative and scrappy. None of them have or make much money. None of them know that she comes from a wealthy family—a fact that she has become skilled at hiding. As a "struggling artist," she feels very accepted in her community. She hears their distaste for "the wealthy" in many of their conversations, and she wants to shrink even smaller. She is terrified she'll be "found out" and not accepted as a real struggling artist. Plus, the things they say about wealthy people don't actually fit what she experiences in her own family. She feels like she doesn't belong in either world—that of her family or her friends—which makes her feel like a fraud in both. Sometimes she wonders if she is a fraud, which leaves her feeling flat, small, and trapped.

While Cassie feels utterly alone in her experience, she is not. There are currently 6.3 million individuals in North America with a net worth between $5 million and $30 million,[1] and an additional 73,000 individuals have a net worth above $30 million (the latter typically defined as "ultra-high net worth"[2] and represents about 1 in every 4,500 people). While the identity experience of someone who is the child of a multi-millionaire may differ from that of the child or grandchild of a billionaire, the challenges faced by Cassie are echoed by many of her next-generation inheritor peers. Cassie is not alone in feeling stuck—but thankfully, there is a way out. Whether you are a next generation family member, someone who loves them (like a parent or friend), or a professional advisor to families of wealth, as you journey through this book, you will learn the following:

- The hidden tripwires to growing up with wealth (and why are they hidden)
- How inner and outer clutter gets in the way of our ability to find our voice and claim our individual life and path, and how to clear that clutter
- How to tap our inner strengths and create the scaffolding to support our growth and flourishing
- What it takes to put it all together and create a uniquely impactful life—one where we wake up feeling ignited for each day and where we can proudly rest our head on our pillow each night, knowing that we are living our own definition of a meaningful life

From Next Gen to Rising Gen

Before we dive in, let's get some terminology straight. *Next generation* vs. *rising generation*—are they synonymous? Is "rising gen" just the more progressive, trendy, or euphemistic way of referring to "next gen"? The answer is no; one term is defined by chronology and the other by psychology. Let's unpack that.

You may be the next emerging generation in your family lineage, but you are not necessarily, and certainly not only, a "next gen." Think about it: The commonly used "next generation" term is a chronological distinction. It only identifies you in relationship to the wealth creating generation in your family—so you become known as a "G2" or a "G3" or a "G4." While your relationship to the wealth creating generation in your family is an important one, you're also so much more than that. If you have this book in your hands, you get to proudly claim yourself as a "rising generation" as well. At its heart, the term rising generation is based on one's psychology—in particular, one's approach to their lives and the challenges and opportunities in front of them. By definition, a **rising gen** is someone who embraces the psychology of growth, possibility, hope, and continuous learning.[3] It embodies a willingness to persevere and find one's own voice and one's own path. And that, my friend, is you.

This book is written for the courageous but struggling, stuck, or directionless rising gen and the heartful parents, advisors, and friends who support and love them. We all need others to help us grow and move through the rough, stuck points in our lives—or the times when we're seeking fresh inspiration—and this book provides guidance for that community. People like Tracey, who want to see the next gens in their lives thrive, but don't know how to best help them.

Tracey is the mother of 24-year-old Avery. Avery's dad has created affluence for his family through the creation and sale of a business, and her older sister has found financial success in her own right. In a family of high-achievers, Avery feels like she doesn't measure up and doesn't fit in. She has attention deficit hyperactivity disorder (ADHD) and says she's only been able to get through school because her parents put a lot of structure around her in the form of tutors and educational aids. Tracey admits that, because of Avery's ADHD and learning differences, she probably protected her daughter too much and didn't allow her to struggle. Now, at 24, Avery finally (and barely) graduated from college and is living in her own apartment, but she is 100% dependent on her parents' financial support. She doesn't know how to budget (or even have any idea how much support she receives from her parents), she doesn't track whether her car insurance is due, or how to read and interpret the lease she signed for her apartment. Tracey can see that Avery is stuck, but every time she tries to broach these sticky topics with her daughter, they end up fighting. Tracey suspects that Avery suffers from a deep lack of confidence and a belief that she won't measure up to the bar of success set by her father and sister so why try? Tracey describes the low-grade panic that continues to grow in her as she projects what her daughter's future looks like if she is not able to untangle some of the knots that are tying her up.

Like Tracey hopes for Avery, these pages will help you understand why false money messages and obscure tripwires of inherited wealth are holding you back. It will help you to see the hidden forces that keep you from feeling your own spark; to clear the clutter so you can let in some fresh, life-giving oxygen; and to create the space to truly claim your flame. But, first, you need to learn a little bit about the clutter that is keeping you stagnant and stuck, unable to see your path clearly. Because if you are anything like Avery and Cassie, you've likely got a *big* clutter problem.

The Clutter Problem

What is the most cluttered space in your home? Your closet? Car? Basement? Garage? How on earth did that space ever get so cluttered? What *is* the clutter?

Really, stop and imagine that place. Look around it in your mind's eye: what is on the shelves, shoved into corners, hidden in the drawers? Where did it all come from? Do you want and need what's there?

When we consider what clutter truly is, there are some attributes that are fairly universal:

- We all have it.
- It accumulates.

- We tend to keep it in private spaces—think closets, not foyers.
- It takes up space we might use in other ways.
- It is the result of keeping things we don't need.
- It is not the important stuff.
- It is a disorganized collection.
- It is not who we are; it is just the "stuff."
- It is the result of what we don't tend to.
- It collects when we hold onto things we don't need or have use for.

Now, again, imagine yourself in your most cluttered room or area. Where do you sit (*can* you even sit)? How does it feel to be there? How easy is it to find what you need? How easy is it to see new possibilities with what's there? Is it light and airy or crowded and stagnant? No room starts cluttered, so where does this stuff all come from and why do we let it accumulate? To answer this—and how it relates to the problems of those with inherited wealth—we have to get even more refined in our understanding of clutter.

Outer and Inner Clutter

Outer clutter is typically the stuff we think of when we think of clutter. It is the stuff in our closet and garage, crammed into our bathroom cabinets and in the backseat of our car. We often default to accepting its existence as a collective nuisance . . . until it either accumulates so great that we eventually have a clearing out day or we move homes or sell that car. Why?

All of that outer clutter that is clogging our drawers and closets is most often the result of inner clutter. Inner clutter? What's that? Inner clutter is all the unconscious patterning and beliefs that we've picked up along the way that inform our thinking and decision-making without us even knowing it. Inner clutter is all of our "shoulds" and "have-tos." It is our "settling" and "can'ts." It is our "what ifs" and "maybe laters." It is our "not good enoughs" and "who am I tos?"

Inner clutter is why we end up staying in relationships too long—and then keeping the exes' old flannel stuffed in the back of our closets, taking up space. It is the empty feeling of questioning whether we are loved for who we are—and then filling our shelves and cupboards with all the stuff we bought to fill that void. (At least we were happy in the moment we bought it.) It is what drives the deal we make with ourselves when we say we'll work more, so that we can get paid more, so that we can buy more . . . when, really, we just all want to know that we matter. That we have value. That we're truly appreciated.

Inner clutter hides in the shadowy parts of our beings the way that outer clutter hides in the shadowy parts of our houses. But, just like outer clutter, inner clutter can be cleared. It is moveable, organizable, shred-able, discard-able, and free-able. And the bonus good news? Once you remove inner clutter it is even easier to clear the outer clutter(!).

But what does all this information on clutter have to do with Cassie (and Avery, and most every other aspiring rising gen family member I've ever met)? Cassie's got clutter. She's got the inner clutter of a belief that she does not belong. She has the confusion around earning money—that she can't, shouldn't, or doesn't know what it would take to be self-sufficient. She feels conflicted in her identity—is she a wealthy inheritor? A struggling artist? Are those two identities mutually exclusive? And all of that inner clutter drives her outer clutter. Her drawers are stuffed with unopened financial statements. She doesn't track her spending and has no idea what her expenses really are. She hides what she has from her friends and then hides from her family the fact that she hides anything from her friends. (She would feel terrible if they thought she was ashamed of what they have created and given to her.) It's a lot of clutter, and she feels trapped by it all. Can you relate? Most rising gen—and the people who love and support them—can. But as stuck as you might feel, there is a way out.

Clearing the Clutter

Beginning to make space for *you* in the midst of all that clutter is a process, a cycle. Defined steps along the path will make the process easier, but the truth is, like any process, it is messy, creative, freeing, frustrating, and amazing. It's all of it. So, you have to get your courage on and be ready. Trust me, it'll be worth it.

Here are the components:

Figure 1.1

Purpose

Overarching the whole process of clearing both the inner and the outer clutter is purpose. But for many aspiring rising gen, the idea of defining their purpose is paralyzing. In fact, for many, they've been told by their parents or grandparents that their highest wish for their kids and grandkids is that they use the resources they have to seek their passion—which, of course, is the precursor to defining one's purpose. What a gift! But, as most 20-somethings (and many next gens who have gotten stuck *feeling* like they're still 20-somethings) can attest to, the very stage when you're being told to find your passion is the same stage when you're least likely to be able to do that. It's the stage when you don't know yourself well enough to have a clue what your passion might be. One's 20s are all about building "identity capital"[4]—the individual collection of resources and experiences that each of us gathers over time and that guides who we are and what we bring to our adult journey. You need time to build your identity capital before you can really know what your passion or purpose might be. But don't worry. You don't have to wait until you've built sufficient identity capital to begin moving through the process of defining what ignites you. Rising gen often find that they can do one of two things to get unstuck.

For some, a sense of purpose comes *as a result of* clearing the clutter. So, if you're truly drawing a blank every time you think about your purpose, first do some inner house cleaning (keep reading to learn how). Often, when you start clearing the inner and outer clutter, purpose inherently starts to become clearer.

For others, it's just about defining what feels catalyzing to them right now. It doesn't have to be your forever purpose, it could be your ideas and musings—the fast fuel you'll read about next—of this moment in your life. Purpose gives us an orientation and sense of direction, a true north to point toward, even if it is just for *this* time in your life. It doesn't have to be your whole life's purpose, but even just having a clear direction for today is enough purpose to ground you and leave you feeling solid and assured.

Answering these questions will help you clarify your purpose, even if only for this stage of your life:

- What gets most of my attention right now?
- What do I get from investing my focus there?
- What is fundamentally important to me at this point in my life?
- Is there a discrepancy between where I'm investing my time and what is fundamentally important to me right now?
- What impact am I uniquely gifted to create?

Regardless of whether you feel paralyzed or catalyzed when you think of purpose, learning to identify and clear your inner clutter will support you to move from ideas (or stuck with no ideas) into action.

Clearing the Inner Clutter

Inner clutter can be identified and removed when there is clarity and alignment in the following:

	What does it do?	What questions does it answer?
Cultivating a Beneficial Mindset	Determines what attitudes we have and how we handle the information around us. *Mindset informs identity.*	What filters do I use to make decisions? Do I feel stuck where I am or can I always find a path for learning and growth?
Adopting an Empowering Identity	Determine how we think of ourselves. *Identity informs our beliefs.*	Who am I? Who do I want to become? How do I think of myself? Do I feel like my parts integrate into a whole or do I feel more fragmented?
Curating Supportive Beliefs	Confirm and support our sense of identity. *Beliefs inform our decisions.*	What do I believe is possible for me? How do others see me? Am I acceptable and loveable for all of who I am? Am I capable?
Making Aligned Decisions	Based on what we believe. *Decisions inform our actions.*	What beliefs am I using to make this decision? Where am I getting stuck? Why am I getting stuck? What would someone who felt capable and confident do in this situation? What decision do I need to make to be aligned with who I am and what I believe?

We'll explore this alignment process in depth in Part II, but for now understand that this work, although it requires commitment, typically yields a sense of relief, and you can trust that you can do it with a good guide.

Clearing the Outer Clutter

When our inner clutter is reasonably well sorted, we naturally want to move to outer clutter (or, as we're cleaning up the clutter, we move from inner alignment to outer alignment):

	What does it do?	What questions does it answer?
Defining a Clear Outcome	Clarifies with conviction what we are working toward. *Defining clear outcomes creates aligned actions.*	What does success look like right now? What does ease, joy, and engagement look like right now? What does satisfaction look like today?
Aligning Your Actions	Action inspires forward movement, which is the opposite of being stuck. *Aligned actions are the upward spiral of the less-cluttered you in motion. Each aligned action affirms your choices and leads to greater freedom, impact, and satisfaction.*	What is the first small step I can take? What is the next step after that? What is the scariest thing I could do? What action leads to a greater feeling of inner freedom?

Creating Systems and Environments to Support Your Success	Supportive systems and environments are like a flywheel that help you continue to move in the direction of who you want to become. *Healthy systems and environments reflect back to us who we are and who we are capable of being.*	What do I need to request to support my success? What do I need to let go of to support my success? What is holding me back? What structures can I put in place that will help me grow?

There is good news and bad news about clearing clutter. The bad news is that it is an ongoing cycle—you are never really going to be done. Your clearing efforts will not always focus on the same topics or tripwires, and you won't end up with the same junk clogging up your drawers, but if you learn to get good at clearing, your reward will be a deepening awareness about the clutter hiding beneath the clutter. Which means, if you wish, you'll always have one level deeper to go. You will get better and better at spotting inner clutter (even as it's forming!) and knowing exactly what to do with it. If you see outer clutter starting to accumulate, you'll know it's a sign to pay attention to the mindsets, identity, beliefs, and decisions that are driving your life at that time.

Once you have begun the heartful work of moving, organizing, discarding, and dismantling the clutter in your life, you're ready for what comes next.

How to Build a Fire

I grew up backpacking with my dad and older brothers in the Colorado mountains. One of the first things you learn when you're in the backcountry is how to build a fire and keep it burning. While it seems like you ought to be able to throw down some logs and light them with a match, anyone who has tried that method (even just for backyard marshmallow roasting) knows it's not that easy. A good fire is a mix of art and science. It must have fast fuel (dried leaves, pine needles, and twigs as kindling), slow fuel (bigger, more sustaining logs), and a spark (provided by a match or something to ignite the quick fuel). And all this needs to be constructed in such a way that oxygen can move through it to feed the combustion—the big logs provide a structure that gives the air plenty of access to the fast fuel and the spark, while still being close enough to the emerging flame so that the logs, too, can ignite when the fire is big and hot enough. *That's* how you get a fire with some real staying power. A little art, a little science.

Igniting and tending the flame inside of you is no different. Right now, there may be a flickering flame inside you. Your flame hasn't gone out—it's still there—but it's starved for fuel and oxygen. It's being suffocated by all the clutter that has accumulated in your life. It needs tending to grow. Or . . . your flame may be awaiting its spark, fast fuel (these are your ideas and musings and your willingness to see these ideas and musings as valuable and worth exploring), and slow fuel (these are character strengths and skills like Growth Mindset, Grit, Mastery-Orientation, Close Positive Relationships, and Foundational Character Strengths, which we'll discuss next and in later chapters). Just like with a good fire, these "big logs" of slow fuel need to be built like scaffolding around your flame. The people who turn their spark into a flame that illuminates their paths and sheds light for others are those who have the right structure in place that is capable of supporting and sustaining their fire through wind and rain.

While scaffolding can (and should) consist of many things—unconditional love, an intrinsic sense of self-worth, the ability and motivation to work, to name a few—in these pages, you will learn what research has shown are the common traits and skills that successful rising gen share:

- Growth Mindset—the belief that a trait (like intelligence or resilience) is malleable and can be developed through hard work, good strategies, and thoughtful feedback.[5]
- Grit—passion and perseverance in pursuit of a long-term goal.[6]
- Mastery-Orientation—being directed toward the attainment of a solution, rather than focusing on the one's failures.[7]

- Close Positive Relationships—the development and maintenance of which is an essential skill that supports all areas of personal growth, including the definition of, and pursuit of, one's ideal self.[8]
- Foundational Character Strengths—the 24 culturally agnostic strengths that form the backbone of human thriving.[9]

With these essential components of a strong structure in place, you can dream big, lean in hard, and begin to accomplish what is significant to you.

The Journey of a Thousand Miles . . .

From where you stand today—somewhere on a continuum of frustrated to stuck or witnessing the rising gen in your life somewhere on that continuum—it may seem like you have a long journey ahead of you. And you do. But take heart from the words of this rising gen:

For so long I was so stuck. And so confused. One day I got so tired of it and I asked myself, "How far could I go if I really tried?" And it was kind of a self-fulfilling process, because when I started taking action, I started getting positive feedback, and that feedback encouraged me further. And then I started feeling better about myself and I got more positive feedback. And then the hard work became something of a habit. For me, working hard at something I find meaningful has become something I really enjoy. It's like a flywheel that just keeps rotating and giving me motivation. That perspective didn't click in until I was an undergrad, but when it did finally click, I realized I had everything I needed to thrive. I mean, it's kind of cliché, but whatever I put my mind to there was a good chance that I could pursue it in a way that I would be proud.

Just like this rising gen, you, too, have what it takes to start your own flywheel spinning. As you've seen in this chapter, there's a lot of commitment and work that goes into becoming all of who you are meant to be. Is it worth the work? Only you can answer that. But I have a feeling that someday, as Future You looks back on the you of today, Future You is very likely to agree that it was absolutely worth the work. So get your courage and grit on, and let's get started.

PART I

Confronting the
Myth of the
Silver Spoon

2 | Poor Little Rich Girl

The McAllister Family: A Story

John McAllister[1] was born to be an entrepreneur. His sharp intellect and gregarious personality made him a natural leader, and his unrelenting drive and vision seemed to give him the Midas touch. Always on the cutting edge and a risk-taker by nature, John cofounded a software company right out of college with two of his buddies that, through years of dedicated work, became wildly successful.

John met his wife Linda in college, and they married soon after graduation. By their late 20s, they had two children—Ben and Ellen. Even though both John and Linda valued family, John wasn't home as often as he would have liked. Managing his rapidly expanding company kept him at the office or on a plane much of the time. Meanwhile, Linda's hands were also more than full, as she juggled the responsibilities of her work as an attorney and the kids' increasingly busy schedules.

John and Linda's dedication to their careers reaped significant rewards. When Ben and Ellen were in their early teen years, John and his partners took their company public, creating a significant wealth event for them all. John and Linda's net worth jumped to $75,000,000, and they began enjoying all the trappings of this next-level wealth.

They built a beautiful vacation home at the beach, and they moved their primary residence to a more affluent part of town. Their large, new home backed to a lake. Having worked hard for this windfall, John loved buying expensive toys for the family—a ski boat for the lake, jet skis, paddleboards, kayaks, the works. Though the kids enjoyed these treats, they also experienced discomfort around their family's increased wealth. Even in this more affluent part of town, Ben and Ellen were known as the "rich kids," and each privately wondered if the other children coming over to hang out at their house really wanted to be their friends or if they were using them for access to the lake and all the fun stuff they had. Additionally, since their father's company employed many people in the community and their last name was well known, both teenagers felt the burden of living in the spotlight, always feeling that people were watching them and judging their decisions and behaviors.

Linda decided to step back from her position at her law firm and dedicate more time to the family's growing philanthropic work, while John continued to work long hours at the company. When he was home for dinner, the kids would often notice how much of his conversation circled around the business. His company got so much of the family's dinnertime attention that the kids joked it was their third sibling. Ben and Ellen knew their parents loved them, but they often felt lost in the midst of their parent's many activities and competing areas of attention.

Having come from modest upbringings, John and Linda were keenly aware how diligently they both had worked to get where they were, and they wanted their children to benefit fully from the fruits of their labors. John and Linda were thrilled they could afford to send their children to high-end overnight camps and the best private schools. What they couldn't give them with their time, they gave them with opportunities.

Not wanting their kids to experience financial strain like they had during their first few years after college when John was investing all his time, money, and energy into the business and Linda was a full-time law student, they decided to pave a far easier path for their kids. They set up trust funds for Ben and Ellen, which would begin to distribute quarterly when each child turned 21. John and Linda figured that if their kids didn't have to stress about earning money, it would free them up to pursue their passions.

During high school then even more so in college, Ben's motivation flagged. He was naturally intelligent, and people had often compared him to his dad. Whenever this happened, Ben got a sinking feeling. He knew there was no way he was as smart or talented as his dad—just look at what his father had created! Ben was sure he didn't have his dad's visionary ideas or his drive, and he was fairly certain he hadn't inherited his father's Midas touch.

When Ben graduated from college, his parents assured him he'd never have to worry about money and encouraged him to travel and pursue his passions. However, at 22 years old, Ben had no idea what he was passionate about, and he felt foolish for not knowing. He assumed it was just another sign that he was not as gifted or as clear-sighted as his father. Ben had some serious inner clutter piling up in his life.

Ben dabbled in several different things throughout his 20s, but he never wanted to be tied down by a nine-to-five commitment. By his 30th birthday, he had yet to hold a significant job.

Ellen struggled in her own ways. She had always wanted to be a teacher, but shortly into her teaching career, she wrestled with the reality that her teacher's salary didn't compare to the trust distribution she was getting. Teaching was hard work and required a lot of hours. It began to feel fruitless to work so much for a relatively minimal financial return. Plus, when she was working, she couldn't join the fun trips that her parents were taking. After just one year of teaching, she decided not to return to the classroom. She considered starting a private tutoring business but didn't follow through to create a business plan or actively take any steps to implement the idea.

By their mid-30s both "kids" had stalled out. They weren't kids anymore, nor were they well-functioning adults. Their lives were full of clutter. The inner clutter of limiting beliefs, narrow mindsets, and self-identities that were more tied up in their parent's wealth than in their own ideas. And the outer clutter of goalless pursuits where their daily action could make them look busy, but both Ben and Ellen knew they weren't gaining momentum on anything that mattered to them. Since they were relying entirely on their inheritances, they were burning through their trusts at a faster rate than their parents had anticipated. John and Linda were confused. They had given Ben and Ellen every opportunity while making sure they never had to struggle. Why weren't they flourishing? Why weren't they using the resources they were given to support the pursuit of their passions—and then doing something meaningful and interesting from a place of joy?

While some of the kids' peers envied them and their seemingly ideal lifestyles, the reality was much more sobering: both Ben and Ellen were miserable. The inner and outer clutter in their lives was suffocating each of them—snuffing out any spark that might try to ignite. As they struggled to find their own paths, each felt increasingly discouraged. They watched as their friends got promotions, got into the groove with their careers, found love, started families. In contrast, Ben and Ellen felt progressively lacking—in direction, purpose, in the things that really mattered. Living in the shadow of their parents' successes and their family name, they felt increasingly unworthy and continued to flounder, developing neither the skills nor the confidence to work hard to achieve something of value to them.

The Hidden Tripwires of Growing Up with Wealth

As illustrated in Ben and Ellen McAllister's story, despite the common myth that people who are born into wealth—"born with a silver spoon," as the saying goes—don't or shouldn't have problems, next generation family members actually face plenty of less overt challenges. Though many of my clients say they won the "family lottery" and were given great advantages growing up, when we start to peel back the layers of a lifetime of accumulated beliefs, fears, and habits, consistent themes emerge from their stories. And these themes often form hidden tripwires on their paths to flourishing. They speak of their fears of failure, feelings of isolation and disconnection from their peers, a lack of motivation, and the heavy burden of worry that they'll never measure up—or worse, that they don't even know who they are or what they want apart from their family's and the public's expectations. While these are not the only tripwires aspiring rising gen experience, they are common ones and can create significant clutter in their lives. We'll explore each of these in a little more depth.

But Who Am I?

If you—or the rising gen in your life whom you care about or support as a client—have ever struggled to find your own voice and uncover or express your individual opinions and ideas, you're not alone. An **underdeveloped or overshadowed self-identity** is one of the most common tripwires of being raised in an affluent family or being gifted with significant wealth at a relatively young age.

Lindsay, a 25-year-old, fifth generation member of an enterprising family described the challenge of finding her own identity in the context of her family's wealth: "It's so strange. I pull up to the Four Seasons in a fancy car, and everyone immediately treats me like I'm somebody. Which feels pretty cool . . . until I remember that I've done nothing to be that cool. So, either I totally identify with my family's money and I have status, or I don't and I'm just me. And, no one would treat 'just me,' Lindsay, like I'm somebody. What's extra strange is I can't even get away from it. I can't find out if 'just Lindsay' is enough for me because as soon as someone finds out my last name, they treat me differently. Sometimes they treat me with admiration, sometimes with envy, and sometimes with disdain—but the way they treat me is rarely based on who I actually am."

If you are the child or grandchild of a highly ambitious and successful wealth creator, perhaps you can relate to Lindsay's pile of identity clutter. If so, you might appreciate knowing that your experience is not an aberration among the rising generation. As Jay Hughes, Susan Massenzio, and Keith Whitaker write in *The Voice of the Rising Generation*, while the transformation of a wealth creator's human capital—the combination of their gifts, talent, and vision—into material wealth is often magnificent, it also can create a black hole for those who live in its wake.[2]

Unfortunately, this black hole can absorb the attention, aspirations, and energies of individual family members, leaving them to feel like their only identity is in relationship to the wealth or the wealth creator. You may have noticed that even the language used to identify the generations within wealthy and enterprising families uses the wealth creator as the baseline (G1, or Generation 1), anchoring the idea that he or she is the beginning of the family line. The challenge or opportunity (depending on your perspective) for most rising generation family members is to ". . . create an effective individual identity strong enough to separate from, yet integrate with, the massive power of wealth itself."[3] While that may sound like a fairly straightforward formula for individual freedom, many of you know that it's not so easy. But it *is* possible—and Part II of this book will help you begin to figure out how, as well as how to disentangle yourself from these other tripwires that follow.

An Unimaginably High Bar

In addition to the challenges of finding your own voice and path, you, or the aspiring rising gen in your life, might feel an **intense pressure to succeed** paired with a **deep fear of failure**. When you're raised in a family where tremendous success is the norm, you might experience intense pressure to measure up to an unimaginably high bar, just like the majority of my clients and those who've participated in applicable research have.

Damon, an 18-year-old, fourth generation, affluent family member described the pressure of growing up in a highly successful family: "In our family, average isn't anywhere good enough. Every generation has done something more impressive than the last. What if I'm just average? Or even just above-average? What if I can't measure up to what my parents, aunts, uncles, grandparents and great-grandparents have done? That legacy is a pretty massive weight."

This experience of an immense pressure to succeed is underscored in Thayer Willis's book, *Navigating the Dark Side of Wealth*, one of the earliest published works that shed a light on the inner experience of inheritors. Willis writes, "Sometimes daughters as well as sons feel driven by their father's big shadow to work as hard as he did (or does), and this pressure may be coming entirely from within. Often, inheritors believe they must do everything better than anyone else. After all, they've been given a big leg-up in life with all their opportunities and wealth. Surely, they think, the cynics of the world would need greater proof from them than from anyone else that they are worthwhile people. Trying to provide that proof, and always failing to live up to your own impossible standards, is one of the darkest corners of the dark side of wealth."[4]

I hear time and time again how this pressure to succeed, to not be the "average" one in the family, creates a massive weight—its own form of inner clutter—and one that is heavy enough to keep many would-be rising gen stuck for years. This pressure to succeed—while in some it may drive them to obsessively chase impossible standards—in others it creates an entrenched fear of failure that—like a self-fulfilling prophecy—has a paralyzing or stunting effect.

A Quiet, Gilded Suffering

In addition to the pressure to succeed and the corresponding fears of failure, **social isolation** is another common experience of growing up with wealth. While this can stem from many sources, I frequently hear stories from clients who question the authenticity of their friendships, internalize the idea that "no one wants to hear the problems of a rich kid," and feel the confusion of society's stereotyping and judgment of who they are because they have inherited financial resources. Especially challenging is social isolation from peers.

Brad's story of his college experience captures this questioning of authentic friendships that often accompanies the rising gen social experience, even when they're in the midst of a crowd: "My family had a really great place in the mountains, and when I was in college my buddies and I would go up there a lot, especially in the winter. At first, I thought it was so cool—I liked feeling like people wanted to hang out at my place. But after a while I started to really question why people wanted to head up to the house. Did they actually like hanging out with me or was it because I had access to a cool, ski-in, ski-out house? It was pretty lonely, not knowing whether these people were really my friends or not."

For many rising gen, questioning the authenticity of friendships is exacerbated by a feeling of being utterly alone in their experience. You, or a rising gen you are pulling for, may relate to how Jared described his own gilded loneliness: "I've been given every advantage, so all I can figure is, the fact that I can't find my way out of a paper bag means I must be really lame. And there's not a friend I have that can relate. There's not a friend I have who wouldn't trade places with me. There is literally no one I can talk to that can help. Even my therapist gets sweaty and anxious when I bring up the topic of money."

Talk about a lot of inner clutter.

Compounding all of this clutter caused by questioning relationships and having few (or no) safe places to hear yourself think outload about these tripwires, you may have experienced another common tripwire, which is in itself a source of isolation: **society's projection of illegitimately gained status**. Culturally, it's common for us to hold up and praise a wealth creator but to discount the inheritor,[5] and you may be on the short end of the stick in that regard. This cultural projection is one that many rising gen unconsciously internalize as confirmation that they are "not good enough." This becomes an embedded narrative, and they may not even know why they have it; if aware of it, they are likely left to untangle it alone.

I often see inheritors deal with this discounting in one of four ways:

- They try to do more and be bigger than the wealth creator in their lives. But when the bar for success is ultra-high, this can be an intensely frustrating proposition.
- Alternately, they determine that the bar for success is too unrealistically high, so why bother? Instead of striving for their own vision of success, they do little to tap their unique potential.
- They experience shame around their wealth and choose to deal with the projection of illegitimacy by distancing themselves from their family and hiding their wealth.
- They live one facet of their lives with their friends and close social circle and another facet of their lives with their family and enterprise-related activities. My clients who do this say they feel like they are living a double life, and that they'd be mortified if their friends found out about their wealth or the prestige of their family.

An example of a combination of the third and fourth forms of discounting was shared with me by a colleague, Mary, a wealth advisor who specializes in working with clients of inherited wealth. Mary described the painful situation of a female client whose identity as an inheritor and identity as a budding restauranteur were in a fight to the death. Having unconsciously internalized some of our cultural judgments about gifted wealth, this client believed she could not legitimately be both these identities. Desperate to carve her own path, the inheritor had moved far away from her family and, in her newly adopted town, started a small café with her own earned money. When the unexpected worldwide pandemic put the brakes on the restaurant industry, this gritty inheritor faced an internal battle: use inherited resources to sustain her little café through this economic storm ... or stay true to her commitment to live only on her own earnings and close the café down. As a thoughtful advisor, Mary worked hard to help this big-hearted and committed client try to resolve this inner conflict so she could make a clear and aligned decision. Ultimately, the client decided that the café not only provided for her current livelihood (and the livelihoods of the people she employed), but it was also the most powerful way she could continue to explore her identity, separate from her family. In an act of brave identity integration, she chose to use some of her inherited money to keep the café operating through the lean pandemic months. The restaurant is now sustaining itself once again, and its owner is one step closer to integrating who she is as an inheritor and who she is as an independent businesswoman.

Most inheritors, however, don't have such a patient and wise counsel as Mary in their corner to help them sort through these very sticky issues of identity, wealth, and decision-making. Instead, when conflicts and questions around self-worth and self-determinism arise, they feel isolated and alone—remaining stuck as the clutter piles around them.

Even with engaged and observant parents and advisors in their lives, this kind of internal clutter can create a suffocating and limiting space for aspiring rising gen. This experience is exemplified by the story shared by a mom, Katherine, regarding her daughter, Megan: "Megan is amazing. I see it in her. She has such a bright light inside of her; she's intelligent, funny, and she's great with people. But I worry about her. She's had three different jobs in the last 5 years and every time she leaves one of them, she says it is because they don't respect her, she can't relate to the other team members, and they don't give her work that is commensurate with her abilities. I could believe it was true if it was one employment situation—but all three? I worry that it's actually Megan. Maybe she doesn't respect and believe in herself. Maybe she doesn't feel like she can be herself and make friends at work. Maybe she doesn't challenge herself to stretch outside her comfort zone and show what she can really do because she's scared of failing. I can hardly even talk to her about it because it so quickly becomes a fight."

I worked with Megan in my private practice, and Katherine's instincts about her daughter's inner clutter turned out to be true.

Any one of the contributing factors offered in this section is enough to cause a sense of social isolation, but taken together, they can result in a rising gen's acute disconnection from others their age and a deep-seated loneliness. Ultimately, the greatest challenge of this tripwire is feeling like you can't authentically be yourself anywhere or share your experiences in a relatable way with anyone. That is a very lonely place to be, especially when others assume that you've got it made.

Where's My Fire?

Not needing to earn income seems like it would be the greatest gift. But as illustrated in Ben and Ellen McAllister's story, when you're a younger person who doesn't need a job to cover your living expenses and you are presented with a dizzying array of choices, **faltering motivation and drive** can follow, creating their own form of inner clutter.

My client Liz had a lot of this type of clutter. She was bright and committed to finding a way to contribute to the world. In her early 30s when we first met, Liz wanted to open a yoga studio in the East Coast seaside town where she lived. She was passionate about yoga, and she had clear ideas about the studio's location, the clientele she wanted to serve, and the type of environment she wanted to create. We worked for many months on a business plan. As the launch date got closer, though, instead of getting more excited she got more deflated and became less motivated to move her plan forward.

When we delved into her low energy and inaction during a coaching session, she revealed that her parents had invited her to go on a multi-month sailing trip that fall and she really wanted to go. She liked the idea of the yoga studio, but the opportunity to sail around the Mediterranean tested her resolve. Well aware that she didn't have to make the yoga studio concept work in order to pay her living expenses, she didn't want to miss out on this enticing travel adventure. Ultimately, Liz dropped the idea of the yoga studio and went sailing instead.

More Money ≠ More Happiness

"Contrary to popular belief, inherited wealth does not conform to common economic theory where an individual's happiness increases when their benefit (like income) is maximized and their cost (like work) is minimized."[6]

If this "popular belief" were actually true, you may indeed feel as if you are in the enviable position that society perceives you to be. However, as illustrated in the stories in this chapter and likely as no surprise to you, many next gen are unhappier than their less affluent peers. As an interesting side note, research shows that while small inheritances can increase well-being, large ones typically do not.[7]

Even though most well-meaning parents and grandparents, aunts and uncles hope that the money they give their family will serve as a safety net and a way to help their relations fulfill their potential, more often the money becomes the very obstacle to that goal. Fortunately, there are proven ways to thread this tricky needle, as you will learn in the chapters that follow. While this negative outcome to significant gifted wealth is common, it's not predetermined. There is a pathway out, and it consists of two main components: shoring up one's inner skills and character strengths and learning how to clear the clutter.

The process laid out in this book will help you—or empower you to help your client, friend, or family member—to dismantle these hidden tripwires of wealth and move meaningfully, gainfully forward. Like Lindsay did.

Remember Lindsay who wondered if being "just Lindsay" would be enough? She tapped deeply into her heart and worked hard at finding her own identity, her individual voice, and her authentic inspiration. After some deep clutter cleaning, she decided to pursue a dream of starting a youth leadership nonprofit. She leveraged her intelligence, her drive, and even some of her family's capital to start up an organization that now has been serving her community for many years. While she still is learning every day how to become the fullest version of a rising gen for herself (and for her family, whom she loves), she no longer feels stuck or wonders if "just Lindsay" is enough.

Similar to Lindsay, you, too, can bust through the myth of the silver spoon, dismantle tripwires, and find your identity, your voice, your inspiration, and your drive. This doesn't mean you have to start a nonprofit or invent some business solution to be fulfilled. Your journey can take countless paths to an unlimited range of goals—what's important is that the goal is truly meaningful to you and you can clear the clutter that has been obscuring or hindering it.

This work begins with more deeply understanding what's unique about inheritors' lives and our definitions, concepts, and narratives around significant wealth itself that enables such suffocating clutter to accumulate in the first place—and then reframing that.

3

Money Versus Wealth

Rich people think they're better than others.
It's not polite to talk about money. (But it's fine to sneakily Google someone's net worth or the value of their house.)
We admire those who make money. We dismiss those who inherit it.
Wealthy people don't have real problems.
Inheritors don't have to work.
If you're rich, you have nothing to complain about.
Money is freedom.
Everything is easier for people with money.
Wealth creators are fascinating.
Wealth inheritors are lazy.
Rich people are out of touch.
Money corrupts.
It is noble to be poor.

Do any of these sound familiar? These are just the tip of the iceberg when it comes to our cultural hang-ups and judgments about money. The roots of our conflicted relationship with money and the people who earn it run deep. In fact, one of the most well-known phrases from the Bible—*"It is easier for a camel to go through the eye of a needle, than for a rich man to enter into the kingdom of God"* (Mathew 19:24)—deals with the moral burden of wealth. While scholars believe that the "eye of the needle" in this passage was actually referring to the name of a narrow gate in Jerusalem's city wall (an easier feat to pass through than a literal eye of a needle), humanity over the millennia has dropped this nuanced interpretation, increasing the generally accepted idea that it is impossible for a rich man to get into heaven. It is, perhaps, no surprise that the subject of wealth is so heavily laden with conflicting, and often unexamined, emotion. Whether you are a "have" or a "have-not," money is an inescapable, deeply charged, and dominant aspect of modern American life.

In fact, our nation's capitalistic underpinnings place money at the forefront of our very existence. We interact with it every day. If not directly, then indirectly in terms of food, shelter, clothing, transportation, lifestyle, profession, opportunities, perceived status—and the list goes on. Its basic function is in facilitating the exchange of goods and services. Like the part of the iceberg that we can see, this transactional nature of money feels easy, uncomplicated, and clear. However, it is what's beneath the murky surface—a mass of belief, identity, and unconscious relationship—that really governs our relationship and our behaviors with money. In fact, it is from this murky place beneath the surface that the number of dollars we have or don't have can feel like it dictates the daily emotional experience of our lives.

At the physical level, money is simply printed paper and metal coins—or, more often today, ones and zeroes on a microchip. It has been nearly a century since American currency left behind its ties to the value of gold. (The United States abandoned the gold standard in 1933 and completely severed the link between the dollar and gold in 1971.) So today, as a society and as a global village, we collectively agree on the dollar's economic value as a shared judgment or "faith" in the strength of the American economy. And that's just the start of our nonphysical, "below the waterline" relationship with money. We then assign traits and values to money, using it as a vehicle for control, an instrument for good, a stand-in for love, a central element of identity, a flag of freedom, a salve for emotional pain—or all of this and more.

Yet despite the tremendous powers we imbue money with, we often are at a loss when it comes to *talking about money*.

As a society in general we are markedly bad at holding meaningful conversations about money and wealth. While this isn't a problem just for the rising gen, affluence tends to increase the difficulty and complexity of these conversations.

Money—Can't Live Without It, Can't Talk About It

Take Trent and Dani and their experience of navigating their prenup. Trent is a G3 in a family with a net worth around $60 million. When he asked Dani to marry him, they both knew they would be expected to go through the process of designing and signing a prenuptial agreement. But every time they attempted to get started, they got into an argument. They wanted to focus on their wedding and envisioning their lives together . . . instead, they had to prioritize discussions about how to handle their assets if they got divorced. Trent and Dani were walking the well-worn path of many rising gen—having to think about their relationship failing right at the time when most "normal" couples would be happily planning their honeymoon.

In my work with the pair, I helped them to slow everything surrounding their prenuptial discussions down and put them and their relationship at the center of the process. We started with conversations about their individual and joint values, the messages they had each been taught (or observed) about money growing up, and how those "money stories" showed up in their adult behavior around money. Little by little, we unpacked some of what was "below the waterline" for each of them:

- As a G3, Trent felt comfortable spending money on a more luxurious life, but as the daughter of a farmer, Dani didn't waste anything, especially money. Sometimes Dani felt judgmental about Trent's spending, and it showed up in snippy comments that could trigger a fight. Prior to our conversations, neither of them had ever considered the unconscious values—in this case, "always be resourceful" for Dani and "there's always enough" for Trent—that were at the root of their disconnect.

- Both Trent and Dani worked—he as a leader in his family's company and she as a nurse—but Trent had access to far more money than he was earning through his employment. Despite both of them contributing to their daily living expenses, Dani always felt less powerful when it came to the big decisions—like where they would live or which vacation they would go on—because she couldn't contribute equally financially. This unconscious power differential resulted in her going along with whatever Trent suggested instead of asserting her own opinion. Once this "below the waterline" dynamic was named and openly discussed, Dani and Trent were able to slow down their decision-making and work together as a team to make sure they had both weighed in on important decisions.

■ Dani worked rotating shifts at the hospital, and she was often home on the days when their house cleaner came, so she typically was the one to pay her. Even though the two lived together, they had never discussed a specific plan for who covered which household expenses—they had just evolved into a system where Trent paid for some things, Dani paid for others, and on the surface, it all seemed to work out. House cleaning was one of the many expenses for which they never discussed a plan. It was a weekly expense, and it wasn't cheap, so it isn't surprising that Dani was quietly resentful that she bore the brunt of this expense just because she happened to be the one who was home when the cleaner came. Given all she and Trent had in their lives, it felt petty to bring it up, so Dani never mentioned it, but it lurked beneath the surface subtly creating discord in their relationship. It wasn't until we began to discuss how the couple wanted to handle their daily finances after they got married that Dani's frustration finally surfaced, allowing us to have a productive conversation.

In the end, Trent and Dani through intentional effort managed to improve their ability to talk about money and finish their prenup. At the conclusion of the process, they both commented to me that they couldn't believe that having to do a prenuptial agreement actually brought them *closer* together. But their challenge in getting to a place of healthy money discourse is more common of a problem than not. Despite the fact that we interact with money every day, our emotional relationship with it—and the number of decisions that get made "below the waterline" in that murky place of the unexamined subconscious—is a significant force in our individual lives, regardless of where we fall on the wealth spectrum.

★ ★ ★ ★ ★

Considering its impact on our daily lives, I find it interesting that money remains a relatively little studied and understood area of psychology. In the introduction of their 1998 book, *The Psychology of Money*, psychologists Adrian Furnham and Michael Argyle write, "There is a rich anthropological literature on the nature and meaning of gifts. There is also interesting and important sociological literature on the behavior of rich and poor people, and the social consequences of a large gap between the two. We know a great deal about the psychology of sex, but the psychology of money is one of the most neglected topics in the whole discipline of psychology."[1] Despite

Furnham and Argyle's comments being written nearly 25 years ago, the topic of money—and especially our personal relationship with it—continues to remain relatively unexplored terrain in psychology and a taboo topic in our culture. As a result, we not only lack a map that might orient us to the interpersonal terrain of money, but we also lack the language to help us even build the map.

"The Limits of My Language Mean the Limits of My World."

This Ludwig Wittgenstein quote perfectly encapsulates our challenge. Humans are meaning-making creatures. One of the most common ways we make meaning is through language. Yet there's a striking lack of vernacular to help us understand what we're talking about when it comes to money and wealth. When I say there's a lack of language, I'm not referring to the hundreds of specialized terms, lingo, and acronyms that dominate the financial and estate planning industries, describing money's many uses, means for protecting it, or ways of investing it. I'm talking about a different sphere: a lack of terminology and common modalities of discussion that could help us describe how we *feel* about money, how it's functioning in our lives right now, and what that *means* to us.

Our Relationship with Money

When I meet with a new client and inquire about their relationship with money, I'm most often met with a blank stare. "Relationship to money? What does it even mean to have a relationship with money?" Many of us aren't taught to think about money that way.

Meanwhile, we aren't nearly as limited by language when it comes to describing how we feel about other important things in our lives. Not even things as complex as the relationships we have with the people closest to us. We have a full spectrum of words to delineate our experience of others—affection to indifference, infatuation to disgust, admiration to distain. When describing a romantic prospect, for example, we might speak of having "a crush," feeling "giddy," "pining for" them, "falling for" them, "obsessing" over them, "dreaming about" them, "desiring" them, "hungering for" them, and so on. We have so many words to capture our complex relationships with other people but no real language to capture our complex relationship with money. The difference is striking. It is said that the Scandinavian countries of Norway, Finland, and Sweden have more than 180 words to describe different types of ice and snow. That's because snow is an elemental component to the culture of these countries. Money is an elemental component to the culture of a country founded upon such a predominately capitalistic system as ours. And, yet, we have no language that specifically maps our relationship to it. Do you find that as curious as I do?

Perhaps this lack of language is partially the result of the evolution from a barter-and-trade system—where two people would agree to a fair value of one product or service for another and make an exchange (which was in sporadic use even up until the end of the American pioneering days)—to our modern-day system where money has become the universal stand-in for all goods or services. In the barter-and-trade system, people were generally exchanging goods and services to get what they couldn't produce or do themselves, but one's ability to "amass wealth" was significantly limited. The production of goods and services tended to be conceptually and practically constrained to what people needed to survive and not much more. In this older economic system, transactions were more "above the waterline" exchanges—easy, uncomplicated, and clear. However, with the advent of money as a stand-in for the value of goods and services, combined much later with the specialization and mechanization that were the results of the Industrial Revolution, and still later with computerization, interconnectivity, and globalization, the ability for people to generate vastly more money than one needs to survive became more possible and widespread. As did generating it in just a few short years (opposed to over lifetimes of a family business or trade guild, etc.). While a sociologist or anthropologist could likely provide more depth to the question as to why we are missing language to understand our relationship with money, I hypothesize that the rapid growth of a general ability (beyond just the ruling class of kings and emperors) to create and hold money—and amass huge wealth—has given rise to a system where money more pervasively equals power and influence within daily life and affects the common psyche. It has taken money from a human-scaled, "above the waterline" transactional system to an emotion- and identity-triggering "below the waterline" realm of unconscious behaviors.

My client Kamal came to me when he was 27 and twisted in knots about his lack of a real job and "not doing anything meaningful" with his life. His mother is a wealth creator who has provided her children with a comfortable lifestyle and ample opportunity. I asked Kamal, "Describe to me your relationship with money." He responded by telling me how much his family was worth and giving a few details about his trust fund. I thanked him, then pressed him again, targeting his relationship with money and how it was affecting his life. He stared at me dumfounded. Then he said, "I don't even know where to begin. . . . For the most part, my mom holds the purse strings. Between my two parents, she's always been the one with a higher drive, and when the business she started really took off, she felt very comfortable being the one to make decisions in our family. She and my dad don't have a great relationship, but I think that they both think it'd be too messy to split up, so they just tolerate each other. My mom and I don't have a very good relationship either. I'm a disappointment to her, and she tries to control my behavior by turning the money spigot on and off, depending on how she's feeling and what she thinks of my current choices. My dad thinks she is unfairly punitive to me at times, and he'll often slip me money to cover expenses. It's all very messy. So, I guess I'd say I don't have a very healthy relationship with money. Or with my mom." It turns out Kamal had a lot to say about his relationship with money—it just took him a number of sessions to learn how to voice it.

If we don't have specific language to map our unique relationship with money but it's an ever-present force in our lives, how *do* we talk about it? As a result of this language vacuum, I've noticed that we tend to borrow the language of human love and loss to describe our attitudes about this inanimate object. We "lust" after money, "pursue" it, "fantasize about" it, "scheme" for it, "obsess" about it, "worry over" and "stress over" it, and . . . we're "heartbroken" when we lose it.

In short, we anthropomorphize money. More than one client has described the experience of "wealth" being like another member of the family. It becomes something that needs to be "protected" and "tended to." One client even said, "We might as well set a place for it at the dinner table. It gets most of our attention anyway."

One last important point about this default setting: Without more effective language and conversation norms to help us unpack our relationship with money, we not only lessen our ability to identify when money and wealth have become negative influences on us, we also significantly decrease our ability to see money's potential to be a force of good in our lives and in the lives of others.

The Concept of Money Versus the Concept of Wealth

Before I go on, I want to distinguish between *money* and *wealth*. I view money and wealth as two distinct but intimately related entities. I see **money** as a resource we engage with every day at the practical, transactional, and sometimes emotional levels. We tend to interact with money at a human scale, that is, in relation to our own material wants and needs. We use money to buy a latte at the corner coffee shop. We pay the cable bill with money. We use money to buy that awesome new sweater. However, when the amount of money we possess extends far beyond our material needs, we have entered the realm of **wealth**. Wealth is represented by the number that shows up on your quarterly financial statements. It's represented by the number of your family's net worth that gets discussed around big, shiny conference tables in meetings with suit-wearing advisors. It's the thing that gets tangled up with your identity when you think to yourself: "We're worth [fill in big number here]. . . ." Separating the conflation of money and wealth in our minds is not only more accurate, but also will help us when we tackle the important work of clearing our clutter—money clutter, identity clutter, and other forms—from our lives, which we'll delve into in Part II. For now, let's explore how the two concepts interrelate.

Accumulated wealth eclipses money. For people who have both, when it comes to our relationship with each, this is most common. Vast wealth takes on superhuman qualities and holds power that impacts individual wealth holders, entire families, and if directed with purpose and acumen, the world at large. Privately held wealth changes our world for the better—and the worse. But, for the rising gen especially, we can't explore the positive power of wealth without first grappling with our daily relationship with money.

Jesse, an estate planning attorney and trustee, described the awakening she had after a meeting with one of her newer beneficiaries: "We had had several meetings at this point, and I thought I was being a good coach for my beneficiary. In our meetings we had talked about the roles of beneficiary, trustee, grantor, and trust protector. We had talked about the assets that were owned by her trust. We had even done a 'Trust Treasure Hunt' exercise where I had her read her trust and we worked together to build her understanding of the concepts and terminology in it. I felt like we were doing really good work. Then, in our most recent meeting, she told me that she understood she was 'wealthy' on paper . . . but that she still had trouble over-drawing her checking account. She couldn't seem to manage the timing of when money came into her account and when it left. And she didn't really understand what I was referring to every time I mentioned her monthly 'cash flow.' Then there were her taxes. Her friends all talked about filing tax returns, but that was something she never had to do, and she didn't even understand the process of it. She was embarrassed. She said she knew it looked like she was an irresponsible 'trust fund baby,' but she really didn't understand how all this stuff worked. I was stunned. I never considered that she didn't understand *how money works.* Here I was teaching her about the more complex aspects of being the beneficiary of wealth, and she didn't even know how to balance her monthly expenses or why she didn't file her own tax returns!"

Jesse shared that she wanted to have conversations with this beneficiary about the impact her wealth could have on her life and also in the lives of others, but Jesse realized that she couldn't even broach that subject until her beneficiary understood the basics of money and developed a conscious relationship to it. Without that, the concept of "being a good steward of wealth" was just another abstract idea that sounded good but had no practical meaning to her beneficiary.

What often looks like a lazy lack of engagement can actually be masking the fact that many rising gen are missing basic building blocks—not only in understanding how money works at the transactional level, but also in being able to reflect on their day-to-day emotional relationship with money. Without these basic building blocks in place, the abstract concept of wealth— including what is most likely an even more intense and tangled emotional relationship than most people have with money—becomes a black box, something that is nearly impossible for a rising gen to engage with without feeling inadequate. In order to have the greatest opportunity for concentrated wealth to be used well—to truly become a force for good in society—we all need to first understand the *differences* between money and wealth, and then we need to support those who have both to build *healthy, skillful,* and *thoughtful relationships* with each. This effort will result in more "above the waterline" thinking around both, which will free up our individual and joint ability to create more impact and less entangled pain around them. Regardless of where one falls on the economic continuum, this honest and reflective work is necessary to find freedom and empowerment. And it is especially important work for those who have amassed (or inherited) enough money to be considered wealthy, and who, as a result, wield more power and influence.

The Paradoxical, Confusing, and Unhealthy Ways We Commonly View Those with Wealth

Culturally, we have a tangled relationship with wealth and with those who have it. We can admire the gritty entrepreneur and celebrate how he or she represents "the American Way." And we can just as quickly despise the wealthy and assume that only those who are willing to be ruthless or unscrupulous get to the top. We can envy the lifestyles we assume the wealthy have and just as quickly dismiss those lifestyles as self-indulgent and wasteful. Stereotypes aren't created out of thin air, so there is likely at least some truth behind the stereotypes we hold about the wealthy, even if making wide assumptions isn't justified.

I was recently at an exclusive beach resort to facilitate a client family meeting. This is a family for whom I have deep affection and appreciation, a family who has built a significant philanthropic organization that is creating positive impact in every community in which a family member lives. My work with this family is—and has always been—deeply meaningful to me. But during the times I was not meeting with the family, I would go about my day in this exclusive beach community—going for runs, getting coffee . . . and, as is my nature, observing those around me. There were moments when I was frustrated with what I saw, starting with the waste: food waste, packaging waste, and so much trash that could be recycled but instead would end up in a landfill. I was saddened at the lost family conversations when I watched parents drink their way through meals, all while their nanny tended to their kids at the table. I was disheartened at scenes of unaware privilege—and, as a result, I had a moment of self-doubt, wondering if I was on a fool's errand with my work and this book. I wondered if my belief that wealth can be an incredible force for good was just a nice idea, but not really how people *are* with wealth.

It is true—not all people with wealth are noble or altruistic and will use their resources and power in meaningful ways. But, momentary self-doubt aside, I can also attest to the significant number of families I know and work with who recognize that their wealth is a privilege and who take *very seriously* their responsibility to give back, enhance the lives of others, invest in organizations that are making a difference in their communities, and create organizational cultures in their family businesses where employees feel respected, supported, and honored for their contribution. I'm proud to work with these authentic, good-hearted people. They've comprised the majority of my interactions with ultra-high-net-worth families. I can't help but contrast these experiences against what—as I mentioned in this book's introduction—is one of the few remaining prejudices our society continues to bless: to pre-judge and have contempt for the rich simply for being rich. Like most complex things, our cultural relationship to wealth and to those who hold it isn't as black and white as we might want it to be.

Wealth isn't all good and worth pursuing at all costs. Nor is it inherently bad and noble to eschew. It's a tool, neutral until its engaged and wielded. And it's a powerful tool at that. The more we can collectively find a right and healthy relationship with it and with those who hold it, the more ability it will have to be a force for a common good. At the individual level, we'll deep dive in Part II's Clutter Clearing process for shining the light on these paradoxes, negative narratives, and unhelpful personal money scripts that are unconsciously influencing our identity and choices. At the societal level, I'll simply say that to simultaneously admire and revile those with wealth illustrates that, collectively, we are operating in the murky place "below the waterline" of this iceberg. So, we have some work to do.

Remember Cassie, the rising gen in Chapter 1 who spent her time torn between a sense of loyalty to her family that she loved and her quest to be seen as a legitimate artist, making it on her own? She spent a lot of time trying to detangle who she was versus who other people thought she was. Wealth has made a lot of her life and creative pursuits possible (or at least much easier), but it also created a lot of confusion about whether she—all facets of her—are acceptable in both communities she cares about. She has struggled trying integrate all parts of her life—as a wealthy inheritor trying to be an artist, an artist trying to gain legitimacy, the granddaughter of a billionaire, and a co-op community member in her funky artist neighborhood. Thank goodness she decided to step on the path of clearing out some of her inner clutter and figuring out what version of herself lay at her authentic center. She's still on her journey—learning to put aside others' judgments of her, finding her own voice and vision, and beginning to question how she can use her financial capital to pursue ideas that may have impact in the communities she cares about most, ideas that are worthy of her immense gifts. I'm grateful Cassie didn't buy into any one stereotype around money or wealth and instead found her own voice and is navigating her own—integrated—course forward.

4

Parenting Without the Worry of Making Ends Meet Should Be Easier . . . Why Isn't It?

Jason's grandfather was a Midwestern titan of business. Through the 1940s, 50s, and 60s, he built significant wealth by manufacturing parts for rail cars, eventually growing his holdings even further when he diversified and acquired multiple manufacturing businesses. He was the kind of man who had the gift of alchemy—he seemed to easily turn lead into gold. While most of Jason's grandfather's four children choose to live in the affluence afforded them by the family wealth, Jason's mother chose a different path. She moved away from her parents and treated the family money almost like a disease—often insisting that her family drive old cars and buy secondhand clothes. Jason described to me how confused and disoriented he regularly felt as a youth when his mom took him to the local Goodwill to buy clothes, but then his grandfather would pick him up on a private plane for an opulent vacation with his cousins. The reasons for this difference were never explained understandably to Jason. As an adult, Jason hypothesized that his mother was trying to protect him and his siblings from the dark side of wealth, but instead Jason ended up feeling more conflicted and pained about money than protected by his mother's actions.

Wealthy parents want the best for their kids—just like any other parent. But too often good intentions are subverted by the complexities and vagaries of this new landscape they are navigating. This chapter helps wealth-creating parents, grandparents, guardians, and family members like yourself to better understand the experience your kids may be facing—which may differ significantly from your own childhood—and how some of your choices and behaviors may be counterproductive to the life and launch you want to provide your children. These same lessons can be extended to those of you reading this book who influence the rising gen, such as professionals who support and serve in various advisory roles. Or if you're a rising gen yourself, the content of this chapter will alert you to ways you can avoid strengthening the tripwires you may have faced or may still be facing when you raise kids of your own.

The Inverted-U: There Is No Such Thing as an Unmitigated Good

There is no contention that money makes life easier. Not having to worry about food, shelter, and the safety of one's family opens up energy to focus on many other areas of growth and the pursuit of purposeful activities. However, recent research indicates that more money increases emotional well-being only to a point, after which, more money can become a stressor in itself.[1] And just as parenting in a situation with scant financial resources is very challenging, parenting in the territory of excess financial resources brings challenges of its own. This concept of the inverted-U—the notion that there is no such thing as an unmitigated good—applies to many material and psychological circumstances that surround emotional well-being.[2] As the ideas goes, all positive experiences, traits, and states have costs that, as they continue to increase, outweigh their benefits. As strange as it may seem to some, this is true of increasing levels of wealth as well.

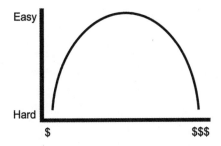

Figure 4.1   The Inverted–U Curve

In my experience of working with affluent families, one of the greatest fears parents have is that they are going to unwittingly "ruin" their children by giving them too much, telling them too much, or making their lives too easy. This is the top concern parents of wealth come to me with. And it's an understandable fear. Currently, 80% of American wealth is new wealth—it has not been inherited from a previous generation[3]—so most parents in this economic demographic are attempting to do something that has not been role modeled by their own parents. And when I talk to many of the rising generation themselves who are now contemplating how to raise their own kids amid affluence, even if they did have some role modeling from their parents, there are still many things these rising gen would choose to do differently.

Unfortunately, high-net-worth parents and grandparents often *do* give their offspring too much and make their lives too easy or support their heirs in inconsistent ways—giving when the wealth-creating generation feels appreciated and holding back or becoming controlling when they don't. Instead of making decisions based on core values and long-term goals that elder generations have for the thriving of their kids and grandchildren, they too often make reactionary decisions based on current emotions and the highly changeable circumstances of the moment. (They are, after all, human and imperfect, with scarce examples to follow and few resources to call out behaviors resulting in unintended consequences.) These inconsistencies compound the stressors brought on in an inverted-U wealth environment.

So, to put us on the path of mitigating these stressors, let's delve into a useful construct for understanding how and why wealth can turn the curve from benefit to detriment in someone's life.

Ages and Stages

To find our way parenting or influencing in this territory of wealth, it'll be helpful to have a framework for understanding what healthy developmental lifecycle looks like. Erik Erikson's theory of psychosocial development identifies eight stages that make up a healthy, lifetime developmental cycle.[4] In each of these stages, a specific psychological need or crisis comes in conflict with a need of society. In order for individuals to grow through a specific stage and into the next stage, they have to resolve the crisis of their current one. The four stages of development outlined next are a condensation of Erikson's theory and its adaptation to individuals within significant families as outlined in Jay Hughes, Susan Massenzio, and Keith Whitaker's book, *The Voice of the Rising Generation*.[5]

Teen Years

The teen years are all about **Focusing on the Self**. This time of life is characterized by moving from dependence to independence and moving from one's family group as a primary social system to one's friend group as a primary social system. This is also a time of increased risk-taking, but without the guardrails of fully formed executive functioning that doesn't develop within the brain until the mid-20s. This is often a time when important lifetime character traits, such as grit and growth mindset, are tested and strengthened through life experiences.

20s and 30s

As individuals move into their 20s and 30s, the most important life themes focused on are **Breaking Loose** and **Building a Nest**. What becomes most significant in moving through these stages are the search for identity, building a career, learning to handle adult responsibilities, and finding a partner. The presence (or absence) of important lifetime character traits (such as grit and growth mindset, among many others) becomes apparent as emerging adults seek to individuate and create their own lives.

40s and 50s

Transitioning to one's 40s and 50s, the focus is on **Looking Around** and **Mid-Life Rebirth.** These stages are often characterized by parenting teens, asking deeper questions about life, and re-inventing the self and one's identity.

60s and Onward

Finally, in the 60s and beyond, key tasks are **Investing in Life, Deepening Wisdom**, and living into the **Twilight Years**. This often looks like experiencing life as an empty nester, redefining and acting upon new or evolved values, the mellowing that comes with life experience and wisdom, and adjusting to the inevitable physical limitations of a declining body.

★ ★ ★ ★ ★

Individuals across the economic spectrum need to find their way through each of these stages in order to experience healthy development across the life-span. As was illustrated with the inverted-U discussed previously, significant financial resources may actually become an unhelpful buffer to this process, impeding growth, engagement, and, ultimately, individual well-being. Let's look at the ways in which wealth can create or exacerbate hurdles to an individual meeting the key challenges of each of these stages.

Focusing on the Self. At a time when building independence and becoming responsible is key, wealth can mute responsibility and accountability, creating a "marshmallow effect" where teens never have to experience the hard edges of their own decision-making because wealth can "soften the edges." Developmentally, when risk-taking is at its lifetime highest, wealth can create a buffer to experiencing the natural (and sometimes very painful) consequences of one's choices, which can impede important growth needed in this developmental stage. Also, at this stage when friends become the central social group, wealth can distort a teen's experience of friendships. Whether it's exposure to only a homogenized social group (i.e., only hanging out with the "rich kids") or peers either discounting them or gravitating to them because of their wealth rather than deeper aspects of their selves, cultivating authentic friendships can be more challenging.

Breaking Loose and **Building a Nest.** At a time when the search for one's identity is fundamentally important, it can be hard for emerging adults to find their own voice and identity in the midst of a significant family that may not only have substantial financial resources but may also have a very recognizable name. This is a stage where individuating and differentiating from one's family of origin is of outmost importance, and yet, significant families—with their higher profile, joint assets, family philanthropy, and joint decision-making—have their own kind of gravity that can keep calling an emerging adult "back home" to engage with the family of origin. A young adult's developing identity can easily get swallowed. Jason, in this chapter's opening story, illustrates this struggle to individuate. As Jason strove to define his own relationship with money and wealth, he remained engaged in some family assets requiring joint decision-making with his family of origin. As a result, he often found himself re-entangled with the confusing money scripts handed down to him by his mom. The 20s and 30s are also the time in life when finding a job, a career, or ways to meaningfully contribute to one's community is essential to growth, yet many rising gen find that having wealth gives them *too many* choices. (Graduate school? Work for the family business? Get an entry-level job? Support the family's philanthropic work? Travel?) They become paralyzed by the possibilities, often taking meaningful action on none.

Looking Around and **Mid-Life Rebirth.** This is a time in life when the hard work of parenting teens can lead to questions (and often disagreements between partners) regarding how to parent based on communicated boundaries and in a consistent way, even more so for those who want to parent in ways leading to natural consequences and learning opportunities for their child. Even when the difficult work of parenting teens begins to ease up as emerging adults move out of the house, parents are left to consider their lives and what's next for them. Life's big questions are revisited. Often, unresolved insecurities from earlier stages can exacerbate the questioning of choices made in those earlier times (such as with one's marriage and career) and can create turmoil and unrest. If marriages run into difficulty, wealth can compound the challenge of considering divorce as a viable option. These stages are marked by questioning and re-examining and often lead to difficulty and discord—which some people avoid by traveling excessively, substance use, and other distractions—but which must be reckoned with in order to find peace and resolution.

Investing in Life, Deepening Wisdom, and the **Twilight Years.** In these stages, worry over the impact of wealth on the lives of children and grandchildren can loom large, causing stress and conflict in family systems. For the wealth creator specifically, questions of identity can become difficult and even threatening. The desire for control may distort decisions about family wealth, family governance, and estate planning. This is also a time when philanthropic and enterprise-related issues of succession and transition priorities may take precedence, but it may also feel like "work" when such obligations may not be welcome. Just "walking away from it all and enjoying retirement" often doesn't feel like an option for the wealthy. This is a time when questions of legacy and impact can rear up larger than ever.

Parenting Well in the Inverted-U: Values, Role Modeling, and Intentional Family Culture

If there is no such thing as an unmitigated good and some amount of struggle is a healthy stimulant for growth, how do parents with financial means begin to think about parenting *well* in this context? We'll get into the nuts and bolts of finding your successful path to parenting in the midst of family wealth in Chapter 12, but for now, let's address three valuable approaches to help navigate this journey.

Decisions Grounded in Values, Not Circumstances

One of the fundamental reasons that parenting amid vast financial resources becomes more difficult is because, when you are no longer experiencing limitations that life circumstances impose on a parent, you have to be very clear in your vision for what thriving looks like for your family and in the lives of your kids. And you have to make sure that your decisions are grounded in your values that inform that vision.

Imagine your teenager comes to you saying he wants to join a traveling youth soccer team. You know participation includes hefty fees. What's the conversation you have with him? *Do* you have a conversation—or just pay the fees knowing you can afford it? In this situation, parents who aren't as financially blessed as you may end up having to say something like, "Paul, I wish we could afford all the fees for club soccer, but we just can't squeeze it into our budget. We'll support you to play on the local team, but if you want to play on this competitive traveling team, you're going to have to find a way to come up with the extra money to pay the travel fees. Maybe get an after-school job and postpone joining if need be." Now, here's what you might say as a wealthy parent who wants their child to thrive but also values imparting a healthy understanding of how money works and the lessons brought by choosing amidst limitations: "Johnny, we know you want to play club soccer. This is a big commitment with significant costs, and it's important to us that you also have buy-in. We're going to request that you contribute 25% of the fees. Whether this contribution comes from saving your allowance or maybe a part-time job . . . we leave that up to you."

Notice the difference between the two responses. In the first example, external circumstances are imposing a limit that is going to force Paul to decide how badly he wants to play on the travel team, and if he decides he does want to, he's likely going to learn some valuable lessons about problem-solving, earning income, perseverance, and commitment. In the second example, Johnny is equally as likely to learn these important lessons, but the limits are being imposed by you as the parent, in alignment with your values, rather than the external circumstances of a limited household budget. It can be a subtle difference, but it's an important one.

Parents who make decisions that are *grounded in their values* and *align with their vision of thriving* for their family members are better able to set, and hold, limits that help their children build important life skills.

Money can solve many problems. As parents, we have to be clear which problems we want it to solve (e.g., food and shelter) and which we want to intentionally *not* let it solve (e.g., anything that removes an appropriate level of difficulty from our kids' lives). We'll get into *why* struggle is important when we delve into the research on Learned Helplessness and Learned Mastery later in the book, but for now, just remember that some level of "desirable difficulty" is essential for individual thriving. Mitch and Kristy's story exemplifies this perfectly.

Mitch and Kristy had "millionaire next door" wealth with a family net worth around $7 million. When their oldest daughter was nearing 16, they wrestled with how to approach a car for her. They had enough money to buy whatever car she would want, but something about that approach felt very uncomfortable to both of them. Having both grown up in families where there was always "enough" but not a lot more, they both had started out with second- (or third-!) hand cars. They each remembered loving the freedom their rusty old cars provided them. They wanted that freedom for their daughter, but they also could see how quickly the "freedom of a rusty old car" could turn into an expectation that "I get what I want." After some work with me unpacking their own stories of their first cars and questioning the reasons they felt it would be beneficial for their daughter to have a car, they were able to get to the root values they felt they learned through their rusty old cars—freedom and responsibility. They could see how just buying their daughter the brand-new car of her picking (and paying for it, the registration, and the insurance) might give her a sense of freedom, but it would rob her of an important mantle of responsibility (and ownership in the process) that a big purchase like this could provide. But buying her a modern-day version of their rusty old cars also wasn't an option—neither Mitch nor Kristy was willing to trade safety for their "clunky teenage car" experience. With a little more digging we came up with a solution: identify a minimum criterion for safety and efficiency (e.g., the car must have anti-lock brakes, crumple zones, and get at least 20 miles per gallon) and a budgeted amount for the purchase under which they would pay 75% and ask their daughter to pay the other 25%. They decided on $15,000 as their budgeted amount. They determined that it was possible to get a recent model year car with all the modern safety features for that amount of money (at that time). It wouldn't be a luxury car, but it would be clean, safe, and reliable. If their daughter wanted something that cost more, she was welcome to come up with her 25% of the $15,000 and the additional amount over that. While it was more work for all of them to approach the car purchase this way, the end result was worth it.

Ultimately, their daughter worked with Mitch and Kristy to research her options, test drove good candidates, and made a decision with her parents' guidance. It took her the rest of high school to pay back her parents for her part of the car, and she later recalled how much she loved and valued her car because it truly felt like hers.

I love this story because it shows wealthy parents making a big decision grounded in their personal values rather than merely reacting to circumstance. Key takeaways are how the couple *questioned the reasons* they felt it would be beneficial to (partially) give their child a major gift in the first place, *unpacked their own stories* of their first cars, and *identified the root values* they learned from their early car experiences. They also gave their daughter realistic *agency through choices within agreed limits.* It's also important to note that this intentional decision-making *took effort;* it was more work for those involved. But by not taking the easy way out, the parents and this rising gen gained so much more.

Positive Role Modeling

It is often said that values are "caught," not "taught." It matters more what kids *see* in our behavior than what we *tell* them their behavior should be. The more honest, gritty, loving, and respectful a parent is, the more honest, gritty, loving, and respectful their children will likely be. But the key is that it has to show up in our daily actions, not our words. What kids mimic isn't who we aspire to be but who we are.

In the early 1960s, psychologist Albert Bandura conducted an experiment where he assigned preschool children to three groups. One of the groups watched adults play quietly with an inflatable doll called a Bobo doll, the second group watched adults play aggressively with the Bobo doll, and the third group had no exposure at all to these adult role models. When the children were then asked to interact with the Bobo doll, only the children who observed the aggressive adults were aggressive with the Bobo doll. In fact, they mimicked what they watched with great precision—hitting, kicking, sitting on it, and smacking it with a mallet, just as they had seen the adults do.[6,7] The level of mimicry is striking (and unsettling).

Since our kids are watching us all the time, there are three ways we can use role modeling to our parenting advantage: (1) making transparent to our kids the things we do every day but that our kids may not see (like struggling with a difficult problem at work and persevering through it— we may do this regularly, but what they see is the successful outcome, not the struggle); (2) paying attention to what we're *not* doing but wish we were (like finding a purposeful and inspiring way to contribute each day); and (3) paying attention to what we *are* doing but wish we weren't (like ignoring self-care or self-medicating emotional pain with food, alcohol, or chronic busyness).

Remember Tracey and Avery from Chapter 1? Avery's mother Tracey struggled with how to support her daughter—who was challenged by learning differences and flagging self-confidence—to find her own path forward while her father and older sister had found success in their own rights. In another layer of that story, one of the many ways that 24-year-old Avery sabotaged her own success was with a regular alcohol habit. When we dug into when and why she would drink, she told me that it was the only time she could "escape the pressure" felt within her. In a separate and unrelated conversation I had with her father, he told me about a recent family dinner where the adult children had both come home for an evening with their parents. He mentioned in an off-handed way that things were tense when everyone first arrived, but conversation was much easier and more enjoyable once they'd all had some wine. From his manner and wording, it was clear to me then where Avery got the message that alcohol was an "effective" means for dealing with tension that she didn't know how to manage.

As parents, role modeling is one of the most powerful tools we have in our tool belt. As illustrated in Avery's story, our kids are highly likely to mimic us—whether the behaviors are ones we want them to mimic or not. One effective positive role modeling practice is to make transparent things you do to learn, grow, and stretch every day, but that your kids may not see. A manageable way to do this is to have dinner conversations where you each share stories from your day, highlighting times when you were challenged by a problem and talking about how you handled it. We often assume that our kids know that we're just humans who also struggle and sometimes get tripped up, but that's often not the case. Especially in families where kids are steeped in the success around them, it is not a big leap for them to assume that their parents have a "magic gene for success" (a gene the children may worry they don't have). Sharing dinner-time stories of struggle, problem-solving, and perseverance—and asking your kids to share the same kinds of stories from their days—normalizes and elevates important traits such as hard work, grit, and growth mindset. This type of intentional and positive role modeling often results in the creation of a supportive and inspiring family narrative that ends up running through the veins of all family members. Ultimately, this kind of narrative feeds a positive family culture—a lived experience of "who we are."

Intentional Family Culture

Related to, and as an extension of, the role modeling parents provide in a family is the family culture they jointly create. The culture of any human system is a combination of its priorities, habits, traditions, beliefs, values, and choices. At its heart, culture represents "who we are" as a family. It answers: What do we stand for? How do we identify? Where do we invest our time? How do we treat one another? How do we treat others outside the family?

Family culture becomes the environmental container that, ultimately, influences individual behavior and choices. This interplay between environment and individual human behavior was captured in 1936 by psychologist Kurt Lewin in this single simple equation: $B = f(P,E)$.[8] Translated, this equation states: *behavior is a function of both the person and their environment*. If we fail to consider how one's environment impacts human behavior, then we are missing an important and powerful lever in supporting successful outcomes for our kids.

All families lie somewhere on a continuum between intentionally designing their family culture and passively defaulting to whatever culture emerges as the result of two individuals originally from different family cultures now partnering to create a new family system. Both situations create consistent behaviors, but families who are more *intentional* in designing their family cultures tend to more reliably generate the behaviors they hope to create. Families who have an unintentional, default family culture are more likely to generate default behaviors (which they may or may not be happy about). No family sets out to raise their kids in a default-based, confusing, and contradictory family culture, but it is often the result if a family doesn't engage in some level of intentional design. Often, where we get tripped up is in outwardly espousing one desired cultural value (e.g. "in our family we work") but then incentivizing another. Liz's story from Chapter 2 typifies this type of conflict between what we say we want for our family and the behavior we actually incentivize.

Recall that Liz was pursuing opening a yoga studio. She'd done the hard work of visioning, planning, and budgeting for her business, and she was ready to move forward into implementation when her mom asked if Liz wanted to join her and Liz's father on a multi-month sailing trip. Liz's father had been a hard-working wealth creator before retiring, and he had always told his kids that he expected them to work and contribute to their own lives. Though Liz struggled to get momentum in a career, she had internalized this message and continued to pursue a livelihood about which she could feel proud. As her parents' wealth had increased, they'd found themselves less able to relate to their old friends and didn't feel like they had any peers who really "got" them. This, combined with the fact that they enjoyed the time they spent with all their adult children, made it easy for them to ask their kids to join them on their adventures. Likely without even realizing it, their compelling invitations created inner conflict for their adult children, especially Liz who had not yet experienced enough professional momentum to keep her grounded and focused on the pursuits of her own life. Despite hearing throughout her years how important it was to work and earn her own way, the lure of accepting her mom's invitation for the free sailing trip trumped her commitment to push forward with her yoga studio.

On reflection, were Liz's parents fostering the family culture they exposed? Were they aware of the critical juncture their daughter was at when they incentivized her lack of follow-through? Parenting is one of the most difficult roles a person can take on, so I don't ask this to criticize but rather to illustrate how our family culture—whether strong and intentional or default and diffused—can have a far greater influence on our children than we may realize.

★ ★ ★ ★ ★

While there may be no such thing as an unmitigated good, it is entirely possible to navigate these tricky parenting waters with grace, grit, and clarity. We'll get into more guidance in Chapter 12, but I hope you've at least seen that we can confront the myth of the silver spoon in the parenting arena as well. Now, on to solutions. Our starting place for thriving—whether we are a parent, grandparent, other family member, rising gen, friend, or influencer—is to internalize the process for recognizing and clearing the wealth-related clutter that can pile up in our lives . . . especially in the lives of rising gen.

PART

II | Clearing the Clutter

5

Money Clutter

Sun is the 32-year-old son of an American success story. His father, who was born in China and immigrated to the United States as a teenager, has a steely work ethic and, in his mid-70s, is still outworking every person in his company. Sun tried to join his father's company after college, but soon found that his father's presence loomed too large, and he was unable to carve out his own place in the business. After several years, he left the company, taking with him his shrunken confidence and a lack of direction for his life. Sun tried to go back and earn an MBA but found his heart wasn't in it. In an attempt to create some space for himself, he moved into one of the family's vacation homes where he thought he could catch his breath and start fresh. That was 7 years ago. And he hasn't held a paying job since.

When Sun talks about his situation, he'll claim that he is "the poorest rich kid [he] know[s]." The majority of his living expenses—including the family vacation home he occupies—are paid for and tracked by staff who take care of accounting and bill pay for the family. He was given a company credit card when he worked for his father's business, and sometimes he still uses that to pay for things he wants or needs (no one has ever told him to stop). But after 7 years of not earning income, he has little of his own money left, and he feels he can't make any decisions about his life without asking for permission from his parents. He has no sense of the funds flowing in and out of accounts on his behalf each month and no idea how much money it takes to support his lifestyle. When he is most despondent, he wonders what it would be like to break free and live by his own mettle, but without any sense of what supporting himself financially requires, the spark of his possibility-thinking quickly extinguishes. Sun jokingly claims he is a "man-child"—a grown man who, like a child, is still supported by his parents and, because of this, needs to get their buy-in for any major decision in his life.

Sun has a lot of clutter, not the least of which is money clutter. One of the four types of clutter that rising gen commonly face, **money clutter** is limiting beliefs and behavioral patterns we hold or follow involving money that are harmful to our overall well-being; for instance, a self-narrative that equates family money with self-worth or shame, or a lack of basic monetary skills such as the inability to budget, track expenses, or understand the concept of credit. Sun's lack of engagement with the flow of money through his daily life has created a pile of money clutter—one so large he can't even imagine his path to independence.

Family Wealth and the Formation of Money Clutter

As I wrote in Chapter 3, I consider money and wealth to be separate but intertwined concepts. When we are using money to pay bills or to purchase things, we can experience it on a human scale. But when the amount of money we have far exceeds our needs (and perhaps also our ability to relate to it), we have entered the domain of wealth.

Unlike money, wealth can be tricky to make sense of on a human level. You may know the numbers—how much your family is worth, how much you are individually worth or in control of, the value of your family enterprise—but what do those big numbers actually mean in your life? When I talk to inheritors or think about it myself, those numbers (as exact and seemingly concrete as they may be) are also, paradoxically, abstractions.

The dollar amounts might evoke a range of contrasting concepts, such as security, power, powerlessness, limitless possibility, suffocating weight. And trying to understand what wealth actually *is* and what it personally *means to you* isn't straightforward. As one client told me, "As soon as I try to understand my family's wealth—what it means to me and how I relate to it, or what others think about me because of it—everything I'm trying to make sense of quickly goes to spaghetti in my head."

I know many rising gen for whom their day-to-day relationship with money is relatively healthy, while their relationship with their wealth is confounding or even unhealthy. But the majority of the inheritors I work with are more like Sun—challenged by *both* their daily relationship with money and their feelings about their wealth. For these clients, we set the concept of *wealth* aside for a moment, and we begin by taking a close look at their relationship with *money*. We look not only at their concepts and feelings about money, but also their resulting actions and patterns of behavior. We do so with a non-judgmental yet clear-eyed view—just trying to map the beliefs, behaviors, and resulting consequences. Awareness and knowledge are powerful tools. Especially to the clearing of suffocating money clutter. In my experience, dealing with money clutter first is a tangible way for an aspiring rising gen to begin gaining confidence and some footing in their lives. Practical wins are gained from lower-hanging fruit. While clearing money clutter doesn't necessarily clear the clutter that surrounds wealth, it's a great start. Very often, the clutter that surrounds wealth is co-mingled with one's identity issues and with challenges around a sense of contribution in the world, so we'll look at the clutter which arises from wealth more closely when we explore those two forms—identity clutter and contribution clutter—in the following chapters.

For now, let's set the groundwork to identify and clear some money clutter of your own.

Sources of Money Clutter

Where does money clutter come from? How does it begin to take hold? As we explored earlier, our culture has a complex relationship with the concept of money. We lack the language to help us name our relationship with it, and as a result, we can easily anthropomorphize money, making it into something that we may not intend it to be in our lives. So while culturally we have a lot of commonly held money clutter, I most often see four specific sources of money clutter in the lives of rising gen family members. The first two sources that I typically witness are the drivers of inner money clutter, and the second two sources are the drivers of outer money clutter. We'll start by exploring the inner sources first.

One of the top sources of inner money clutter that the next generation within wealthy families has is **confusing and disempowering "money scripts"** handed down (mostly) from parents or grandparents. These money scripts are overt or inadvertent messages that create confusion about what money is and what it isn't. No one intends to pass on confusing messages about money to their kids, but like many beliefs and attitudes that transmit through generations, our (often unexplored and unconscious) ideas about money and wealth get transmitted as well. We'll see examples later in this chapter.

As a result of these money scripts, many inheritors also have a second source of inner money clutter—an **unconscious (and often unhealthy) relationship with money and wealth**. This may take many forms (including both under-identifying and over-identifying with money and wealth, which we'll look at more closely in the next chapter), but it usually results in a lack of engagement with money as a tool in their lives. This inner clutter is exemplified in a comment made by a rising gen client who was on the journey to clearing her own clutter when she admitted to me: "I just don't know the value of a dollar. I'm embarrassed to admit this, but it's true. I don't pay attention to how much it costs to buy coffee, how much we spend when we eat out, or how much I spend on groceries. I literally never even look at the receipt or pay attention to the total. If you asked me how much it costs for me to live each month, I couldn't even give you a ball-park guess."

This lack of engagement with money as a resource and tool leads to an outer source of money clutter, **underdeveloped personal money management skills**. Like the previous story of Sun, the inability to track cash flow, live within a budget, or make a financial plan to support an idea is a behavior that ends up limiting the possibilities a rising gen can act on or even imagine for their lives.

Finally, compounding the underdeveloped personal money management skills is the **unconscious and unintentional infantilization of next gens** that often results from having highly competent professionals handling all aspects of money and wealth in their lives—from filing taxes to paying bills to tending to the personal and business accounting for the family. While this may feel like a benefit (who wants to deal with filing taxes every year?), it keeps aspiring rising gen from understanding how money works and taking ownership of building personal money management skills that will serve them—and their pursuit of independence—well.

You can see that money clutter, like all clutter, has both inner and outer elements. As I mentioned in Chapter 1, the most effective way to start to clear a pile of money clutter is to tend to your inner clutter first and then tackle the outer clutter. This requires getting real about the mindsets and beliefs you have about money (inner clutter) and then by developing healthy and consistent habits and behaviors in how you interact with and manage your money (outer clutter). As a reminder of this clutter clearing process, revisit Figure 1.1 in Chapter 1.

In the next three sections, I'll walk you step by step through first the inner work then the outer work my clients do to identify their money clutter and to clear it, forging in its place an intentional, empowered relationship with money. If you are a parent, grandparent, spouse, professional advisor, or other influencer who is reading this book, I'd encourage you to engage in the exercises included here—and in the next three clutter-clearing chapters—yourself. While these exercises have been designed for the aspiring rising gen in your life, we could all probably clear out a little more of our own clutter. The more you clear for yourself, the better able you'll be to support the rising gen you care about to do the same.

Inner Work: How Healthy Is Your Relationship with Money?

Regardless of how much money any of us does or doesn't have, we *all* have a relationship with money. Whether our relationship with it is one of scarcity or abundance, freedom or invisible strings, easy flow or tooth-and-nail fight, or even joy or pain, in our culture, we interact with money on a daily basis.

Being honest with yourself about how *you* feel about money is a must if you want to develop a positive, empowered, and decluttered relationship with both money and wealth. Many terrific resources are available to support you on your inner journey with money. Two of my favorites are *The Seven Stages of Money Maturity* by George Kinder and *The Soul of Money* by Lynne Twist. But even before you turn to a new book, the simplest way to jump-start a more conscious relationship with money is to reflect upon your current lived experiences with it.

Shining a Light on Your Hidden Money Relationship

Often our mindsets toward, identities about, and beliefs regarding concepts in our lives get all intermingled with each other. While we know that part of clutter clearing is teasing out how one's mindset informs their identity, their identity informs their beliefs, and their beliefs inform their decision-making, to get started it's less important to understand whether what you're dealing with is a "mindset," an "identity," or a "belief" and more important just to shine a light into the dark corners we often don't explore.

Following are several reflection questions to help you do this. I recommend taking an active approach: consider getting out a favorite pen and a journal—or your tablet or laptop if that's more your style—and carve out time to reflect and write your responses to these questions. I strongly encourage giving yourself the space to deeply consider each query before reading further. I assure you it will be time well spent. And it will make the rest of this chapter's content even more useful.

1. What are the first adjectives that come to mind when you think about money?
2. If money were a person, what characteristics would it have? Is this someone you would choose to be friends with?
3. What are the most common feelings that arise when you think of money (they may show up as something you feel in your body, a picture, or an emotion)?
4. On a scale of 1–10 (with 10 being super easeful), how easeful does money feel to you?
5. What stresses you out when you think about your relationship to money?

Reflect upon your answers and consider if there are any themes or patterns that have emerged. Did an answer surprise you? When completing this exercise, was your overall feeling positive and uplifted or negative and heavy? Remember, for most of us, the majority of what drives our relationship with money are deep, below-the-waterline mindsets, beliefs, and messages that we have internalized and likely do not even know are there. Pause for a moment and pay attention to how you are feeling. The first step to clearing clutter is recognizing that the clutter exists. The emotional tone you have after completing this exercise can help you begin to shine a light on the money relationship quietly at work in the corners of your mind.

Uncovering Your Money Scripts

Now that you have more clarity around the overall emotional tone of your relationship with money, the next step to transforming that relationship is to understand your money scripts—the messages about money that have been handed down to you from your parents, grandparents, other family members, or society-at-large. These beliefs around money may feel prescriptive—like you ought to embrace them without question. Or they may be ideas that you heard touted as important, but then you may not have seen actually practiced in your family. Some scripts may be implicit and others explicit. Some may be helpful and others limiting or damaging. The Money Messages© is a tool[1] designed by 21/64, a nonprofit training and family facilitation firm. This tool, designed for multi-gen families, is a resource that can help you identify the money scripts that may be at play for you (see the Appendix A for where to find this, as well as a host of other helpful 21/64 tools). Following is a list from that tool of some of the "scripts" mostly often claimed by rising gen:

> It's your responsibility to give back.
> Be grateful for what you have.
> We don't talk about money.
> You'll never have to work.
> We made sacrifices so you could have this.

You may see how some of these commonly held Money Messages are driving your own relationship with money, and you may also experience others not listed here. I often hear other money scripts from clients as well: "We put our pants on one leg at a time, just like everyone else." "Money is a tool." "Follow your passion; don't worry about earning money." "Inherited money ruins lives." "Your value does not lie in your bank account—you have so much more to offer." What other money scripts can you think of that you heard or internalized growing up?

★ ★ ★ ★ ★

Now that you've read through these common money scripts once, revisit the list (including all of those you've added) and consider the following questions and instructions. As with the previous exercise, you'll get the most benefit from this exploration if you take the time to write your answers.

1. Circle all the money scripts previously listed that you believe impact your relationship with money.
2. Are there ones you've heard or experienced in your family that aren't on this list? If so, write them down as well.
3. Do you find any of these scripts to be unhelpful? If so—and if you'd like to pluck them out of your mind like a weed out of a garden—please strikethrough or mark those.
4. Are there any of these messages that, as a conscious and engaged adult, you'd like to plant and let grow in your mind? Put a star next to those.
5. Please also consider and note money scripts that trigger conflicting feelings within you. Your experience of this might be similar to Cassie's at the beginning of Chapter 1. For example, you might feel an uncomfortable contrast or disconnect around how you have internalized and adopted a particular money script as compared to how you hear that same message and attitudes about it expressed by your coworkers, acquaintances, and even friends and family. You might put a question mark next to these and come back to them after you've complete a round or two of the seven-step clutter clearing process presented later in this chapter.

Once you have clearly identified which Money Messages or money scripts best reflect who you *want* to become in your improved relationship with money, write them down on a notecard or sticky note. Place them where you'll see them each day. Give yourself the daily opportunity to bring into your conscious awareness if and how you are aligning your actions with the intent of that message. While the value of the exercise on the previous pages lies mostly in intentionally bringing to surface and evaluating your money scripts, you may be surprised at the transformative power of such a seemingly small step as taping up a reminder.

★ ★ ★ ★ ★

By reflecting on the quality of your relationship with money and the money scripts that you've inherited or assimilated in one way or another—and by proactively choosing to release those that no longer serve you and accentuate those that do—you'll have taken significant action on your way to building a positive and engaged relationship with money. Next, we'll use the insights you gained in the previous two exercises to actively begin to clear your inner money clutter.

Clearing Your Inner Money Clutter

Remember from Chapter 1 that we have a seven-step clutter clearing process, with the initial four steps designed to clean out inner clutter:

---

1. Cultivating a Beneficial Mindset

Mindset informs identity. It determines what attributes we hold consciously or unconsciously and how we handle and process the information around us. This first step of Cultivating a Beneficial Mindset means we become aware of what filters we use to make decisions. To reveal the mindset we're using we answer telling questions like, "Do I feel stuck where I am or can I always find a path for learning and growth?"

↓

2. Adopting an Empowering Identity

Identity informs our beliefs. It determines how we think of ourselves. The second step of Adopting an Empowering Identity challenges us to answer questions like, "Who am I? What criteria am I using to define who I am? Who do I want to become? Does the way I define myself support who I want to become?"

↓

3. Curating Supportive Beliefs

Beliefs inform our decisions. They confirm and support our sense of identity. The third step of Curating Supportive Beliefs asks us to consider questions such as, "What do I believe is possible for someone like me? Am I capable? What would I need to believe in order to feel capable?"

Figure 5.1

4. Making Aligned Decisions

Decisions inform our actions. We make decisions based on what we believe—what is right, what is possible, what is realistic for the person we believe ourselves to be. The fourth step of Making Aligned Decisions challenges us to address questions like, "What beliefs am I using to make this decision? What would someone who felt capable and confident in this situation do? What decision do I need to make to be aligned with who I am committed to be?"

Figure 5.1   (*continued*)

Based on this process, and using the insights you gained from the exercises you just completed, following is a series of Reflection Questions to help you identify and clear some inner clutter money in your life. With this exercise and all the clutter clearing exercises to come, if you can't answer a question right now—if you literally draw a blank and don't know what you'd respond—don't get frustrated. Set it aside and move on to the next question. Try coming back to the question or questions that had you stumped after finishing this book. Remember, this is a cycle, and you'll have more clarity and insight as you move through the process.

Beginning to gain clarity on what mindsets, beliefs, and parts of your identity are operating beneath the surface will help you to see where you are making decisions that are aligned with what you *want* to create in your life and where you might be defaulting to unconscious patterns and beliefs. Give yourself permission to release the old patterns of thinking and beliefs and make room for what you intentionally want to cultivate. It can be as simple as telling yourself, "This is no longer the thinking that I want to have, and I don't have to be beholden to it. I can discard it, like clutter from a closet. While that may take me seconds or days or even years to fully release, I am starting that process right now. I'm freeing

	Reflection Questions
STEP 1. Cultivating a Beneficial Mindset	Thinking about the emotional tone I experience in my relationship with money (from the previous exercise), how might that emotional filter be supporting or sabotaging the mindset I have around money? *(For example, you may have an overall negative feeling toward money and have been able to identify that you feel controlled by it. Being able to name that as an unhealthy filter through which you've been experience money is a form of taking ownership of your filters and clears mental space to imagine an alternative, beneficial one—a first step toward changing your mindset around money).*
	When I consider the money scripts listed previously, what was the most positive and empowering message I identified? How might I use that empowering money script as a filter to guide decisions in my life?
STEP 2. Adopting an Empowering Identity	What is[are] the most important aspect[s] of myself that I want people to know and experience?
	How often do I feel like people see me for that (above) versus my last name or my financial situation? In what situations have I felt like people do see me as that (above)?
	How do I think of myself? How integrated or separate are money and wealth to my identity?
	If you stripped wealth from my life, what would remain about who I am? Is that pleasing and exciting to me? Terrifying?
STEP 3. Curating Supportive Beliefs	What do I believe is possible for me?
	Am I capable? If I put my mind to learning or doing something, do I believe I can accomplish it?

Figure 5.2

Reflection Questions	
STEP 4. **Making** **Aligned** **Decisions**	When I consider how I interact with money in my life, where am I getting stuck? Why am I getting stuck?
	What money skills would I need to build in order to get unstuck?
	What would someone who felt capable and confident with money do in this situation where I am getting stuck?
	What decision do I need to make to be aligned with who I am and who I want to become?

Figure 5.2   (*continued*)

myself of this inner money clutter that I have uncovered, named, and stuck a pin in." Start imagining your more positive, healthy, empowering answers to these questions even if you are not sure how you will actualize those answers yet.

For example, my client Sun took this process to heart in his efforts to create a more aware and healthy relationship with money. In doing his own inner clutter clearing work, he realized that he felt distinctly different about the money that he had earned versus the money that came to him from his family. He was able to discern that he had a distinctly more positive feeling toward his earned money—and he wanted more of that feeling. That awareness helped him to recognize that, while life was easier living on his parent's dime, the ease wasn't worth the satisfaction and freedom he felt when he had his own money. While Sun is still a work-in-progress, actively decluttering his relationship with money, he says he feels "less stuck" than he has in a long time.

You, too, can become less stuck. You can discard damaging inner money clutter to give space to come up with empowered, positive answers to all those questions. To envision who you *want* to be in your relationship with money. Once you have created a sense of inner alignment about who you are and who you want to become, it's much easier to tackle the outer clutter that might be getting in your way of taking action.

Outer Work: Mastering Your Money Skills

After the inner work of exploring your current relationship with money and the relationship you want to have, your next step is to do the outer work of building skills and habits to operate effectively with money on a daily basis.

Becoming financially aware, capable, and confident is essential if you want to overcome the infantilization that is often the unfortunate by-product of having a team of professionals oversee your family's financial life. Getting educated about how to responsibly manage your money—like learning almost anything new—requires a willingness to lean into discomfort and stick with the process.

Many of my clients tell me that they know they *should* create a budget, but since they really don't *need* to, they keep avoiding the task. Often, when we finally dig in deeper, they reveal that they don't actually know how to get started in the first place. If budgeting (or any personal financial skill) feels intimidating to you, you are not alone. The truth is, the *need* to budget is far less important than the reason for learning how to—which is that doing so will help you build a conscious, practical, and human-scale relationship with money, and ultimately, with wealth. This will give you a more engaged seat at the table of your own life. *That's* why it's well worth your time and effort to lean into the challenge of up-leveling your fiscal savviness.

Aaron is a perfect case study for the power of clearing outer money clutter through building his financial skills. Aaron is married with two little boys. He is a massage therapist and has a small practice, but he does not earn enough to cover their living expenses. He loves being a dad and is okay with not maximizing his earnings right now while his boys are little. His partner Maria was once a practicing nurse but quit her job when they had their children. While they have always been able to cover their financial gap by using the distributions from Aaron's trust, they never had a sense of financial security because they didn't understand how to track their cash flow or create a livable budget. In addition, to feeling the strain from occasionally running out of money in between scheduled trust distributions because they didn't plan well, Aaron also felt shame that he couldn't provide financial stability for his family. After clearing some inner money clutter around his shame and his money script that "men should be providers," it became clear to Aaron that he *could* be a provider for his family; he just had to learn how to manage his resources better.

Aaron started by making the commitment that they were going to learn how to live within their means. This required that he and Maria understand what money came into their household and where they spent it. They were initially intimidated by some of the computer-based programs for budgeting, so they started by making a simple tracking sheet on a piece of paper that captured how much he earned through his massage therapy practice and how much they got from his trust distribution. They then asked his family office team to begin sending him his credit card statement (since he had never received nor paid the bill himself). Next he learned how to download his monthly bank statement. With these documents in hand, he and Maria took pen to paper and made a rough sketch of where they spent their money.

While the process was arduous at first, they began to see their patterns for spending and how their unconscious habits (like eating out most nights) added up. Ultimately, they created a tracking sheet in Excel that helped them to see (and also interact) with their cash flow. In an effort to make "living within their means" something they both were invested in, they decided to create a monthly financial "date night" where they would update their income and expense spreadsheet together. Over time, they began to get a feel for what they could and couldn't spend money on if they didn't want to exceed their monthly income. Through this process they found that, instead of feeling restricted, they actually felt like they had more freedom than ever. It turns out, the systems they created to track their cash flow helped them to clear a big pile of money clutter and started them on a path to feeling more engaged and empowered with the resources they had.

All adults need basic proficiency in a few fundamental money management skills. Proficiency. Not perfection. But which skills? I've drawn from research the core financial skills that emerging adults—especially those from affluence—should build in order to clear their outer money clutter and become skilled, confident stewards of their financial resources. These are widely regarded as the most relevant and important:[2]

- How to save (even if there's not a pragmatic reason for you to save)
- How to keep track of money (using a program or app specifically for this purpose, or even just creating a simple spreadsheet)
- How to get paid what you are worth (a skill that can be especially difficult to master if you have supplemental financial support)
- How to spend wisely
- How to talk about money

- How to live on a budget
- How to invest
- How to exercise the entrepreneurial spirit
- How to handle credit (knowing what "good" credit is, knowing your credit score, and knowing how to increase your credit score)
- How to use money to change the world (even if it's just your little corner of it)

As you consider the previous list, circle the top two or three skills that you either feel most inspired to learn more about or that you feel would be most important to learn. Who in your family or family advisory team could you ask for help in building the skills you picked? Remember, sometimes you might be asking one of your parents or advisors to *start* doing something (like making sure you're the one to receive your credit card statements) and sometimes you might be asking them to *stop* doing something (like being responsible for paying all of your bills). Next to the skills you circled, write one action step you could imagine taking to start learning about that skill. Don't expect to master these skills overnight. Just like Aaron and Maria, empower yourself to take the first, easiest step you can—even if that means starting with a pen and paper despite the fact that there are fancy software systems that would do the work for you. Everyone has to start somewhere when learning something new. Right now, your goal is just to challenge yourself to learn and begin practicing the skills you've identified. Once you've developed some confidence with your first picks, work your way through the list. Be sure to reach out for support as needed, be it from family members, family advisors, or through self-study with some of the resources listed in the back of this book. If asking someone for help, go to someone you trust or who comes recommended and be aware that they may be very surprised to hear what you don't know about money (you could even bring this book along as a reference). Have some thick skin, but don't let anyone shame you. You are making an important effort—one you can be proud of.

Clearing Your Outer Money Clutter

Similar to our inner clutter clearing process, here are the steps to effectively clear outer clutter:

5. Defining a Clear Outcome

Defining clear outcomes clarifies with conviction what we are working toward. It makes it possible to align our actions with a defined end goal. The fifth step of the process, Defining a Clear Outcome, asks us to consider questions like, "What does success look like? What am I aiming to learn, do, or achieve?"

6. Aligning Your Actions

Aligned actions are the upward spiral of the less-cluttered person in motion. Action inspires forward movement, which is the opposite of being stuck or directionless. The fifth step of Aligning Your Actions challenges us to ask such things as, "What is the first step I can take? What is the scariest thing I could do right now? What action leads to a greater feeling of inner freedom?"

7. Creating Systems and Environments to Support Your Success

Healthy systems and environments reflect back to us who we are and who we are capable of being. They are the flywheel that helps us to continue to remove friction in our lives so that we may move in the direction of who we are becoming. The seventh and last step, Creating Systems and Environments to Support Your Success, asks us to consider these questions, "Where do I need support? What do I need to let go of in order to be successful? What supportive structures—or scaffolding—will help me grow?"

Figure 5.3

Based on this process and using the personal financial skills you circled previously, following is another series of Reflection Questions that will help you begin to clear some serious outer money clutter:

Reflection Questions	
STEP 5: **Defining a Clear** **Outcome**	What does success look like right now? What is the outcome I'm trying to achieve? *(Think of Aaron's story—the first outcome he defined was to "live within their means.")*
STEP 6: **Aligning Your** **Actions**	What is the first step I can take? *(For example, if the clear outcome you identified is to begin to keep track of your money, then a first step you might claim could be to download a financial app—like Quicken or Mint—that can help you build this skill).* How will this action lead to a greater feeling of inner freedom?
STEP 7: **Creating Systems and** **Environments to** **Support Your** **Success**	What help do I need to support my success? *(Think about the professionals or trusted advisors in your life. Who do you feel comfortable with? Who might you ask to help you achieve the outcome you named?)* What do I need to let go of that is getting in my way? What scaffolding—or systems of support— will help me achieve this outcome? *(Be creative. Remember Aaron and Maria's monthly financial "dates.")*

As with the inner clutter clearing process you did earlier, once you've answered these questions, you can start letting go of those harmful outer money behaviors that you've identified as "getting in the way" and start moving toward the empowering "clear outcome" you've decided. Remember, this doesn't have to be your forever outcome. Just one clear objective you want to achieve at this point in your life. Set a date by which you will take your first action. Hold yourself to it. After some time has passed, repeat this seven-step clutter clearing process to yield fresh answers and further actions.

Your willingness to engage in both the inner and outer work of clearing money clutter will set you on the path to developing your right relationship with money and wealth. And *this* is your ticket to both a greater sense of personal freedom and to generating optimal impact with your time and resources. Get started now. Your future self will thank you.

Integrating It All: Finding Your Right Relationship with Money

Your right relationship with money is a healthy, positive, self-actualized, and personally meaningful one. However stuck or dissatisfied you may feel today—or the rising gen in your life may seem to be—this right relationship is not only possible but already forming as you read these pages. When you have taken practical, intentional steps to clear some of your money clutter, you let the oxygen in and make space in your life for this new relationship to grow. Consider some of these aspects of the healthy, balanced money relationship that is waiting for you.

First, a key word is this phrase is *your.* This right relationship with money is unique to you. No one gets to define it for you—not your parents, not the wealth creator in your money story, not society, not me, not your therapist or support team.

Second, "right" indicates a balanced and satisfactory relationship—not perfection. Remember the stories of both Sun and Aaron in this chapter? Neither one of these men "have it all figured out"—they were (and are) both just taking the next step . . . and then the next after that . . . in clearing their own money clutter. Their processes haven't been pretty, and their paths haven't been straight, but they are actively engaging in something that, at one point, felt impossible to each of them.

Third, a relationship is a living, moving thing—it changes over time. What constitutes a satisfactory, balanced relationship between you and money today can—and probably should—look very different 10, 20, . . . 40 years from now. Cultivating your ability and tools to take ownership of this relationship and care for it will enable you to adapt better in the future.

Finally, for some, a right relationship may also mean turning your attention outward to the needs you see in your community and the impact you feel you could create with the time, talent, and treasure that you have. We'll explore this possibility in Part IV, as I invite you to consider more deeply what "an impactful life" means, but as always, this aspect of your healthy money relationship is up to you.

6

Identity Clutter

Harper is 27 years old and a third-generation member of a family whose net worth is about $30 million. Smart with her budgeting, she is able to live on the public servant's salary she earns as a social worker. Harper leads with her heart and heeds her calling to work with underserved and marginalized populations, dedicating long hours at an inner-city health clinic. All her clients live below the poverty line, and her coworkers seem to have an "eat the rich" mentality.

Deep emotion clouds her voice when she tells me about the turmoil that arises within her whenever she hears her colleagues discuss their distaste for the wealthy. She weighs their perceptions of rich people against her actual experiences. She adores her family and admires the priority they have always placed on using their wealth to address pressing needs in their community. In fact, her drive to become a social worker was born out of her family's commitment to bettering the lives of the less fortunate. Still, she acknowledges that she is also embarrassed by her family's wealth and frightened that she'll be unmasked as "rich" at work. She wonders if these uncomfortable feelings would vanish if she asked her parents to just give away her inheritance.

Harper has a classic case of identity clutter. When she considers creating distance from her family's wealth, she feels disloyal to the family she loves. And when she tries to fit in with her work friends and chosen social circle, she feels guarded and, ultimately, inauthentic. It's a no-win situation that leaves her feeling untethered and somehow unfaithful in both worlds.

85

Identity—"Who Am I?"

The most important, enduring, significant relationship we will ever have in our lives is the relationship with ourselves. At the very core of the relationship we have with ourselves is a definition of self that we have constructed (or others have constructed for us and we've accepted). That definition of "self" is our identity. Remember the famous psychologist, Erik Erikson, whose work we explored briefly in Chapter 4? He was one of the first researchers to take an active interest in the formation of one's personal identity. He defines personal identity as a foundational organizing principal of development which evolves throughout the lifespan.[1] It is how one sees oneself, and it includes an individual's experiences, relationships, values, beliefs, and memories. Since, according to Erikson, the formation of identity is something that happens across a lifespan, don't feel like you have to have it figured out today. That said, Erikson also believed that one's teens and 20s, in particular, are very important years for establishing an authentic sense of identity. He felt that the stage between youth and adulthood is an important period for personal exploration and a time for each person to create his or her own life.

Erikson's belief was that this process can't be rushed and it also can't be passive or, worse, stalled. Remember that Erikson's research showed that in order for an individual to grow and evolve through each of the eight life stages, they needed to wrestle with and resolve the crisis of their current life stage. It is through this cycle of "crisis and growth" that one builds what sociologists refer to as identity capital.[2] **Identity capital** is the sum of who we are. The collection of our personal assets. It is the result of the investments we make in ourselves. It is the degrees, jobs, test scores we accumulate, but it is also the way we engage in the world—how we speak, how we solve problems, who we present ourselves to be.

In her book, *The Defining Decade: Why Your Twenties Matter—And How to Make the Most of Them Now*, clinical psychologist Meg Jay describes why this process of crisis and growth is so important. She writes, "Researchers who have looked at how people resolve identity crises have found that lives that are all capital and no crisis—all work and no exploration—feel rigid and conventional. On the other hand, more crisis than capital is a problem, too. As the concept of identity crisis caught on in the United States, Erikson himself warned against spending too much time in 'disengaged confusion.'

He was concerned that too many young people were 'in danger of becoming irrelevant.' Twenty-somethings who take the time to explore and also have the nerve to make commitments along the way construct stronger identities."[3]

So, it is both the crisis *and* the commitment that are important. Together they create the opportunity for you to activate the cycle of knowing yourself ever more deeply and using what you learn about yourself to engage with and impact the world around you. This is true regardless of who you are and what you were born into. Learning how to move through each stage's crisis and growing into the next stage is essential for the healthy development of individuals, regardless of their economic demographic. And while having too little financial security can pose one set of challenges to a path of healthy development, having too many financial resources can pose a different set.

Family Wealth and the Formation of Identity Clutter

Becoming who we are is tough, lifetime work. Becoming who we are when we are raised in the shadow of a big-thinking wealth creator gives rise to its own unique issues—sources of clutter that can make this fundamentally important task of identity formation even more difficult. I see three major sources of identity clutter creating problems for aspiring rising gen:

- The wealth creator in your life has generated a level of affluence and influence that few people can achieve, and those **shoes feel too big to fill**. It can be difficult to find your own voice and path when the bar for success has been set unimaginably high and you're trying to decide if just being a good, solid contributor at an ordinary job is "good enough."
- **Over-identifying with family wealth**, meaning that the concept of "wealth" in your life is either something that you consider a fundamental part of who you are or is highly associated with how you are perceived in the world.
- **Under-identifying with family wealth**, alternately, you work to distance yourself from the concept of "wealth," trying to ignore it like you might ignore the antics of a poorly behaving relative.

For the latter two bullets, if you can't imagine your life without being wealthy, or if you think your life would be better if you didn't have to deal with or associate with family wealth, you're probably somewhere on this continuum between these two poles. Let's dive a bit deeper into each of these three sources of identity clutter.

The High Bar of Success

As of the class of 2022, there have been a total of just over 300 football players inducted into the Pro Football Hall of Fame.[4] When you think about the people who have been inducted into the Hall of Fame, how often have you wondered if one of their kids was also going to be a Hall of Famer? If you're like most people, you probably don't immediately assume that just because someone has the genetic predisposition, the drive, the professionalism, the opportunities, and the commitment (as well as probably some degree of luck) to be highly successful and recognized at the top of their chosen field, that their kids would have all these same characteristics and would (or should) also be able to clear that exceptionally high achievement bar. Yet the majority of rising gen I talk to feel that, to some degree, they are "a failure" if they are not able to fill the very large shoes of their parents or grandparents. Feeling like you *should* be able to capture lightening in a bottle the way that the wealth creator in your life has leads to a very limited space in which to define success for yourself. And does that definition of success really let you explore and build your *own* identity capital? Does it build the most unique and magnetic version of you that you can bring to the world? Let's underscore the point with a few more statistics about the Pro Football Hall of Fame.

In 2020, there were 73,712 athletes who were National Collegiate Athletic Association (NCAA) participants in college football.[5] Of those, approximately 16,000 athletes were eligible for the draft, and only 254 athletes got drafted. That's a mere 1.6% of NCAA (all divisions) football players who got drafted to the National Football League (NFL). In the history of the NFL, approximately 28,000 players have ever played a snap, and only 363 of those players have been elected into the Pro Football Hall of Fame.[6] Additionally, of those 28,000 players, there have only been 280 father-son combinations who have both played a snap in a pro game.[7] Only 1%. Of those 280 father-son combos who both played a snap in a pro game, just 13 involved at least the father or the son ultimately becoming a Hall of Fame player. There is not a single example of both a father and a son player who have both been elected into the Pro Football Hall of Fame.

When you think of it this way, can you let yourself off the hook for not following in your parent's or grandparent's footsteps and filling their shoes? Can you give yourself a little more room to breathe and discover how *you*— with your unique well of identity capital—can create your own definition for a life of engagement and impact?

Over-Identifying with Wealth

In their seminal white paper, *Acquirers' and Inheritors' Dilemma: Discovering Life Purpose and Building Personal Identity in the Presence of Wealth*, James Grubman and Dennis Jaffe describe both over-identification and under-identification with wealth.[8] For inheritors who over-identify with family wealth, their sense of self may be fully tied-up in what someone else has created, not what they are creating themselves.

This is dangerous because over-identification with familial wealth creates a vacuum of "self" that can sabotage confidence, sense of capability, and intrinsic sense of worth. See if you notice evidence of this in the following real-life story of a newly minted college freshman from a well-known family, as she relates how she ended up with a single room her freshman year at college: "Within the first month, I knew that the roommate thing just wasn't going to work out. When I mentioned it to my mom, she called the university and said I needed a single room immediately. Before my roommate even knew what was happening, I had moved out and taken all of my stuff with me. I guess she forgot what my last name was—she didn't know who she was dealing with."

As this young woman pridefully told me this, I sensed the power she equated with having a last name that made things happen. Internally, however, I wondered if she realized that this was a missed opportunity for her to communicate with her roommate or her resident advisor on her own to address and try to resolve her concerns with the roommate situation. Despite her mom's well-intentioned actions, this next gen relied on her wealth and her family's name to solve the problem for her. Remember how earlier we explored the unintended consequences of parental behaviors that remove an appropriate level of struggle from their children's lives? How doing so inhibits a child's natural development? Projecting forward in the case of this client, if she is not willing or able to tackle difficult situations in her own right and with her own skills, she is likely to become highly dependent on the wealth and status that her family provides, a situation likely to leave her stagnant in her pursuits and unfulfilled in her life.

Under-Identifying with Wealth

On the other end of the continuum, though, are inheritors who under-identify with their wealth. This carries its own pain. Harper, who you learned about at the beginning of this chapter, is a classic example of this under-identification with wealth. Harper is disheartened by the prospect of disavowing her family's legacy, of which she is quite proud. Yet she repeatedly wonders if that is the only way to free herself from the confusion that wealth creates in her life.

It is not. In fact, it likely wouldn't work. When she suggested she might feel better if her parents gave away her inheritance, I told her that it wouldn't magically resolve her inner conflict. I went on to say, "Your family will always be your family, and your family will always have a lot of money, whether or not you personally do. One day you may decide to give every dime of your inheritance away, but even that is unlikely to create the liberation you seek if you don't first do the hard work of integrating your family's wealth into your own healthy sense of self. It is your job and yours alone to find *your* right and balanced relationship with the legacy of which you are a part. From there, you can freely, joyfully make thoughtful choices about your money and your life."

As if riding a teeter-totter, you may feel as if you vacillate between over-identifying with your family's wealth and under-identifying with it, depending on your life stage and the particular circumstances. For example, if you're hanging out with the people you went to boarding school with, you may strongly identify with and perhaps feel proud of your family's wealth. But if you're just out of college and working at a starter job with peers who are barely scraping by, you may tend to under-identify with it.

Either way, the ultimate goal is to transition from having *wealth be a focal point* to having *wealth be a tool*. A tool for what? Well, that's up to you.

But in order to get there, you probably need to clear a bit of that clutter first.

Clearing Your Inner Identity Clutter

By now you've had some practice with the seven-step clutter clearing process (as described in Figure 5.1) through the money clutter work you did last chapter. You'll see that this process remains the same for each of the four forms of clutter you tackle—money, identity, relationship, and contribution—it's just the reflection questions that differ slightly. Consider the following Reflection Questions for identifying and beginning to dislodge your inner identity clutter that is stifling your growth.

I encourage you again to act on this process with intention and thoughtfulness; take dedicated time to reflect on and write your answers to these questions. It is helpful to remember that our identity is not like a coat that we can put on and then take off. Identity is core to who we are and also deeply intertwined with our family of origin. But that doesn't mean we're stuck with every part of our identity that we've inherited or unconsciously adopted over time. Looking more closely at the inner identity clutter you may have gathering in the dark corners of your mind and heart will give you the clarity to begin to really move out some clutter piles. Then, you can align your mindset, identity, beliefs, and decisions (Steps 1–4) of who you want to be with the outcomes, actions, and support systems (Steps 5–7) to help you make it so.

When I first began working with Lindsay (from Chapter 2), she wanted to start a for-profit private school, a model she imagined would attract investment dollars rather than charity dollars and one that others might replicate. In our first session I asked her to describe her definition of success. Lindsay's definition of success contained having vacation homes, the ability to travel, not having to worry about money, being respected, and being a leader. When I asked her how she would define fulfillment, she was stumped. She said to me, "I never thought about that. It's confusing because our culture definitely sends the message that success is measured in financial terms. But for me, maybe that's not actually true." As we delved into the topic further, it was clear that for her father, financial success and life fulfillment *were* one in the same. He loved his work, he was a skilled leader, and he was able to generate significant wealth through the business he created. But from Lindsay's perspective, once she was able to reflect on it, success was defined in financial terms, whereas fulfillment fulfillment was defined through impact.

This dissonance was a form of inner identity clutter for Lindsay. (See Step 1 in Figure 6.1.) Her dad was fulfilled running a successful business that resulted in the ability to have vacation homes, to travel, and for his family not to worry about money. But for Lindsay, who—because of her father's success—didn't have to worry about money, fulfillment looked different. She wanted to work with kids, education, and leadership development. Once she was able to separate her father's definitions from her own, she realized she wasn't driven to make money. She was driven to create impact. Which is, ultimately, what the youth-focused nonprofit she later built has done.

Reflection Questions

STEP 1. **Cultivating a Beneficial Mindset**	How do I define success for myself? How do I define fulfillment? What is similar or different in the two definitions? What components of each definition are most supportive and beneficial to me and my ability to thrive? *(This is the mindset that will be most empowering to you.)*
STEP 2. **Adopting an Empowering Identity**	Between over-identifying and under-identifying with wealth, which one do I lean towards more often? What part of my current identity would I need to let go of or evolve in order to experience more balance and authenticity in my daily activities? What is most core to who I am? Where and how do I share those core attributes each day? *(This is the identity that you most want to embrace and express).*

Figure 6.1

Reflection Questions	
STEP 3. Curating Supportive Beliefs	In what situations do I feel most capable and competent? Do I believe that I have what it takes to create meaningful impact with my life? Why? What belief is most generative to who I want to become? *(This is the supportive belief you want to adopt and use in your decision-making. For example, you might choose to believe that you are capable and complete, perfectly designed to live a life of flourishing and impact. If you believed that, what possibilities might you see that you don't see now?)*
STEP 4. Making Aligned Decisions	When I consider how I show up in my life, where am I getting stuck? Why am I getting stuck? What skills or competencies would I need to build in order to get unstuck? What would someone who felt capable and confident in who they are do in this situation? What decision do I need to make to be aligned with who I am and who I want to become? *(This is the decision—or decisions—you can use to define the outcomes you want to create. Think about the belief you named in step 3. What decision could you make today that would affirm the belief you stated? In that example, could you take action without needing to "fix" or adjust yourself in order to be "ready"?)*

Figure 6.1 *(continued)*

Clearing Your Outer Identity Clutter

Taking insights from your previous inner clutter clearing, carve out some time and space to respond to the outer identity clutter questions in Figure 6.2.

Reflection Questions	
STEP 5. **Defining a** **Clear Outcome**	What does success look like right now? What is the outcome I'm trying to achieve? *(Imagine what it would feel like to be wholly, unapologetically you in all facets of your life. What would that look like?)*
STEP 6. **Aligning Your** **Actions**	What is the first step I can take? How will this action lead to a greater feeling of inner freedom? A greater feeling of deep authenticity? *(Naming the first step you can take—and how it will support your growth—will help you get into action).*
STEP 7. **Creating Systems** **and Environments** **to Support Your** **Success**	What help do I need to support my success? What do I need to let go of that is getting in my way? What systems of support—or scaffolding— will help me achieve this outcome?

Figure 6.2

Soon, this seven-step clutter clearing process will start to feel more natural. For now, if it still feels awkward or like you're lacking the "a-ha's" you were hoping to have, just hang in there. It'll come.

Early in our work, Jairaj struggled to have clarity on any outcome he wanted to create. Jairaj was the son of a high-drive, tech entrepreneur mom, a woman with a big intellect who had generated significant wealth for her family from the initial public offering of her company. When we tried to do a vision exercise, he kept describing big ideas like "start a business," and "trek through Europe." I told him those were great ideas if they were really the outcomes he wanted to achieve, but that I had the sense that he was naming what he thought he *should* do, not what was really most meaningful to him right now. He paused and said to me, "The truth is, if I could just not feel such pervasive anxiety every day, I'd probably be better able to even consider what I actually want to do in my life." That insight was the golden nugget we needed to begin clearing some clutter. To Jairaj, this seemed like a petty outcome to name. To me, this was shining a light on the clutter that was obscuring Jairaj's ability to gain traction in his life.

After giving himself permission to let go of how he thought others would want him to answer, Jairaj's authentic, stated outcome became: "To experience more peace in my daily life." (See Step 5 in Figure 6.2.) It was his goal "for now" in his life. Based on this outcome, we were able to define specific steps he could take to increase his self-care, notice what circumstances triggered his anxiety, and get the professional help he needed to more consistently experience the peace he was seeking—and as a result create the space to think and dream.

Creating a Positive Wealth Identity

Clearing your identity clutter means you look at those big shoes and decide it matters more to wear your own comfy shoes than to try to clomp around in shoes that don't fit. It means getting off the see-saw of over- or under-identifying with your family's affluence and finding out how to integrate who you are and what you have in a healthy, honest, and thoughtful way. Letting go of who you have been in order to make room for who you are becoming is scary work. But it's so worth it.

★ ★ ★ ★ ★

"Let me fall if I must fall. The one I will become will catch me."
— *Attributed to Baal Shem Tov*

★ ★ ★ ★ ★

The result of all this identity clutter clearing will, hopefully, be your ability to create a positive wealth identity. Here are five elements that professional advisors in the family wealth advising field agree comprise a positive wealth identity:[9]

- A sense of personal security and self-esteem
- A lifestyle that is balanced and derives pleasure from the appropriate use of wealth
- The ability to trust other people in intimate relationships

- Acceptance of stewardship of wealth for future generations
- Financial awareness and capability in managing wealth

Take a moment with your journal or laptop to reflect upon each of these statements. Which one, if any, do you feel you have nailed? Which one(s) do you struggle with the most? Pick the one from the list that you feel most compelled to work on first. What is one action you will take to begin to build competency in this area of positive wealth identity? Consider the resources listed in the Appendices for further support.

★ ★ ★ ★ ★

In Harper's search for her own positive wealth identity, she doesn't have it all figured out yet, but today she is way less confused than she was when we started working together. After doing a lot of identity clutter clearing work, she decided she could start to integrate her "two selves" by having an open conversation with her parents about her struggles in feeling comfortable with the wealth in her family. She was surprised by how much both her parents reflected back to her times when they, too, felt uncomfortable as they navigated the terrain of wealth. She hasn't found anyone at work that she feels safe sharing with at this point, but as she continues to find her way, I have confidence that she'll either feel safe enough to be her full self at work, or she'll find another organization in which she can have impact *and* be her full self. And if someday she decides to give her full inheritance away, I know she'll be doing it with her eyes wide open, from a place of clarity and conviction.

Your Hyper-Agency Superpower: Aligning a Positive Wealth Identity with Empowered Action

Hyper-agency is the recognition that you have the ability to determine the conditions and circumstances of your life instead of merely living within them. It is a state of being where you experience a heightened sense of control and empowerment, which you channel to take decisive action in your life. When I talk about hyper-agency, many rising gen tell me that this sounds like a superpower they'd love to have.

In the context of affluence, sociologists Schervish, Coutsoukis, and Lewis[10] take this one step further. They use the term hyper-agency to describe the special responsibility and opportunity that the exceptionally fortunate experience *because* of being wealthy. Of course, having the special responsibility and opportunity of wealth doesn't automatically translate into the ability to use your wealth and privilege in positive and productive ways. Knowing *what* you want to impact and *how* to do it takes curiosity, a willingness to stretch, and a desire to grow. The upshot is, when you act from a place of hyper-agency, you engage this superpower to support you in using your wealth to determine the conditions and circumstances of your life rather than just living within them. But also, as a rising gen, when you align this hyper-agency with your positive wealth identity, you'll start to realize that, like Spider Man, you too have a "Spidey-Sense"—the ability to recognize when your unique gifts and skills could really make a difference.

Getting there, however, takes doing the work you're doing now— clearing your clutter and learning to integrate your family's wealth story into your life. You can then use this superpower to claim your voice, your life path, and create impact that is meaningful to you. Now *that's* the power of finding your positive wealth identity and right relationship with wealth.

7

Relationship Clutter

"Love and belonging are irreducible needs for all people. In the absence of these experiences, there is always suffering."
—Atlas of the Heart, *Brene Brown*

Rebekah was the daughter of an entrepreneur. Having grown up alongside her dad's ever-increasing success, she was fairly comfortable with her family's wealth and also confident in her place in the world. Despite a relatively healthy self-identity and a positive integration of her family's wealth story, she yearned for the experience of living in a place where her last name didn't mean anything to anyone. When she left for college, she chose to go out of state in order to get that experience she was seeking. During her first semester at college, she met someone she really enjoyed, and they dated for most of that term. While she wasn't hiding her family story, she also wasn't forthcoming with it—she was just enjoying experiencing life untethered to a recognizable name. As winter break approached, Rebekah and her boyfriend decided they wanted to spend time together over the holidays and Rebekah invited him to join her family for a ski vacation. Rebekah tells the story: "Honestly, I enjoyed this guy so much, and I thought he was the real deal. He was my first college love. I hadn't even thought that my family's situation would matter that much. When we arrived at my parents' mountain house, I watched him start to shut down. It was clear that he was overwhelmed and having some sort of internal struggle. I tried to talk to him about it, but he didn't have much to say. After a couple of days he said he thought he should leave. When I asked him why, he said he wasn't 'my kind of people.'

I was hurt and also stunned. I let him leave and that pretty much ended it right there. He took a shuttle to the airport, and we didn't reconnect when winter break was over."

Rebekah was fortunate because she had a strong sense of self and was easily able to see that her boyfriend's hang-up about wealth had nothing to do with her personally. That said, she recalls how much his comments stung—and left her feeling less confident about her "acceptability" in future relationships.

Do I Belong Here?

The feeling of belonging is at the heart of every flourishing relationship, regardless of whether the relationship is with your best buddy, a colleague you look up to and admire, your circle of peers, or the love of your life. In fact, it is such a strong human drive that we'll often try to experience it by any means possible—even if that means contorting who we are to receive others' approval and acceptance.[1] Yet, according to researcher and sociologist Brene Brown, in the end, "hustling for approval and acceptance"[2] ends up becoming obstacles to the very experience of true belonging that we're seeking. In her book, *Atlas of the Heart*, she describes belonging this way: "True belonging is the spiritual practice of believing in and belonging to yourself so deeply that you can share your most authentic self with the world and find sacredness in both being a part of something and standing alone in the wilderness. True belonging doesn't require you to change who you are; it requires you to be who you are."[3] Powerful words. A sentiment echoed by one of my rising gen research participants as she described her relationship with her longtime, no-doubt-about-it best friend:

I have one friend who has known me since the day I was born. She's the one person [with whom] it has never felt like work to be who I am. With her, there's nothing to hide or shield her from because we grew up together. We've walked through life together. She has a similar family situation to mine. Our grandmothers picked each other to be the godmother to each of our own mothers. We've had three to four generations of connection. Not of bloodlines, but of family relations. So there's a deep sense of trust from the get-go that I never had to work at building with her. But that hasn't been true in other relationships.

While sometimes it comes easily, more often than not, the work of learning to trust that you can be your full, multifaceted, authentic self takes a lot of courage, intentional effort, and trust, a challenge even more keenly felt if you are very affluent. This kind of pursuit isn't for the faint of heart. And as you can see from the definition of belonging, finding your way to true belonging in a relationship with someone means you have to first authentically be yourself. Thankfully, you've courageously gotten to work clearing a lot of dusty, stagnant clutter in the previous two chapters, so you're well on your way on that front.

Whether romantic or plutonic, long-lasting relationships are both based on a foundation of true belonging and fueled by a sense of relational intimacy. Intimacy is created and deepened by what researchers Jane Dutton and Emily Heaphy call *high-quality connections* (HQC).[4] These connections are social interactions that can consist of many different behaviors, but the basic DNA of this important relational currency is to engage with another in a way that shows they are important; to support someone else or feel supported in doing something meaningful; to build trust through communication and actions; and to play together.[5] HQCs are fundamentally important to healthy relationships because, biologically, they engage our "calm-and-connect" system, triggering a host of chemical reactions that intensify the feelings of connection with another.[6] Barb Fredrickson, a psychologist specializing in research on positive emotions, refers to these moments of connection as "positivity resonance"—a phenomenon where one person's brain is literally syncing up with another person's brain. The feeling is intoxicating for a reason—it signals that we are in a safe relationship where we belong and can let down our guard. The rising gen research participant mentioned previously went on to describe this kind of relationship where she could truly be herself and get that sense of deep connection:

This friend and I have been friends for so long, and we've built a habit of being there for each other in very real ways. Thankfully, I also now have deep and loving relationships with people that I've met more recently, but my relationship with her is what helped me understand what real friendship is. When it comes to needing someone to "help bury the bodies," she is always going to be there. There was never a question in my mind whether she was truly my friend or not. I feel really lucky to have had that experience from early on in my life. I never questioned her intentions. I never wondered whether I needed to hide something from her. And I never felt I needed to filter some story from my family life so I didn't sound like a jerk complaining when I know that I'm too lucky to be complaining about anything. She gets it. And she gets me. Her friendship has been a game-changer in my life.

The bond that this rising gen has with her friend models the true belonging and relational intimacy of the robust, healthy, authentic relationships that are essential to our thriving—ones that all rising gen can build with some effort. Wealth aside, it can take the courage of a lion at times to do the self-work and the relational work needed to experience these types of rich, rewarding, and enduring relationships. And as you've seen in the domains of money and identity, wealth can complicate this process in ways that create another pile of clutter.

Family Wealth and the Formation of Relationship Clutter

Many rising gen describe experiencing a type of loneliness that, from the outside, often surprises people. How could someone who "has it all" be lonely? But as exemplified by Rebekah's story, wealth can complicate relationships—both friendships and romantic partnerships—and leave rising gens questioning their intrinsic value, feeling misunderstood, and being the recipient of other people's projections of wealth and the wealthy. In my work and research, I generally see wealth complicate relationships in three major ways, each of which creates its own type of relationship clutter.

If you've ever found yourself **questioning your intrinsic value** as a friend or a spouse, you're not alone. Like Ben and Ellen McAllister in the opening story of Chapter 2, it's not uncommon for rising gens to experience at least an undercurrent of wondering, "Do they like me for *me* or because I have the best toys?" One of my research participants described his experience with this form of clutter this way:

When I turned 21, I received some money from my grandfather's passing, and I bought a house. It was a nice house, just off campus. It ended up becoming the hangout for my [athletic] team—nobody else had a house at that time. I always made sure the fridge was stocked with drinks and there was plenty of food around. It was a great hang-out spot. I paid for all kinds of stuff—not just the stuff at my house. I also took people on camping trips and other fun things like that. I think it's at that point that I started to recognize those feelings of "I wonder who is hanging out with me because of the things I have?" I think some of those people were friends with me for genuine reasons, and I think other people just enjoyed the ride. I'm grateful I at least started to pay attention to the question of who my real friends were.

In Buddhism, there is a concept of a "near enemy." A near enemy is when something is close to the thing we are attempting to cultivate (in this case, authentic relationships), but there are subtle differences that make it so that instead of helping us make progress toward that thing, it actually becomes an obstacle to that thing. Being able to discern true friendships from their near enemy is a skill and attunement you can build. Clearing your relationship clutter will help you get there.

Another form of relationship clutter that is common is **difficulty being fully authentic** as you wonder when (and if) to share your family story during the course of a developing friendship or romantic relationship. I often hear rising gens claim that they've learned the hard way that there is a time in a relationship when it is too soon to share (meaning, you don't yet have enough relationship capital to know if the other person can really hold, honor, and respect the information you're sharing with them) and a time when it is too late. One rising gen I worked with was so terrified of the impact that wealth could have on her relationship that she didn't tell the father of her baby (they were not yet married) about her family story until he came to her, excitedly letting her know that he had just completed the paperwork so they could get a house as a part of the affordable housing program in their city. With a lot of support, they were able to navigate integrating her family wealth into their relationship, but he often said he thought it would have been easier to come to terms with if she would have told him sooner. There is not one right time to share information about your family and their wealth story, but the more relationship clutter you clear and the more attuned you are to what makes a true friend or an aligned partner, the easier it'll be for you to know when—or if—to share.

Finally, the last major source of relationship clutter that I see most commonly is that of **unequal power dynamics** that get created because of wealth. Sometimes this starts as benign as wondering if you should be (or if others are expecting you to be) the one to pick up the tab when your friends go out for coffee (because you can afford it, right?). This unequal power dynamic often extends into significant relationships and marriages which, when unexplored, can create obstacles to building a balanced, mutually supportive lifetime partnership. One client, Karina, described to me her dismay after she and her fiancé moved into a house that was purchased by her trust for them: "I don't understand it. I feel like we're so blessed to be able to live here. And we picked this house out together. My parents got behind the idea because it is going to be a great investment. But Dan's attitude about it— and, actually, about a lot of things—has changed since we moved in. We had this leak in the bathroom shower—it's totally the kind of thing he could fix. But he wouldn't. He still hasn't. We've been fighting a lot more."

Karina's story is quite common. It is likely that her fiancé didn't feel like the house was really his (and, technically, it wasn't—it was owned by her trust), and so he didn't want to invest time, money, and effort into it. In their case, the house turned out to be the catalyst for Karina and Dan breaking off their engagement. It's just one example of how wealth can create unseen power dynamics. For instance, it is common that the parents who hold the purse strings to have a strong influence in the decisions that a couple makes regarding where to live and what type of house to buy, among other decisions. This kind of strong influence can undermine a couple as they try to establish themselves and their own balance of relational power. As another example, recall the story of the engaged couple Trent and Dani from an earlier chapter, where Dani—the less affluent of the two—had "always felt less powerful when it came to the big decisions," because she couldn't contribute equally financially and therefore wouldn't weigh in fully at times. So, for rising gen especially, unequal power dynamics between peers, friends, generations, or couples can lead to some pretty weighty inner and outer clutter. Luckily, this source of relationship clutter, just like all the others, can be mitigated with awareness, courage, and action.

Clearing Your Inner Relationship Clutter

You can see that wealth can take what is already big lifetime work and add another layer or two of complexity. But fear not, by now you've had some practice with the seven-step clutter clearing process (Figure 5.1), and hopefully, you can see that there is a way out to the clean, fresh air or less cluttered relationships. Consider the Reflection Questions in Figure 7.1 for identifying and beginning to remove the inner relationship clutter that may be getting in the way of the deep sense of belonging that will support you to thrive.

	Reflection Questions
STEP 1. **Cultivating a** **Beneficial** **Mindset**	Who are the people that, when I spend time with them, I feel most fully myself? Most fully alive and supported?
	What qualities do these people—or these relationships—have? What is it about these relationships that helps me to feel fully myself and deeply supported?
	What relationships do I have that feel like "near enemies" (close, but not actually true and genuine friendships) to the authentic qualities and relationships I've just described?
	Based on these insights, what do I consider to be the most important qualities for a true friend to have? In other words, how will I know when someone is in the relationship for me and not for what I have or the experiences I can provide? *(This is the friendship filter—the mindset—that will be most empowering to you.)*
STEP 2. **Adopting an** **Empowering** **Identity**	Do I believe I have more to offer than the "stuff" or influence I have? Why?
	What are the qualities I bring to a relationship that make me a true friend or partner?
	Who am I in a relationship? Try to create an identity statement. *(This is the identity that you most want to embrace and express).*
	"I am . . . [refer to the authentic qualities you bring to a relationship from the above question]."

Figure 7.1

Reflection Questions	
STEP 3. **Curating** **Supporting** **Beliefs**	Do I believe that it is safe and acceptable for me to bring my whole self—and all of my life stories—to the relationships in my life? Why? What would need to change for me in order for me to feel I could have strong, true relationships based on the whole "me"? What belief about relationships would help me attract more of the kinds of friendships I want to have? (*This is the supportive belief you want to adopt and use in your decision-making*).
STEP 4. **Making** **Aligned** **Decisions**	When I consider the relationships I currently have in my life, where am I getting stuck? Why am I getting stuck? What skills or competencies would I need to build in order to feel a deep sense of belonging in my relationships? What would someone who felt capable and confident in their relationships do in these situations in which I often get stuck? What decision do I need to make to be aligned with the relationships I want to cultivate in my life? (*This is the decision—or decisions—you can use to define the outcomes you want to create*).

Figure 7.1 (*Continued*)

Bret's story typifies how inner relationship clutter can be cleared to create a more fertile soil in which relationships can grow. Bret's parents owned a working ranch. Growing up he spent most summers there. He loved spending his days with the ranch hands—tending to the horses, learning how to handle cattle, and feeling like a part of the crew. During the school year, he lived with his parents in an affluent neighborhood and went to the most elite private school in the city. When we met, he was in his early 30s and still had not had a significant, sustainable romantic relationship. And he claimed he didn't really have any good friends. Bret is gregarious, a great storyteller, and incredibly intelligent. He is the kind of person that people love to be around, but he kept everyone at arm's length. He had been raised to be skeptical of others and question what they wanted from him—an approach he told me that he'd adopted as second nature throughout high school and college. But when he talked about the cowboys at the ranch, it was clear that he felt differently. When we dug into his experience there, he said that while they knew his family owned the ranch, they never pandered to him. They expected a lot from him, and they respected that he lived up to their expectations. We were able to use that lived experience as a template to help Bret begin to build a new, conscious mindset (Step 1) about relationships he wanted to cultivate in his life. And while he still has a skepticism about others, he also has been able to forge a few genuine relationships, all built on the same qualities he valued in himself and in the bonds he experienced working with the cowboys on the ranch (Steps 3 and 4).

Clearing Your Outer Relationship Clutter

Based on the insights from your inner clutter clearing above, now focus your mind and heart on the outer relationship clutter questions in Figure 7.2.

Sandy's story illustrates how you can use the outer clutter clearing work to create energizing behavioral patterns and supportive environments that expand into healthier, more authentic relationships.

Sandy is a 50-something, divorced, second generation family member from a very wealthy Midwest family. She had been raised doing all the "right" things that someone of her social standing, raised in the 1960s and 1970s did—she belonged to the country club, she supported local charity events, and she held fundraisers at her beautiful home. She never went to college, and she never had a "job." She always said how blessed she was, but the light in her eyes was always dim when she said it. It turns out that she was financially blessed but very emotionally isolated. We first started talking because she was worried about her adult children and whether they were going to "launch" or not. But our initial conversation revealed that she had more pressing issues than her adult children—she was painfully lonely.

Reflection Questions	
STEP 5. **Defining a** **Clear** **Outcome**	What does relationship success look like right now? What is the outcome I'm trying to achieve? *(Imagine what it would feel like to be wholly, unapologetically you in the relationships of your life. What would that look like? What would be different from how you experience relationships today?)*
STEP 6. **Aligning** **Your Actions**	What is the first step I can take? How will this action lead to a greater feeling of belonging and connection? *(Naming the first step you can take—and how it will support your growth—will help you get into action).*
STEP 7. **Creating** **Systems and** **Environments** **to Support** **Your Success**	What help do I need to support me on my journey? What do I need to let go of that is getting in my way of feeling deeply connected to others? What support systems—scaffolding—will help me experience more of the types of relationships I've determined that I want? *(Think about where you spend time or what you spend time doing—are these activities that truly represent you? If you find yourself doing things that "people who are like you do," but it's not actually what lights you up, you are not likely to meet people who will fit you like a hand and a glove).*

Figure 7.2

Sandy was constantly surrounded by people in her community, but she didn't have any real friends. So she had a lot of connections, but no real HQCs. She was missing the positivity resonance and feeling of relational safety that HQCs provide. Because role modeling is so important, before we could turn our attention to her adult kids, we had to do some clutter clearing work with Sandy herself. Luckily, she was up for the challenge. After some emotional "digging in the dirt" and some deep self-reflection, Sandy was able to recognize that she did know what qualities in relationships really mattered to her and she did have some people in her life that she thought, with some genuine conversations and relationship-tending, could be true friends. Her biggest challenge was building out the systems to support her success (Step 7). She was going to have to branch out and do new activities or invite the people she wanted to deepen relationships with into new situations, so she could experience herself and those around her in new ways. She'd always loved cooking, so she courageously invited one of the women she knew from her country club to join her in an eight-week cooking class. It was different for both of them to interact in this new way, but they found they thoroughly enjoyed each other and began to build a friendship that wasn't just based on circumstances, but based on a mutual investment of time and care. After a while, Sandy realized that she felt more alive when she was laughing with her new cooking friend then when she was doing all the things to "look right" in other parts of her life. Her journey has taken a lot of effort and a willingness to be vulnerable, and there is a lot about what she's experiencing that she's still trying to understand. But Sandy is finding that she's getting better at discerning which relationships genuinely resonate with her versus when she is just playing the part of a socially connected "happy and blessed person." It has meant letting go of some of the relationships and activities she used to invest a lot of time in, but she's finding that even though she is alone more often, she's less lonely.

Being *All* of You—The Path to Joyfully Being with Someone Else

Deep, true, authentic friendships and romantic relationships help anchor us. They mirror back to us that we have value for who we are and not what we have. These kinds of relationships are fundamentally important to our well-being and to our ability to pursue a bigger, bolder version of who we are.[7] They give us a safe container to cultivate the best of ourselves and the courage to bring who we are into the world. They're not just a "good to have". . . . they're a "must have." So it's important, resuscitative work to clear the clutter inhibiting them.

Considering how instrumental close, positive relationships are to our well-being, it is not surprising that thriving rising gen universally name the presence of such relationships in their lives as an important theme. The power of becoming who you are means you're also more likely to attract someone who values who you actually are rather than who you're projecting yourself to be. In this way, clearing your relationship clutter and clearing your identity clutter are intrinsically interconnected. Like an upward spiral, the more you know who you really are, and the more you accept and celebrate who you really are, the more you will be *seen* for who you really are and attract people who love *that* person. So, thankfully, all the clutter clearing you've been so heartfully doing throughout your journey with this book will only help you to more easily find—and be in—healthy, supportive relationships.

After years of clearing out her own relationship clutter, Rebekah eventually met and married someone who is a great fit for her. She has a robust community of friends and professional colleagues who value her for all of who she is and the multifaceted perspective she is able to offer. While she occasionally will say that she's "temporarily forgotten herself" and gotten entangled in some inner dialog or a relationship that isn't totally supportive to her, she's quick to notice the signs that clutter is building up again and use strategies to "get back to herself," feeling strong and confident in her relationships, feeling like she belongs.

8

Contribution Clutter

Opportunity is missed by most people because it is dressed in overalls and looks like work.

—Thomas Edison

Trevor, now in his 50s, grew up with a dad who was a successful businessman in the farm equipment industry. With a net worth around $25 million in the 1970s, his father had created a level of wealth that no one else in their community had. In his teens, Trevor remembers his dad telling him, "You'll never have to work. This business has taken off, and you'll have more money than you need for your whole life." Trevor internalized this message, making his way through high school and college, but never considering any tangible goals beyond that. He graduated college and began his life—enjoying that he didn't have to hustle for a job the way so many of his peers were. He struggled through his 20s, marrying and divorcing, dabbling with drugs and alcohol. It wasn't until he was in his 30s—depressed, alone, and without any meaningful direction for his life—that he began to question whether it really was a privilege to never work. He looked around at his college peers, and they all seemed to be progressing in their careers, building their lives, making purposeful decisions. Trevor was stuck. He had never even considered how he might want to use his skills or any way that he could contribute to his community or the greater world. He had considered it a gift that he

111

didn't have to work to support himself. But he'd never considered that there might be reasons *other* than income to work.

Why Work

A common definition of work is "an activity involving mental or physical effort done in order to achieve a purpose or result." The *Cambridge Dictionary* defines work more specifically as an "activity, such as a job, that a person uses physical or mental effort to do, usually for money."[1] Whether you're working for an end result or working for money, work—or, more broadly, contribution—matters. While it is not always the case, often rising gen don't need to earn money in order to cover the expenses of their lives. So, it naturally begs the question, if you don't *need* to earn money to live, why work?

To start with, we're wired to be productive. We're wired to experience the satisfaction of our actions having a resulting impact. From very early in life, infants show delight in being the cause of events—dropping a ball out of a crib, turning a light switch on or off, shaking a noise-making toy and seeing the reaction of the adults around them. With the right support and structure, young children will illustrate their natural inclination for concentrated effort.[2] Evolutionarily speaking, our species would not have survived if we didn't learn to find value in being productive and finding ways to contribute to our tribes. Abraham Maslow, the psychologist most well-known for his study of the progressive fulfillment of psychological needs that lead to one's ability to express their full potential (known as "Maslow's Hierarchy of Needs," or sometimes more colloquially "Maslow's pyramid"), describes the value of contribution this way: "Self-actualizing people are, without one single exception, involved in a cause outside their own skin, in something outside of themselves. They are devoted, working at something, something which is very precious to them—some calling or a vocation in the old sense. They are working at something which fate has called them to somehow and which they work at and which they love, so that the work-joy dichotomy in them disappears."[3] While the reason to work may be different for a rising gen than someone in another economic circumstance, the value of working—of contributing in some meaningful way—is the same as it has been for all people since the beginning of time. It's part of our humanness.

Not only are we wired for work, but work—when it is aligned with our skills and interests—is also a source for happiness. It increases our well-being. Arthur Brooks, a Harvard Business School professor who teaches business students about happiness, illustrates how well-being is enhanced through work (and other important components) in these simple equations:[4]

Subjective Well–being = Genes + Circumstances + Habits

Habits = Faith + Family + Circumstances + Work

Brooks distills a significant amount of psychological literature in his equations, and while they are simplistic, they are accurate and, I think, quite useful. Let's break them down:

Subjective well-being is the term social scientists have agreed upon to describe someone's overall level of life satisfaction. **Genes**, in this equation, refers to the heredibility of our level of happiness—our happiness set-point. Whether we like it or not, it turns out that our genes play a strong role in our baseline happiness (by one study, somewhere between 44% and 52%).[5] **Circumstances** refers to the situations in our lives that impact our happiness. While there is no clear agreement on how *much* our life circumstances impact our subjective well-being, there is agreement that, in general, circumstances only sway our baseline happiness temporarily, not permanently. So according to Brooks' first equation, since we can't change our genes and the transitory circumstances of life don't greatly impact our long-term happiness, what lever can we pull to increase our overall level of life satisfaction? Enter our **habits**. And as well see in the next paragraph, according to Brooks' second equation, integrating work as one of our regular habits is part of the happiness equation. Brooks writes, "I am convinced that . . . enduring happiness comes from human relationships, productive work, and transcendental elements of life."[6]

In Brooks' second equation, we see this connection between work and overall life satisfaction as he lays out the fundamental components of our habits. First, **faith** refers to any structure (religious or philosophical) through which you can ponder the questions of life and "transcend a focus on your narrow self-interests to serve others."[7] **Family** has a broad definition including both the people we're related to and those we've picked to be in our lives. At the end of the day (and as we've seen in the previous chapter), social connection is deeply connected to happiness.[8] Finally, there is **work**. One of the central findings in happiness literature is the importance of human productivity and creating a sense of purpose in one's life. As you may have guessed given that the title of this chapter is "Contribution Clutter," the definition of work does not have to be as narrow as the *Cambridge Dictionary* defines it; it can be creating impact and achieving results without necessarily holding a corresponding job title or having to earn money to do it. According to Brooks, the key to making this component of the equation tip the scales toward greater well-being is that you have the sense that you are *earning your success* and *serving others*.

It can be as simple as a summer job. Remember Mitch and Kristy from Chapter 4? They were the parents who were trying to figure out how to help their almost-16-year-old daughter Taylor have ownership over her new car. Prior to purchasing the car, Taylor had decided to get a job at a little local market about two miles from their house as a way to earn each money toward her car. She rode her bike to and from the store without (too much) complaint and found that she enjoyed both the freedom of getting herself there and home and also the feeling of accomplishment that came from earning her own money. While she started off making minimum wage, she was quickly seen as responsible and reliable and the store owner gave her a raise within the first 6 months.

Taylor worked at the market all through high school (eventually driving her car instead of riding her bike), and it was clear that she enjoyed the feeling of earning her own money while also serving the needs of the market's owner and customers. Later in this book we'll get into how contribution can help us to transcend into truly creating a life of impact, but for now, let's focus on basics of the role of work in our lives and how family wealth can make the path to meaningful contribution more cluttered.

Family Wealth and the Formation of Contribution Clutter

It seems like eliminating the need to earn income to pay basic expenses would be the greatest gift ever. Yet, as many rising gen will tell you, removing the economic imperative to work makes it significantly more difficult to find a path of meaningful contribution. Which is, as we've learned, an essential component to a rewarding and well-lived life. Complicating that path, I tend to see three major sources of contribution clutter in my work with rising gen.

The first source of contribution clutter comes from often well-meaning parents and grandparents who, having toiled to get to the top themselves, may encourage their rising gen to **"go find your passion"** rather than putting effort into work and earning income. This is a fine goal, but the problem is, rising gen are often told to go find their passions at a time in their lives—typically their 20s—when they are least likely to know how to go about doing that. As we explored in the chapter on identity clutter, it's a time when they haven't built a deep-enough well of identity capital (the individual collection of resources and experiences that we gather over time that impact how we engage in the world)[9] to guide them toward what their passion might be. The risk of this situation is that you may get stuck *seeking* and not learn to *commit*. Remember, it is both the ability to explore and the ability to buckle down that increase the kind of self-knowledge that will, eventually, lead you to understand yourself—and the world—well enough to know what your passion might be. Getting stuck in the seeking becomes a death-blow to learning to work. As one 31-year-old rising gen client, Gabrielle, shared with me, "By the time I realized I had stalled out, all of my friends had careers they had been progressing in for a decade. I was too embarrassed to get an entry-level job but had no marketable skills for a more advanced job."

Gabrielle went on to share more of her story, which illustrated a common second source of contribution clutter—**becoming a hobbyist**. Gabrielle disclosed, "Ultimately that's how I ended up working for my family's foundation. But honestly, that doesn't require much of me. It feels more like 'make-work' than a real job. I like being able to say that I have a job when people ask, but inside I know that I don't have that much to do and I don't have any real autonomy. It's the kind of job that I can *not* pay attention to for weeks at a time and it doesn't make a difference. Honestly, at least the way that I'm doing it, it is not that rewarding." Gabrielle is highlighting the important relationship between the effort we put into something and the meaning we get out of it.

In their book, *The Voice of the Rising Generation*, Jay Hughes, Susan Massenzio, and Keith Whitaker define work in a way that highlights why Gabrielle likely feels so flat about her job. They write, "Work is any activity that challenges you and tests your abilities, that requires your dedication, and that also meets the true needs of others."[10] Gabrielle had become a "family foundation hobbyist"—someone who could dabble in the work, but it didn't test her abilities or require any roll-up-your-sleeves-and-get-your-grit-on dedication from her. She was likely creating positive impact for others through the foundation's gifts, but she was not engaging in the work in a way that was meaningful to her. She wasn't engaging in a way that would challenge her to grow.

Finally, another common source of contribution clutter is **the pull (and the trap) of the leisure lifestyle**. So many people spend so much of their time trying to earn more so that they can get to that pinnacle part of their lives when they can retire and do whatever they want. Unfortunately, the research shows that those who disengage in productive activities in their retirement don't fare well when it comes to health and longevity.[11] And the same is true on the other end of the age continuum—unemployed and under-employed 20-somethings tend to have higher levels of depression than their peers.[12] So the pull of the picture-perfect leisure lifestyle can soon become a trap. As Hughes, Massenzio, and Whitaker put it, "The reason that vacations, or retirement, or relaxations in general—fun as they are—are truly worthwhile is because they provide a pause from work. When we work, we get tired. We need a break. But if you never work, then you really never enjoy a break. In such a situation, going from one vacation or fun activity to another can start to feel like drudgery. It is like a weekend that never ends. It becomes as boring as any dead-end job."[13] This was the exact experience of my 24-year-old client, Lucy, who, having not yet "found her passion" and uninspired by any job prospects, was dabbling with the idea of just fully embracing a leisure lifestyle. After getting back from a 2-week vacation to Maui she told me this: "I was really looking forward to this vacation. I had all of the places I wanted to go planned out and I had a stack of books I envisioned myself reading on the beach. The first couple of days were really fun. But, honestly, after a while it just felt like I feel when I'm at home—I read when I wanted to, ate when I wanted to, watched TV, took naps. It all sounded like a perfect vacation, but it was no different from my daily life. Except I was at the beach. That part was nice, I guess."

Not having the *financial* need to work does not remove the *human* need to work. Contribution is wired into us and we're happier when we're challenging ourselves to build our skills. We're happier when we're leaving our own mark. It's validation that we matter. And it's a sense of connection to something bigger than ourselves. Let's look at how you can clear some of the clutter that may be getting in the way of your ability to contribute.

Clearing Your Inner Contribution Clutter

By now you're starting to get this seven-step clutter clearing process down and hopefully you're also seeing some results from your hard work. The following Reflection Questions are designed to help you spot where you may have some contribution dust bunnies hiding in the corners of your mind. Let's see if we can't clear some of that inner contribution clutter out.

Reflection Questions

STEP 1. Cultivating a Beneficial Mindset

When was a time that I fully committed myself to something (a job, learning an instrument, a chess club, dancing lessons, etc.) and I experienced the satisfaction of hard work?

What were the qualities of that experience (e.g., the people, the rewards, the internal feeling of accomplishment) that made it so valuable?

What, if any, are the negative or disempowering connotations I have with work that would be helpful to shine a light on? *(Consider the work experiences [paid or unpaid] you've had—did you ever feel undervalued? If you ever thought your contribution didn't matter, what did that feel like? Or if you suspected that you were only given the job because of your last name, what thoughts and emotions did that generate?)*

Based on these insights, what is the mindset I want to adopt regarding work and contribution? What would be the most beneficial and empowering mindset I could create? *(This is the mindset that will help you transform your relationship to work/ contribution, transforming it into an activity that feels intrinsically compelling.)*

Figure 8.1

Reflection Questions	
STEP 2. Adopting an Empow- ering Identity	Do I believe I have what it takes to create a genuine impact through my concerted efforts? Why do I believe this? What qualities do I have that I know will support my success? Who am I as a contributor? Try to create an identity statement. *(This is the identity that you most want to embrace and express.)* "**I am . . .** [refer to the authentic qualities and skills from the question that you bring to the work you engage in]."
STEP 3. Curating Supportive Beliefs	What do I currently believe about the role of work and contribution in my life? Is it important? Is it worth pursuing? Do I feel supported and excited by these beliefs? Why? What holds me back from fully committing myself to work I care about? What belief about work would help transform how work feels to me? *(This is the supportive belief you want to adopt and use in your decision-making.)*
STEP 4. Making Aligned Decisions	When I consider the work experiences I've had to date in my life, where have I gotten stuck? Why have I gotten stuck? What skills or competencies would I need to build in order to feel confident in pursuing a profes- sional field or interest area I care about? What would someone who felt capable and confident in their capabilities do in this situation in which I often get stuck? What decision do I need to make to be aligned with the impact I want to create with my time and talent? *(This is the decision—or decisions—you can use to define the outcomes you want to create).*

Figure 8.1 *(Continued)*

The concept of work can be a complex one. Culturally, we have a lot of confusing messages about work embedded in our collective belief system. We celebrate those who work hard, while also pointing to greater leisure in one's life as a marker of success. We work all our adult lives aiming for the day when we can retire and "do whatever we want." Our relationship with work—like our relationship with money—is complicated. It's no wonder it feels like it should be satisfying to not *have* to work, but then it feels empty when we don't do something meaningful with our time.

Remember Liz, the rising gen from Chapters 2 and 4 who wanted to start a yoga studio but ended up abandoning her plan when her mom invited her on a multi-month sailing trip? When she embarked on her inner clutter clearing process, she found that she had a lot working in her favor when it came to her relationship to work and contribution. She had watched her father work hard and enjoy his career, and she wanted the same for herself, so she had a beneficial mindset around work. Though she did admit that, at times, she worried that a successful yoga studio would give her less freedom with her time, a Step 3 limiting belief that did require a little clutter-clearing effort. Once her limiting belief was identified, Liz did the work to create a more empowering belief where she could consciously name her conviction that she could engage meaningfully with work, while still making time for life adventures. Despite some reservations, Liz had an empowering identity when it came work. She had put significant effort into her studies at college and knew she was capable of achieving much when she put her mind to it. While she was nervous and felt like she was really stretching as she wrote her yoga studio business plan, she also believed she had what it took to be successful (Steps 1, 2, and 3). For Liz, the place she got stuck was in her decision-making. When it came down to it, she wanted two things—she wanted to find success in her own right *and* she wanted to have the flexibility with her time and her travel schedule to do fun things with her parents. It is this kind of buried ambiguity that can sabotage the best-laid plans. She had to dig deep to find this conflicting decision (going sailing when she had planned to launch her business) so that we could shine a light on it. Then she could determine which was the higher goal—working toward her own vision or having freedom to travel—and align her future decisions to that (Step 4). While Liz did not end up ever opening a yoga studio, after her sailing trip she did get actively involved in the management of one of the family's business acquisitions, a role that required her innate community-building skills, afforded her some flexibility, and challenged her to develop her own unique leadership style. Ultimately, even though it wasn't a job she first pictured for herself, it has become a role in which she has found a lot of satisfaction.

By working the inner clutter clearing process and answering these questions for yourself, like Liz, you too can remove what's inhibiting your ability to see and choose your path to meaningful contribution.

Clearing Your Outer Contribution Clutter

Based on the insights from your previous inner clutter clearing, now roll up your sleeves and try focusing on the outer contribution clutter questions in Figure 8.2.

Once you start doing this outer clutter clearing work—actively and with intention—you'll begin to see its elements reinforcing each other and the flywheel effect it can generate. To pick up on Liz's story again, she not only had some inner clutter when it came to the conflict in deciding what she really wanted, she had some outer clutter that she needed to clear as well, systems and environments she'd been allowing to hinder her success. Ultimately, what Liz figured out was that she needed to ask for her mom's support. As much as Liz's mom loved spending time with her daughter and enjoyed having Liz as her "adventure buddy," in order for Liz to be able to fully engage in work that challenged her, she needed to focus more of her attention on work than travel. As a result of doing some sincere clutter clearing and being able to identify what she needed, Liz was able to lovingly and clearly ask for her mom's support and tell her why it mattered (Step 4). Liz's mom had never even considered that her invitations to travel were becoming an obstacle to her daughter's growth. The two of them sat down and identified two adventures they wanted to go on in the next year, working together to plan them so that Liz could prioritize her work and still make time to play.

Integrating It All

This chapter is entitled "Contribution Clutter" because there are so many ways to engage in meaningful work in your life and to use your gifts to

	Reflection Questions
STEP 5. **Defining a Clear Outcome**	When I imagine a situation where I'm thriving—feeling engaged and challenged—what components are present? What am I doing? What am I not doing? What is the outcome I'm trying to achieve? *(Imagine what it would feel like to be "firing on all cylinders"—experiencing the intersection of high challenge meeting your high level of skills. What would that look like? What would be different from what you're doing today?)*
STEP 6. **Aligning Your Actions**	What is the first small step I can take? How will this action lead to a greater feeling of engagement and impact? *(Naming the first step you can take—and how it will support your growth—will help you get into action.)*
STEP 7. **Creating Systems and Environments to Support Your Success**	What help do I need to support me on my journey? What do I need to let go of that is hindering my ability to feel confident and competent? What scaffolding will help me move from feeling stuck to feeling like I have what it takes to actively pursue a vision of thriving and having impact? *(Think about who you surround yourself with and what you do day-to-day. Is this supportive to who you want to become? Would it be helpful to hire a coach, set up a home office, or engage in an educational program?)*

Figure 8.2

impact the people and world around you. It all can be contribution, even if it's not formal, compensated work. For some people, the term "work" is too small—it means a paid "JOB" and that is just not for them.

If that's you, it's fine. You get to define what contribution means to you.

Just don't get stuck *contemplating* how you might contribute and never actually *committing* to action. If you find yourself getting queasy at the idea that as you get into action you might stumble and skin your knees, it's okay. Faltering and failing are all part of the path to success. In fact, learning to tolerate the discomfort of failure—and then learn from it—is a fundamentally important skill for all of us to build. So don't let fear of failure stop you from taking action, from taking a chance on yourself. Remember, learning to work is essential to our well-being and happiness. It's in our DNA. While a formal job may not be your path to self-actualization, there are lots of non-traditional ways to engage and contribute that will support your growth and have positive impact beyond you.

It matters less *what* you do and more *how you feel* about what you do. Whether you choose to pursue paid work outside of your family, actively engage in your family's philanthropy or enterprise, volunteer in your community, or engage in social entrepreneurship—that's up to you. What matters most is that your relationship to what you do is positive, that you feel challenged. Accountable. That you have considered what your highest and best use is and have been thoughtful in applying your gifts and skills.

If what you're doing feels like "make-work" or like it doesn't require you to really stretch and grow, it's probably not going to feel very satisfying either. But if you apply yourself, working hard at something meaningful to you, your contribution can become—as the successful rising gen at the beginning of this book said—"something of a habit" and "like a flywheel that just keeps rotating and giving . . . motivation."

Trevor, the rising gen whose successful father had told him he'd never have to work in his life, eventually ended up discovering that even though he didn't *have* to work, he *wanted* to work. But he hadn't been able to get to the place of being intrinsically motivated to work until he'd completed some pretty serious clutter clearing. It was in that process of self-reflection and exploration that he realized that, while his dad thought he was giving his son the gift of freedom to not work, Trevor's unconscious translation was that his dad must not think him *capable* of meaningful work. With this as the backdrop in his 20s, no wonder he didn't strive for anything. Once Trevor was able to reframe this part of his self-narrative, he started gaining traction in his life. Today Trevor has a thriving psychotherapy practice where he supports many other rising gen to successfully find their way—just as he eventually did.

The Big Logs for Your Fire: Human Thriving and Your Unique Spark

9

The Science of
Human Thriving

"Psychologists have scant knowledge of what makes life worth living. They have come to understand quite a bit about how people survive under conditions of adversity. However, psychologists know very little about how normal people flourish under more benign conditions ....Whatever the personal origins of our conviction that the time has arrived for a positive psychology, our message is to remind our field that psychology is not just the study of pathology, weakness, and damage; it is also the study of strength and virtue. Treatment is not just fixing what is broken; it is nurturing what is best ....And in this quest for what is best, positive psychology does not rely on wishful thinking, faith, self-deception, fads, or hand-waving; it tries to adapt what is best in the scientific method to the unique problems that human behavior presents to those who wish to understand it in all of its complexity."

—Martin Seligman and Mihaly Csikszentmihalyi,
American Psychologist, 2000

As we move into another level of solutions for rising gen, their families, friends, and advisors to dispel the myth of the silver spoon and give the next generation of the affluent the tools and support they need for a life of thriving and impact, we are going to draw on validated research from the field of positive psychology. *Wait,* you might say. *We're going on a detour into pop psychology and mantras of rainbows and butterflies?* No. And for the tools that follow to be most effective, it's important that you understand why.

"Happiology" Versus the Science of Human Thriving

Let's get this on the table from the get-go: the field of positive psychology, despite its upbeat name, is not merely the study of happiness. It is not about putting a big, yellow smiley face on all of life's circumstances, ignoring the dark corners of our minds where doubts and fears reside. It is not about positive affirmations and pasting over life's difficulties with fabricated optimism. It is not a "happiology." Nor is positive psychology "pop" psychology (short for "popular psychology," which is often nonprofessional and based more in myth than science), a self-improvement fad, or just about using positive thinking. So, what is it?

The field of positive psychology is the scientific study of human thriving. It's about what goes right in life, about what makes life worth living—from birth to death and everything in between.[1] It recognizes that both the good and the bad in life are genuine aspects of the human experience and that it is as important to effectively learn how to navigate life's difficulties as it is to learn to joyfully celebrate life's wins.

In my experience—both personally and professionally—positive psychology provides a powerful chest of tools to support the growth and thriving of both individuals and their families. We'll get into some of those tools in the coming chapters, but for now, let's lay some groundwork, starting with how we define flourishing.

While many notable scientists have described and researched frameworks for defining well-being, one of the most accessible definitions for human flourishing is the contribution of Martin "Marty" Seligman. Often referred to as the "father of positive psychology," Seligman has challenged the field of psychology to give equal attention to understanding human thriving as had been historically dedicated to understanding human suffering.[2] In his book, *Flourish: A Visionary New Understanding of Happiness and Well-Being*,[3] Seligman defines **human flourishing** as containing these five components, which spell out the easy-to-remember mnemonic PERMA:

- Positive emotion—Encompassing the idea of things that feel good—the "pleasant life." This component includes, but is not limited to, happiness and life satisfaction. It also includes positive emotions such as pleasure, ecstasy, comfort, and warmth. We pursue positive emotions for their own sake, not as a means to an end. We pursue them because they feel *good*.

- Engagement—This is all about complete absorption in an endeavor. People often describe having lost track of time when they are fully engaged. It generally shows up when we're involved with something that requires both a high level of skill and is very challenging. This is often referred to as "flow state."[4]
- Positive **R**elationships—Relationships (the good ones!) are the cornerstone of well-being. Engaging in positive, kind, and giving relationships provides one of the single most reliable increases in well-being.
- **M**eaning—Meaning can only be defined by you, but at its heart, it is about experiencing your own sense of worth and value while also serving a purpose greater than just yourself.
- **A**ccomplishment—Accomplishment can be measured both in short-term achievement (running your personal record at a recent race) and long-term achievement (completing your PhD or dedicating many years of your life to a cause that matters to you). People who pick goals and pursue them over months and years tend to report higher levels of life satisfaction.

While you don't have to have all five elements of PERMA working for you at all times, the more you invest in developing each component, the higher the level of well-being you'll progressively experience. We'll get into more specifics about *how* you actually do that in the coming chapters. But do you remember the rising gen from our discussion of relationship clutter who described how her no-doubt-about-it best friend had influenced her life? That's a great picture of human flourishing germinating from one of these components—positive relationships. Here are a few other examples. They show what some of these components of flourishing can look like in the lives of thriving rising gen.

Expressing accomplishment:

Accomplishing both of those big goals—earning a spot on a Division I team and graduating with honors—have given me the confidence to know that I can figure most things out. I'm confident based on my past experiences that I can take most any leap. When I come to a ledge and I decide I'm going to jump, I know I can do it because I have done so successfully before.

Expressing engagement and positive emotion:

[Many of my extended family members] have just accepted the family's money. They haven't done much with their lives and to me that feels like settling. Do

I fantasize about just [accepting the money and] being provided for? Absolutely. Do I think it would be satisfying? No. It absolutely wouldn't. What I'm doing [in charting my own course] is hard work. I'm grateful I have some financial resources that have allowed me to pursue creating this business, but at the end of the day, I know it is mine to make happen. It's hard and, right now, it's all consuming. But the work is satisfying. And no one can take that away.

Expressing meaning:

My advice to any rising gen would be to make yourself proud. There is so much to be said for how often we're trying to make other people proud, and there is something to be said for setting small goals, learning every day, and making it all mean something to you. How you create a wealthy/rich life that has nothing to do with money. This is how you make the path to feeling good about yourself, and then the money is just a tool.

Each of these quotes have been taken directly from my research interviews with successful rising gen family members and illustrate the lived experience of facets of PERMA in their lives. These examples of thriving reveal a promised land that can also be yours. Where your life burns bright with purpose and fulfillment—lighting your path forward, motivating you on.

★ ★ ★ ★ ★

Now for those of you who are science buffs like me, you're going to love learning next about how positive psychology became a formalized field of study and why it's going to provide us with such powerful tools for navigating family wealth and creating an impactful life. And for those of you who started yawning as soon as you read that sentence, feel free to skip ahead to Chapter 10 where you'll find ways to begin gathering the "big logs" that will provide the long-term fuel of your own thriving.

A Field with a Long Past and a Short History

It is said that psychology is a field with a long past, but only a short history.[5] Meaning, the field of psychology has only formally existed for a little over 100 years, but the questions that are at the root of the field are ones that philosophers, theologians, and common people have wrestled with for millennia. The same can be said of positive psychology. While the field of positive psychology is relatively new (officially founded in 1998), the questions that have guided the research and application in the field have been asked throughout human history.

For thousands of years, dating back to Confucius and Lao-Tzu in the East and the Greek philosophers in the West, thought leaders have been asking what constitutes a good life, what conditions support human thriving, and what it means to be happy.[6] Embedded in these ancient inquiries are questions regarding the role of character, virtue, and strengths—all topics that live at the heart of the field of positive psychology today. But what has now become the study of positive psychology hasn't always been separate from the topics traditionally studied in the field of modern human psychology—and what's interesting is why.

The roots of modern psychology date back to the 19th century when the field had three missions: **to cure illness, to make the lives of all people more productive and fulfilling, and to identify and nurture high talent**.[7] When you consider the field and practice of psychology today, do you even think about those latter two missions? Likely not.

After World War II, the focus of psychology in the United States began to shift. Due to the creation of the Veterans Administration (now Veterans Affairs) and the National Institutes of Mental Health—which were created to address the grave needs of veterans returning home with mental health issues after the war—government funding began to flow to (1) research that was focused on understanding human suffering and (2) to practitioners who treated human suffering.[8] A widespread refocusing resulted, amidst which the other two components of the field's original mission were left behind.

While the narrowing of the field's empirical lens to assessing and curing individual suffering was detrimental to the study of well-being, this era did produce incredibly valuable work. It was in this post-WWII era that both the *Diagnostic and Statistical Manual of Mental Disorders* (DSM),[9] sponsored by the American Psychiatric Association, and the *International Classification of Diseases* (ICD),[10] sponsored by the World Health Organization, were established. Both these resources helped to create a common practitioner language and agreed-upon criteria for diagnosing disorders, making it possible to leverage research available in the field to treat or cure some mental illnesses that were previously considered intractable. But, while the tight focus of the field in the 20th century following WWII had been extremely valuable, it was incomplete.

As stated in the preamble to the constitution of the World Health Organization, "Health is a state of complete physical, mental and social well-being and not merely the absence of disease or infirmity."[11] Embedded in this definition is the implicit recognition that *health is not just defined by the absence of disease, but it is also about the presence of wellness.* By extension, mental well-being is not merely the absence of mental illness, but the presence of psychological well-being. This larger sphere was what had gone missing in psychological research and application. And it's what grew to become known today as the field of positive psychology.

The Birth of Positive Psychology

The field of positive psychology was formally born in 1998 when Martin Seligman gave his seminal presidential address to the American Psychological Association, challenging the field of psychology to give equal attention to understanding human thriving as had been historically dedicated to understanding human suffering. As a result, the increase of research money and subsequent attention paid to topics addressing well-being has exploded since the early 2000s. This increased research has expanded our knowledge of what supports human flourishing significantly. Thank goodness for that, because it is this body of science that we're going to be drawing on to help you move from your clutter clearing process to beginning to design your own path of flourishing and impact.

A Tool Chest for the Rising Generation

How might the lens of positive psychology be helpful in creating a new paradigm for members of the rising generation in affluent families? For one, research continues to mount that the cultivation of human strengths and virtues can act as buffers against mental illness.[12] In fact, positive psychology's version of the *Diagnostic and Statistical Manual of Mental Disorders* was created in what is called *Character Strengths and Virtues: Handbook and Classification*[13] (CSV), a reference book dubbed "the manual of the sanities."[14] The CSV is important because it gives a classification system of strengths and virtues— giving equal weight to that which supports our well-being as has previously been given to that which hinders it. Now that you've cleared some major clutter and you're ready to start—intentionally—constructing your own path to thriving, we're going to pull from this "manual of the sanities," the field of positive psychology in general, and, specifically, from my own research on rising gen who are flourishing and creating impact.

What is in store for you next is a research-based, practical framework to help you thrive.

10

Big Logs: Growth Mindset, Grit, Mastery-Orientation, Close Positive Relationships, and Your Foundational Character Strengths

"I would rather that my spark should burn out in a brilliant blaze than it should be stifled by dry-rot.
I would rather be a superb meteor, every atom of me in magnificent glow, than a sleepy and permanent planet."

—Jack London, *How to Build a Fire*

Pierre did not consider himself to be smart. Not smart the way his dad was smart. Or the way he perceived his siblings to be smart. But he did know how to work hard. Pierre grew up in a very small East Coast town, and his father had built a successful enterprise distributing wholesale food to restaurants. His family's net worth was around $10 million, a sum that was big enough to make Pierre feel small. Pierre came from a big family with a strong focus on their faith. His siblings had all gone to college and most of them were married now, but school just didn't fit for Pierre, so he started working construction in their little town. Pierre's parents loved their big family and enjoyed sharing their resources with their kids—his dad always said it was just his way of "softening the rough edges of life" for his children. Pierre got married in his late 20s, and he and his wife had a little boy, whom he loved. It was seeing himself through his toddler's eyes that jarred him awake, and at the age of 31, he started to question why he seemed to have stalled in his life. He realized he wanted more for his son than the life he, himself, was living. Pierre was also wise enough to recognize that if he wanted something different for his son, he needed to role model something different to him.

Pierre knew he smoked a little too much pot and openly admitted that this habit dulled his drive and dampened his enthusiasm for stretching out of his comfort zone. He often said that he knew he should quit, he just hadn't found a compelling reason to do it yet. After a fair bit of clutter clearing to try to understand how he got to be in his early 30s and feeling so directionless, he realized he didn't have any vision for his life. He didn't have a spark. Besides knowing how to work hard, he didn't have confidence in himself. He felt helpless to make the kinds of changes that would get him moving toward some goal in life. He was holding on to old baggage about not being smart enough, which had grown into a feeling of not being good enough, which had become the belief that he wasn't capable enough.

Pierre looked at each of these piles of clutter one by one, and over time, he cleared them out to create some room for himself. He began to show an interest in hydroponic farming and found that the local community college had a class on the topic. Pierre had found a reason to self-medicate a little less and stretch out of his comfort zone a little more. He still had some work to do in order to set himself up for a different future, but he had cleared enough space to let a new vision take root.

★ ★ ★ ★ ★

Before Martin Seligman gained fame with his research on human flourishing, he was studying, among other things, depression. The year was 1967, and as an extension of this research focus, Seligman and fellow psychologist, Steve Maier, were testing their theory of "learned helplessness." This original research concluded that animals (dogs in this case) that experienced a low-level electric stimulus would give up trying to escape that stimulus if they discovered they could do nothing about it. (An important note if you love animals as much as I do, Seligman writes about his early misgivings about animal studies[1] and, as an animal lover himself, he writes how he always "took his own medicine"[2] first—administering the low-level stimulus to himself and also taste-testing the dog food they were given. He humorously writes that the dog food was worse than the stimulus.[3]) In essence, the animals learned to become helpless because their circumstances taught them that nothing that they did would impact their situation, so they began to passively accept it. Even after the experiments were over, these animals experienced ongoing negative effects such as depression and the inability to exert effort in subsequent challenging circumstances.[4]

Over the years, I have heard many advisors who work with significant families talk about the "learned helplessness" of next generation family members. How, when faced with trying to create their own path, earn income in their own right, and find an identity separate from that of their families, the gravitational pull of family dynamics and family financial support are too great, and they become helpless—unable to escape the black hole that sucks the oxygen out of the aspirations of so many individual members of affluent families. Like the dogs in the 1960s experiments, these next gens give up trying to "escape" and just succumb. This research finding and the concept of "learned helplessness" is one that, in the past, I have shared with my own clients in an attempt to highlight the pull of passivity.

The problem is, it's not true.

Decades later, when advances in neuroscience allowed for a more refined understanding of the neurobiological mechanisms at work during a so-called helpless experience, Seligman and Maier's continued research revealed something startling: *Helplessness is actually not learned. Instead, helplessness is our default state, and it is control over our circumstances that can be learned.*[5] This is big. Continued research by many in the field has demonstrated that animals and humans alike can be "inoculated against," or become psychologically resistant to future helpless experiences. It turns out, we are *all* born with a helpless orientation, and it is through overcoming developmentally appropriate doses of difficulty and adversity that we build competency and resilience over time.

The headline news here is that it is actually not *helplessness* that is learned, but *mastery* that is learned.

What does this mean for you or the rising gen your care about? Having experiences that challenge you and in which you learn to overcome difficulties can keep you from feeling helpless in the face of future stressors. Put another way, appropriate challenges can teach you how very capable you are. Developing the habit of mastery by tapping into innate (even if not often used) character traits and building supportive skills when facing difficult life events can serve as a buffer against helplessness and its spirit-crushing cousins of depression, anxiety, and passivity. These traits and skills are the "big logs" we talked about in Chapter 1. These logs create a scaffolding for the ignition of your unique spark and provide the ongoing slow fuel to keep your internal fire burning throughout your lifetime.

After learning of this new research regarding helplessness, I became curious: If it's not helplessness that is learned but mastery (as the result of experiencing manageable levels of adversity), is there a common set of character traits and skills that support the growth of a thriving rising gen? In other words, could there be a set of specific things you could work on to help jump-start and speed your process toward capability, confidence, and impact? Grateful for the many practitioners who came before me who interviewed inheritors and published insightful work on their lived experience, but not finding any existing empirical research that answered this question, I set about conducting it myself.

A Key Question: What Traits Do Successful Rising Gen Have in Common?

As I considered the research I wanted to conduct on the lived experience of adult children raised in affluent families, I found myself asking questions like these:

How can someone, particularly someone who's grown up with or inherited significant wealth, avoid the tripwires that many of their peers stumble on?

Why is it that some of my clients are quickly able to adopt new thinking and take aligned action in their lives, while others really struggle to even identify their own voice amidst the cacophony of other voices?

What do well-intentioned parents who are raising their kids in the context of wealth need to know or do to help set their kids up early on for successful, fulfilling lives?

Is there a set of character traits and skills that engaged advisors could guide their client families to focus on in order to support the future success of their rising generation family members?

Despite the fact that the stereotypical floundering inheritor makes for easy internet news click-bait, I knew from experience that there are also many rising gen who are happily and quietly going about thriving in their lives and building paths of impact. Sure, they experience difficulties and setbacks like all people do, and sometimes their difficulties and setbacks are related to their unique financial situations. But I had witnessed many committed and generous adult rising gen who were doing the important work of figuring out how to be in healthy relationships, how to parent well, what work and contribution looks like for them, and how they could impact their communities. But what did this quiet army of thriving rising gen have in common?

Determined to get answers to these questions and based on what I was learning about positive psychology and observing in the field, I came up with and tested a hypothesis. I posited what could move rising gen from helplessness to learned mastery, then interviewed thriving rising generation family members, eager to better understand which character traits and skills they had acquired to support their successes.

By focusing on the upper end of development within a population (a research approach called exemplar methodology), I explored if and how often these wealth inheritors had experienced feelings of helplessness that can show up among children in affluent families. I also wanted to learn more about the specific inner traits and external experiences that supported these rising gen in creating lives filled with autonomy, contribution, and engagement.

My in-depth, interview-based research supported my original hypothesis, yielding this equation:

Helplessness → Learned Mastery = Growth Mindset + Grit + Mastery−Orientation/Experience(s)+Close Positive Relationships

In other words, the path from helplessness and passivity to learned mastery and agency over one's own life is paved by cultivating a Growth Mindset, developing Grit, employing a Mastery-Orientation, and experiencing Close Positive Relationships. While not every research participant exhibited every one of these traits and skills, overall, they all had a strong stable of them. And while a Growth Mindset, Grit, Mastery-Orientation, and Close Positive Relationships aren't the only factors that contribute to success, they are *undeniably significant ones.*

Speaking of other factors that support thriving rising gen, an important note: In this chapter you will not only read about the traits and skills I researched, but also about a specific classification of 24 positive psychology-defined character strengths and virtues. The latter is one of those potential "big logs" that I *didn't* include in my study—but I wish I had. So even though you won't see this factoring into my previous equation, I think a quick discussion of them is worthy, and we'll explore that further later. For now, let's dig into each of the four critical aspects I named for helping you—or the rising gen you care about—move toward a place of personal agency, freedom, and purpose.

The Big Logs

Take a moment to inhale. Exhale. Ahhhh. Can you feel how easy it is to breathe now that you've cleared out some of that stagnant, dusty, no-space-for-you clutter?

Having a little more elbow room and enough fresh air to feed even the smallest spark, it's time to bring in the big logs and build the scaffolding for your future fire. Let's look at how these "big logs"—Growth Mindset, Grit, Mastery-Orientation, Close Positive Relationships (and, in the next section, Foundational Character Strengths)—create the internal structure so that the "tinder" of your ideas have the support to become a stable fire. A fire strong enough to ignite powerful change, either in your own life, your community, or in the world. While this chapter is written especially for the rising gen, if you're a parent or a trusted advisor, the following content will be useful to you too. It'll not only give you an understanding of what traits and skills will support the success of the rising gen in your life, it'll also prepare you to soak up the practical tips and wisdom outlined in Chapter 12 (for parents) and Chapter 13 (for trusted advisors).

To get us started, let's define one other important term from the previous equation—learned mastery. We've already defined the concept of helplessness; the antidote to helplessness is **Learned Mastery**. Mastery teaches us that we have personal agency, that we have the ability to act of our own accord to change the circumstances we're in (or at least change our response to the circumstances we're in). Mastery is a skill (or I might even suggest that it is a skill that can become a habit) where we develop the ability to consider and try various actions in response to negative events. Mastery can help buffer against helplessness and its negative after-effects because it reminds us that *we have control.* We are not at the whim of our circumstances. This approach can be learned—it just takes discovering that we can meet and overcome appropriate doses of hardship along the way.

Now that we've defined the goal—adopting a lifetime approach of Learned Mastery—let's unpack those big logs that will help you get there. For each of these big logs, in addition to descriptions and advice for cultivation, I've also included quotes from my research interviews to give you an inside peek at the lived experience of other thriving rising gen.

Growth Mindset

A **Growth Mindset** is the belief that a trait (like intelligence or resilience) is malleable and can be developed through hard work, good strategies, and the ability to receive and integrate thoughtful feedback.[6]

Growth Mindset is a character trait, and like all human traits, it is partly inherited and partly developed through individual action and environmental support. While some people naturally approach life with a Growth Mindset more often than not, others are naturally more inclined to experience life with a fixed mindset.

Carol Dweck, the researcher well-known for her work on Growth Mindset, suggests that if you have a fixed mindset, you tend to think that intelligence and other traits are static.[7] Based on this view, you're more likely to avoid challenges, get defensive, give up easily, perceive significant exertion toward a goal as a sign that you're not talented, ignore constructive criticism, and feel threatened by others' accomplishments. In sum, you are very likely to achieve less than your potential. Whereas, if you're naturally predisposed to a Growth Mindset, it's typically the opposite.

The good news is, regardless of where you land on the growth-to-fixed mindset continuum based on your genes, you *have the ability to increase* how often you experience life with a Growth Mindset. All it takes is awareness and choiceful action.

Cultivating a Growth Mindset

According to Dweck, simply learning about the concept of a Growth Mindset can begin to impact how often you adopt this mindset.[8] Awareness of this trait can begin to change your approach to challenging situations, receiving feedback, and your willingness to try something new where you know you'll feel out of your depth. I remember my disappointment when I received my first graded paper soon after I had started my MAPP graduate degree. At that point, it had been two decades since I had last been in grad school and written an academic paper. I'd invested immense effort to write a good, strong paper, and I was excited to get mine back from the professor. When I received my graded paper and saw how many comments and notes of constructive criticism were covering its text, I teared up. It took one of my wise classmates to remind me that all those comments were actually a sign that my grader saw potential in me and invested his effort to help me become a better writer. In that moment I was reminded that I could choose to have a fixed mindset (seeking to prove that I was smart by getting nothing but congratulatory comments) or I could choose a Growth Mindset (open to receiving feedback that would help me become an even better, more powerful writer). We all have that choice every day.

If you have a Growth Mindset, wherein you view intelligence and other advantageous traits as qualities that can be developed, you're more likely to embrace challenges, persist in the face of setbacks, appreciate effort as essential for mastery, value constructive criticism as an opportunity to learn, be inspired by others' achievements, and, thus, work toward higher and higher levels of personal accomplishment. Here is a short, three-question survey designed by Dweck to help you assess where you land on the fixed-to-growth mindset continuum;[9] I encourage you to take it right now:

Using a 6-point scale (1 = Strongly Agree; 6 = Strongly Disagree), rate how you feel about each of the following statements:

- You have a certain amount of intelligence, and you can't really do much to change it. (Your Answer_____)

- Your intelligence is something about you that you can't change very much. (Your Answer_____)
- You can learn new things, but you can't really change your basic intelligence. (Your Answer_____)

Add up your answers. A lower overall score leans more toward fixed mindset and a higher score leans more toward Growth Mindset. Where do you land? Try not to judge your answer—similar to the clutter clearing process you undertook in the last part of this book, understanding where you're at today is an important part of being able to make changes to who you want to become tomorrow.

If your score is on the lower end, or the description of a fixed mindset lands uncomfortably close to home, don't fret. Here are a couple of simple steps you can take:

- **Actively seek feedback.** Ask teachers, bosses, advisors, and family members, "How am I doing? Where do you see that I could improve?" And when someone tells you something you don't want to hear, take a deep breath and remind yourself that the people who really care about you will invest in you by giving you feedback. It's a gift, and you can receive it as such.

- **Learn to love the process of learning.** Sometimes learning feels . . . hard. It's work. Learn to recognize that when something gets hard it doesn't mean that you're not capable. It means that *this* is what learning feels like. Celebrate it!

- **Don't shy away from difficulty.** Just because you've never done something before doesn't mean you don't try. Want to play a new position on your lacrosse team? Ask for the chance. Interested in graduate school? Put yourself out there and apply. Want to try for the open seat on your family's board of directors? Throw your name in the hat. Opportunities come to those who ready themselves and know when to act. Learning to take on difficulty will help you be ready when the opportunities you desire arise.

These habits will help you build a Growth Mindset. Since a Growth Mindset is a key link between helplessness and mastery, it's worth figuring out how to embrace feedback and to keep putting yourself in situations where you are challenged and learning.

Growth Mindset—Rising Gen in Their Own Words

. . . *[In] high school, I partied a lot and didn't get great grades for a little period of time . . . . My dad, who came from a good family but was pretty much a self-made person, had some real heart-to-hearts with me and said, "Get your [expletive] together." [And that had an impact on me.]*

. . . *My uncle played an important role, [because of some challenging family experiences in my youth], which, as a teenager, made me uncomfortable and angry. I remember my uncle sitting me down at one point and giving me a lot of feedback about how I was showing up in the family and gave me some tools of how I could be better. And I think that was really hard to hear. But I had such great respect for him that it meant a lot that he even took the time to give that feedback."*

. . . *[So much of it is] about attitude. When you fall down and you fail, you can look at it and say, "I'm no good . . . why did I even take that risk? I'm embarrassed. People are laughing at me." Or you can say, "You know what? I gave it my best. And I know that there are going to be lots of times that I try something and I fall down, and I'm gonna be embarrassed . . . But if I have my goals and my vision set on something that I aspire to, it's going to require that I continually try to learn how to stretch. And stretching is going to result in failing—and those are the times that I'm going learn the* **most.** *" I think a lot of people, certainly myself included, believe that I've learned a lot more through failures than I ever have successes. And I think that attitude is so important. I think you have to learn that.*

Grit

Another one of the big logs that is key to your long-term success is that of Grit. **Grit** is defined as maintaining passion and perseverance in pursuit of a long-term goal.[10] Interestingly, a Growth Mindset supports the cultivation of Grit by helping us view obstacles and setbacks as learning opportunities rather than signs of failure. In this way, adopting a Growth Mindset is supportive to becoming grittier. As you might imagine, having a Growth Mindset can serve to keep you in the game—enabling you to maintain focus and effort over time. In contrast, if you're insulated and protected— not encouraged to challenge yourself, test your limits, and receive feedback from others—you're less likely to stick with something with both passion and perseverance. In short, you'll miss out on opportunities to build Grit.

According to Angela Duckworth, the psychologist well-known for her research on this character trait, it's helpful to think about what Grit *isn't* in order to understand what it *is*.[11] Grit is not talent. It is not intensity. It is not about being gifted at something. Grit is about single-focused persistence despite the inevitable setbacks and difficulties. Gritty people aren't necessarily smarter or innately better. Gritty people just work harder.

★ ★ ★ ★ ★

Nothing in the world can take the place of Persistence. Talent will not; nothing is more common than unsuccessful men with talent. Genius will not; unrewarded genius is almost a proverb. Education will not; the world is full of educated derelicts. Persistence and Determination alone are omnipotent. The slogan "press on" has solved and always will solve the problems of the human race.

— President Calvin Coolidge

★ ★ ★ ★ ★

Cultivating Grit

Encouragingly, Grit (like a Growth Mindset) can be learned. First, it's helpful to know how gritty you are today. On her website Angela Duckworth has an interactive Grit Scale that'll give you a score of where you land on the grit-o-meter. You can find it here: https://angeladuckworth.com/grit-scale/. Your score will be given to you on a scale of −5, with 5 bring the grittiest. If you find that you're interested in increasing your level of this important character trait, Duckworth suggests these four steps to growing grit from the inside out:[12]

1. **Find what you're interested in.** A terrific first step to cultivating Grit is to identify an intrinsically motivated long-term goal. Something *you* really want to accomplish. Something that matters to *you*. Music, sports, writing poetry. It doesn't matter what it is, it matters that you care about it enough to stay interested in it, even when it gets hard.

2. **Practice it.** Remember, gritty people aren't smarter or better than others. Gritty people just work harder and practice more. Pursue what you're interested in with focus and determination. Love the violin? Practice with consistency and focus. Want to become a better writer? Write every day and challenge yourself to publish. Interested in running a marathon? Figure out a step-by-step training plan and get into action by taking your first jog

around the neighborhood. As you stick with your goal despite the inevitable bumps in the road, you will build and strengthen your grittiness.

3. **Find your purpose.** Gritty people have both a strong interest in something and the intention to contribute to the well-being of others. When these two things intersect, this is purpose. We'll get into this more deeply in Chapter 11, but for now, on your journey to become grittier, hold onto the idea of exploring not only what interests you, but also what might support others.

4. **Cultivate hope.** There is a special kind of hope that coexists with Grit. It is the kind of hope that relies on our understanding that *our own efforts* will make tomorrow a better day. It's not just about hoping for a better outcome tomorrow; it's about actively taking the steps to create a better outcome tomorrow. This kind of intrinsically motivated hope gives us the unshakable self-knowledge that we will always get up one more time than we fall down. This is the kind of hope that gritty people have.

Finally, it's helpful to recognize that you don't have to be gritty in every domain of your life. In fact, time and bandwidth will be natural limiters, forcing you to pick the areas you want to pursue. That said, once you have learned that you *can* be gritty in one area of your life, it's much easier to apply those same skills to other pursuits.

Grit—Rising Gen in Their Own Words

For me, it was passing the bar exam. I went to a prep school for high school and boarding school, and I went to college, and even the graduate school I got into—you could say there might've been some help from family reputation at any of those stages. I don't know how much there was, maybe none at some of them, but maybe some. If I had any doubts, the bar exam was the one thing that the graders weren't going to be looking at anything except the answers I put down on the paper. [My passing]—that [was] all me. When I finished it, I thought, "I think I could do anything. Anything I decided to put my mind to, I really think I could do it. Give me enough time, I'll put in the effort, and I'll get there eventually." I just felt like I wished everyone could have that kind of encouraging experience.

. . . I just nibbled away at [my goals] and didn't stop until things were different. I watched that [growth] in myself as I've become more self-aware of that creative process in me. [What I focus on is] birthed within me and is inner directed.

Mastery-Orientation

The next big log to put on your stack is Mastery-Orientation. The benefits of pursuing a Growth Mindset and cultivating Grit are that they will work together to support you in your pursuit of, and engagement with, one of the key ingredients of unshakeable confidence—mastery experiences. We explored the idea of learned mastery earlier; having a Mastery-Orientation is part of the process of building the skill of learned mastery. A **Mastery-Orientation** is when an individual focuses on attaining a solution rather than ceasing to persist due to the potential for failure.[13] You can see how Growth Mindset, Grit, and Mastery-Orientation all work together to promote your personal growth and engagement.

Every experience you truly invest yourself in, whether it's learning an instrument or new language, challenging yourself in school, stretching to get a meaningful role in a community organization or within your family enterprise, or something else altogether, can be a "mastery" experience. Having a mastery experience doesn't entail becoming a virtuoso, it just means you are committed to the process of learning and growing. Writing this book, for example, has required immense commitment, care, a willingness to learn, and an openness to accept feedback. From its inception, it has required a Mastery-Orientation from me. And at its completion, despite the fact that I'm unlikely to make it into the history books as one of the greatest authors of all time, there is no doubt that it will have been a mastery experience for me.

Every mastery experience you engage in will help you build your confidence. And research shows that this will not only serve to boost confidence in that specific activity, but it will also support your self-assurance in unrelated activities over time.[14]

When faced with challenges or failure, Mastery-Oriented individuals focus on finding a solution and seeking to learn from the causes of failure rather than perseverating on the failure itself. In fact, once someone creates the habit of orienting toward mastery, they often don't even perceive themselves as having failed. I often hear those who are clearly Mastery-Oriented say things like, "Yeah, that one didn't work out, did it? We learned a lot about what makes for a bad deal on that one." Or "Failure? We didn't fail. But we did gather a lot of data about what *not* to do next time." You may notice this in the stories of the wealth creator in your family. In my experience, wealth creators rarely see failure as failure. Instead, they'll see it as a learning experience, or they might not even note it at all.

Cultivating Mastery-Orientation

Building the habit of engaging in mastery activities generates an upward spiral. Because you become more likely to stick with challenging tasks, you increasingly understand that you are quite capable. This belief in your own capabilities is called self-efficacy, and it becomes the flywheel that supports a lifelong habit of achievement and the pursuit of mastery.[15] Remember, mastery isn't about perfection. It's about the pursuit of learning, growing, refining, improving, and continuously deepening confidence in your abilities. Build your Mastery-Orientation with these ideas:

- **Take stock.** You may have mastery experiences in your past that you have overlooked or forgotten. Stop and consider times that you have challenged yourself with something new and approached the experience with the intent to learn and grow and continuously improve. Recognizing the situations in which you've already built this skill will help give you confidence as you face your next chosen challenge.

- **Learn to reframe.** When faced with a new, difficult endeavor, learning to reframe the situation is a powerful aid. Instead of focusing on how you might feel if you fail, focus on what you're learning every step of the way. Ultimately, this will make every new summit you climb a worthwhile one—whether it's a knock-it-out-of-the-park success or not. The value will be in the journey, not in the final destination.

- **Notice your confidence.** Building self-efficacy—the belief that you are capable—is one of the beautiful outcomes of having a Mastery-Orientation. Take note of how your confidence continues to build as you face each new challenge with an openness and the desire to learn. Every new experience puts a deposit in your "confidence bank," a bank you'll be able to pull from to fund bigger and bolder ideas in your future.

Think about your life. Where have you had mastery experiences? In sports? Art? Learning about a particular period in history? The strategic thinking needed for gaming? As I've shared, research shows that when you experience self-efficacy in one domain of your life, that feeling of self-efficacy is likely to transfer to higher degrees of success in other domains of your life.[16] What experiences from your past can you mine right now as you build the foundation for your future successes?

Mastery-Orientation—Rising Gen in Their Own Words

[Every one of] these big goals have given me the confidence to know that I can figure most things out. Even when things don't turn out like I expected, I know I can figure it out. I'm confident based on past experiences that I can take this leap, I can jump off this ledge, because I have done so confidently before.

[Running my division of the business has] given me a lot of confidence in terms of . . . managing people and processes, and really understanding where people are coming from—and how to put them in the best role and make them successful. I haven't always felt like I knew what I was doing, but I trusted I could find my way. And that confidence is self-fulfilling—the more confidence I have, the better decisions I seem to make.

Close Positive Relationships

The fourth big log that will provide important scaffolding as you build your future fire is that of Close Positive Relationships. The ability to develop **Close Positive Relationships** is an essential skill that supports all areas of personal development, including the definition of and the pursuit of one's ideal self.[17] Meaning, when you have great friends who love you for who you are, you're more likely to dream about who you want to become, and they'll support you to get there. These are the kinds of friends we could all use more of. Not only will good friends help you dream about who you want to become and give you a safe home to be authentic, but a wealth of research has shown that close relationships are just plain good for you. Research shows that people who report being in good relationships have higher levels of both physical health and emotional well-being, regardless of the presence of life stressors.

Interestingly, research has further indicated that as important as it is for people to have social resources to support them when things go wrong, it is also important for people to be able to share with others when things go right.[18] The latter contributes to a process called "capitalization," which greatly expands the beneficial impact of good news or a positive event. Like many other rising gens, you may have experienced a double-bind when trying to tell your friends about your life. If you mention what's not going well, your friends might suggest or imply that you shouldn't have anything to complain about. (You come from a wealthy family, after all.) Meanwhile, if you mention something good that has happened, your friends might respond with envy or judgement that you seem to get all the breaks. Viewing this as a no-win situation is one of the many reasons that rising gens often feel lonely or isolated.

Many of my clients tell me they have very few, if any, close relationships where they can fully be themselves. This is heartbreaking to hear. If you're like the rising gen I typically talk to, this isolation may also be compounded by internal family norms to not discuss the family wealth with others. You've likely also come up against plenty of external negative stereotypes about "rich" people as well as the myth of the silver spoon—the misconception that the more money you have, the fewer problems you experience and the happier you are. While you may describe your life like many of my clients— that you have all your material needs and most of your material wants met— you may receive painfully mixed messages about love, money, and relationships.

Less-than-ideal relationships can raise fundamental questions of worthiness such as, *Am I loveable? Are **all** parts of me acceptable? If all the "trappings" went away, would I still be attractive to you?* For those with unearned wealth, these questions become even more complicated around friendships and romantic partners. You may wonder if these people are attracted to you as a person, or if they are attracted to your money. You're not alone in these questions, but there are things you can do.

Cultivating Close Positive Relationships

One of the most important things you can do to help set yourself up for good, healthy, and supportive relationships is to clean up your own relationship clutter first (if you skipped the exercises in Chapter 7, you might start by going back and working through those). It's essential to learn how to tell the difference between true friends and those who are enamored with your or your family's status. Start by getting clear about what works and doesn't work for you in your relationships and then you can move on to building more of the relationships you want. Use these ideas to help deepen your insights on the quality of the relationships in your life:

- **Your ideal self.** One of the traits that makes great friends great is that they give us the space to envision and become our ideal selves. They don't keep us small, or ask us to be someone we're not—they dream with us and then provide the support for us to live into those dreams. Who do you have in your life that plays that role for you?

- **Be a good friend.** Another trait of close positive relationships is that they allow us to "capitalize"—to celebrate what's good as much (or more) than we commiserate when things are bad. One way to get good at knowing if you're in this kind of relationship is to *be* the friend you want to have. The more you show up this way, the more you'll get insight as to whether your friendship has the depth to be truly authentic or whether it remains more surface and situational.

- **Ask your parents.** Although you may not have considered this before, it's likely that your parents, at some point in their lives, also have experienced the challenges of trying to find true friends who accept them for who they are. Are you comfortable asking your parents how they have navigated (or continue to navigate) the minefield of disingenuous friendships? They might have valuable insights to share.

Each one of the successful rising gen I interviewed for my research told me that they had at least one person who undoubtedly cared about them for who they are and not what they own. False friendships and superficial romantic partnerships can be difficult to detect, but over time, you'll build the skill for discerning true friendships and unions and nurturing those.

Close Positive Relationships—Rising Gen in Their Own Words

*I was married twice—you heard that right—twice in my twenties. I couldn't pick a good mate to save my life. I see now that it was because I didn't really know myself. I was so confused about what wealth was in my life and who I was "supposed" to be because of it. It took me hitting my own emotional rock bottom to finally realize that I needed to get to know myself. In my thirties, I met the man who is now my husband—and his love of **me** has only helped me to deepen my self-knowledge. Today, I really do get that I'm not my family's money, I am my own person. It took loving myself—and then having someone love me for me—to really get that.*

I think what it made me think of was growing up and having people razz me, or worse, for being "the rich kid." That sort of label. I didn't know where that was coming from, what information they had and whatever. But I grew up in a community where my family was somewhat prominent. Then I went off to boarding school for high school. From the time I left my hometown, I was in a community where it didn't really matter so much. Where I wasn't known, labeled, whatever. So that was really great because it helped me to feel what authentic friendships felt like. At that age, I don't think I could have figured that out still living in my hometown. It's funny because I really wanted to go to this school and [getting away from my hometown] wasn't the reason I wanted to go. That was not something I was thinking about at the time. Looking back, I see that I was able to build friendships based on who I really was, not on who people perceived me to be. Then, when I went back home, I was more mature and more able to discern true friendships from false ones. It turns out that was really important for my confidence and development.

Foundational Character Strengths and Virtues—A Final Big Log

Now to the last big log—the framework addressing character strengths that I didn't include in my research but wish I had. Luckily, there are literally thousands of intelligent researchers whose work we can refer to as we build out this particular big log to support your success. So even though this wasn't a factor in my research, I feel it is a science-based addition and worth including here—especially given that my years of experience of supporting clients' development using a framework of character strengths has been resoundingly positive.

Foundational Character Strengths are based on 24 culturally agnostic character strengths that social scientists say form the backbone for our cultivation of human thriving. Research shows that a person's increasing awareness and use of character strengths in human development and interpersonal relationships is associated with increased life engagement;[19] higher relationship satisfaction;[20] a heightened experience of flourishing;[21] and elevated work engagement, work satisfaction, and the experience of feeing like one's "work is a calling."[22] Which all means, the focus on—and growth of—one's Foundational Character Strengths is a well-researched way for fostering more of what makes life feel vibrant and enriching.

But what exactly are character strengths? In general, *character strengths* are positive aspects of your personality that impact how you think, feel, and behave.[23] Character strengths are human traits and like the other traits we've explored in this chapter, the presence of any one of these strengths in an individual is partly due to genetics and partly due to environment. So, while some people may be born braver—or more grateful or kind—than others, with awareness, intention, and choiceful action, we all have the ability to develop further bravery, gratitude, kindness, or whatever strengths we've decided are important to us. In other words, you can increase your character strengths.

The empirical framework underpinning these 24-character strengths is relatively new; the *Character Strengths and Virtues Classification and Handbook* was published in 2004.[24] However, the cultivation of character strengths is based on two ancient ideas: (1) that we can improve character through mindful action and (2) that this mindful nurturing of character strengths can result in greater happiness, fulfillment, and meaning.

Cultivating Foundational Character Strengths

An easy way to get started in understanding your character strengths is to take the free, validated VIA Character Strengths Survey at (www.viacharacter.org). This assessment is based on the empirical 24-strengths framework, which is rigorously researched and open-access (they encourage researchers and practitioners to use it). The VIA Character Strengths Survey is the only scientific assessment of character strengths that exists at this time. The 96-question assessment takes 15–25 minutes to complete and produces a complimentary report that rank orders your character strengths from strongest and most naturally present for you (we call these *signature strengths*) to the ones that are least active in your day-to-day actions. I recommend that you take it—now if possible—to increase your self-awareness. It will not only help enhance the efficacy of the remainder of this book, but also reinforce your confidence that you have your own inherent strengths to draw upon in life.

Once you know what your Foundational Character Strengths are, there are many resources on how to enhance and use them (see Appendix A). However, here are a couple of easy ways to get started:

- **Accentuate signature strengths.** Signature strengths are typically the top five strengths in your profile. These strengths are viewed as most essential to who you are and are qualities that are especially energizing and natural for you to use. Once you know what your signature strengths are, try noticing all the ways you use them each day.

- **Use strength-spotting.** Strength-spotting is the act of intentionally noticing what people are doing when they are at their best. You can build your character strength awareness by both noticing what *you're* doing when *you're* at your best and by noticing what your friends and loved ones are doing when *they're* at *their* best. You don't even have to know what their official Foundational Character Strengths are—you can just pay attention to what they do most naturally. Then you might casually say something about it. *("David, I love your zest—you make every life adventure more fun.")* By calling out their character strengths, you help enhance awareness and appreciation as well as amplify that strength for others. People may then start doing the same for you, creating a mutually reinforcing upward cycle. This is especially helpful in teams and family groups.

- **Grow a strength.** It's just as important to know that you can grow a strength that is not innate to you as it is to use the strengths that are most natural. Look at some of the lower character strengths on your report—is there one you'd like to try cultivating? All it takes is understanding what that strength is about (see Appendix A for a list of some of my favorite books and tools for deepening your knowledge) and then focusing attention on growing it. It is most effective to focus on growing one or two strengths at a time. I recently decided I wanted to grow my strength of "appreciation of beauty and excellence" (one of my lower strengths), so I got in the habit of watching the sunrise each morning. I started each day with slowing down and appreciating the natural beauty that was all around me. Soon I found myself pausing to notice beautiful things in all my surroundings.

Knowing what your Foundational Character Strengths are—and learning to use them intentionally and effectively—is the last important big log to stack up as you begin to intentionally create your path to thriving.

Using Your Big Logs to Create the Scaffolding to Support Your Thriving

Now it's time to put it all together. Here's the great news: The support for your unique path to a fulfilling life is already within you. Whether strongly assembled or waiting for your loving attention, the big logs of your lifetime success—Growth Mindset, Grit, Mastery-Orientation, Close Positive Relationships, and Foundational Character Strengths—are yours to build upon. It takes awareness, choiceful action, and a commitment to grow. Remember, while you may be a next gen by birth, you have the power to distinguish yourself and thrive as a rising gen. As you consider how you can move beyond your default position as a next gen and actually become a rising gen—someone who embraces the psychology of growth, curiosity, and resilience—you've got all the tools you need right here. These five big logs— rather than being more clutter around you, weighing you down—are proven to be what rising gen like yourself can rest upon and use for support. They can buttress you and fuel you through tough times and new opportunities. They take genuine effort to build, but it's an effort that will pay you back handsomely.

As you're thinking about getting started, here are some ideas to give you traction:

- **Achieve some quick wins.** Begin with the logs (or just one of the logs) you think are easiest for you. Look through the ideas for cultivating that particular "big log" and commit to getting started. Allow it to be messy, don't worry about perfection, and be open to the struggle that can accompany learning something new.

- **Hold yourself accountable.** Have a way to keep yourself accountable, like a calendar where you track your goals, or by journaling your progress, or by asking for support from a friend, therapist, or coach.

- **Don't go it alone.** As you work to integrate these big logs, you don't need to do it by yourself. Share what you're working on with a friend or professional you trust. Be willing to receive their feedback and don't hesitate to celebrate your wins with them.

Remember Pierre from the start of this chapter? Pierre ended up signing up for that class at the community college. He had a teacher who really believed in him and challenged him to go further than just that one class.

He eventually completed an associate's degree and walked across that community college's graduation stage with great pride. It had taken him clearing out some serious clutter to even be willing to get started, and in the process of earning that degree, he had challenged himself to put in place some of his own big logs for lifetime success. The last time we talked, his little boy was eight years old and thriving, Pierre was writing a business plan to fill a market gap for a hydroponic facility in his small town, and he was proud of the role model he had become. That's a far cry from where he was when we met and he was feeling small, stuck, and helpless.

PART IV

Creating a Uniquely Impactful Life

11

From Spark to Flame: Ideas That Ignite You and Impact Others

Peter is a professional musician, a *New York Times* best-selling author, and the co-chairman of a private foundation worth more than one billion dollars. He is the second generation of affluence in his family. While he is the son of one of the wealthiest people on the planet, his parents decided not to give their three adult children significant inheritances. In fact, Peter has said that despite being a part of a family with great wealth, he has lived much of his life like "a working stiff," a situation he doesn't begrudge in the least, acknowledging that, growing up, he was given love, attention, strong values, and the privilege of opportunity. In his words, his job has been to make "the best of a good situation." Peter says his life circumstances were truly a "luck of the draw"—or, as his dad always said, he and his siblings had won the Ovarian Lottery (maybe you can relate?). Peter is not one of my clients for whom I'm using a pseudonym, like others you've met earlier in this book. Peter is his real name—and his father is Warren Buffet.

As the youngest child of Warren and Susan Buffet, Peter had a front-row seat to one of the most significant stories of wealth creation ever. In his book, *Life Is What You Make It: Find Your Own Path to Fulfillment,* Peter writes about the importance of one's personal developmental journey on the path to becoming who you are. He shares his perspective that "at the individual level, our development is aimed at the self-respect that can only come from earning our own rewards. Our goal is the peace of mind that derives from choosing our own lives, pursuing the destiny that feels truly like our own."[1] And complementary to this inner journey is our potential for outer impact. "At the level of society, our most meaningful progress is that which brings us to the point of being able to give back . . . directing our work *outward,* toward the common good, rather than for private gain is a way of giving back. Stretching beyond our comfort zone to engage in a wider world is a way of giving back."[2] Ultimately, this requires more than check writing. It is tough work that requires you to stretch, grow, fall down, get back up, and keep learning. Peter is an exemplar in not only finding a positive wealth identity, but also in learning how to create what he calls "an enrichment loop"—an ongoing cycle where we find that when we give of ourselves, we get back from the world, and we discover that we have yet more to give. Peter has engaged in this enrichment loop through the NoVo Foundation that he and his wife, Jennifer Buffet, cofounded. He has also found ways to use his love of music and his life story to spread the idea that each of us—regardless of our circumstances—has the capacity to engage in our lives in ways that make a difference. He writes, "Let me be clear: I believe *all* of us should be proud of our lives, because making a life is the one profound and sacred opportunity shared by every person ever born. *Life is what we make it.* No one else can do it for us; no one has the right to tell us what it ought to be. We make our own goals. We define our own successes. We don't get to choose where we start in life; we *do* get to choose the kind of people we become."[3]

Engaging in your own inner, personal developmental journey is the all-important beginning. But it doesn't have to be the end. By this point, you're hopefully seeing things more clearly than when you began this book, now having cleared some clutter and begun developing important traits to increase and sustain your happiness. What's next, if you feel ready and inspired, is the invitation to get curious about how you might channel your life experiences, built skills, innate talents, and spark of ideas to create impact outside of your own life. In other words, how you might combine your identity capital with your social and financial capital to engage and even ignite change in your community or in the world.

Igniting Your Fire—Fast Fuel

At this point you have almost everything you need to start a nice, big, sustainable fire. Almost everything. You've now cleared some space (clearing your inner and outer money, identity, relationship, and contribution clutter); gathered up the big, slow burning logs you'll need to sustain your fire (developing your traits of Growth Mindset, Grit, Mastery-Orientation, and Close Personal Relationships, as well as your Foundational Character Strengths); and built those big logs into a structure that is both sturdy and spacious (adopting these concepts and practices into your life). But as every skilled camper knows, those big logs won't catch fire on their own. They need some fast fuel and a spark. We'll get to the spark in a minute, but for now, your fire is going to need some fast fuel—tinder, dry leaves, or wood chips—that will ignite quickly and get hot enough to begin the slow burn of those big logs. What is fast fuel in this analogy? Your ideas, dreams, and inspiration. The things that—when you've got clutter-free space to move in, fresh life-giving air to breathe, and a felt-sense of how gritty, capable, and loved you truly are—light you up. You know what I'm talking about—these are the ideas that not only capture your attention, but they make your heart race a little, too. Hopefully, now that you've cleared out some of the "*not you*" clutter, you're starting to notice more and more of these ideas and musings fluttering around in the "*truly you*" spaciousness of your big heart and brain. But if you're still wondering where your "muse of inspiration" is and why she hasn't crossed your threshold, maybe it's time to consider some good sources for fast fuel.

Collecting Your Fast Fuel

A good starting place for collecting usable fast fuel—for creating favorable circumstances where new ideas have the chance to percolate up and grab your heart by its strings—is *novelty*. It is necessary to challenge the current status quo of your life, to leave the familiarity of your day-to-day routine, in order to grow. It turns out that the need for exploration, for curiously seeking new, challenging, and novel perspectives and experiences is a fundamental—and irreducible—human need.[4] Remember, part of how you build a solid bank of identity capital is to both explore *and* commit. Exploring too much without ever digging in and taking action on something you care about can leave you wandering and feeling irrelevant. Committing to something without ample exploration can leave you feeling rigid and uninspired. The rising gen that is able to balance curiosity followed by active engagement has the winning formula.

In fact, research shows that a predictable pattern takes place before someone hits a "hot streak"—bursts of high-impact work output clustered together in close succession.[5] Before a hot streak, people tend to explore a wide range of topics, styles, and ideas, but then become notably more focused as their hot streak heats up. Once their internal fire starts to ignite, they focus their attention and start to produce. And I mean *really* produce (hot streaks are aptly named). But it is the combination of exploration and then actively beginning to apply what you've learned in a focused way that sets up the conditions for a hot streak. Taking time to explore—to expose yourself to new people, new places, and new perspectives is invaluable.

If you're curious about how much of an explorer you are, try assessing yourself on this Exploration Scale by Todd Kashdan and colleagues.[6] Using a scale of 1–5 (where 5 = Strong Agree and 1 = Strongly Disagree), rate yourself for each of these statements:

- I view challenging situations as an opportunity to grow and learn.
- I am always looking for experiences that challenge how I think about myself and the world.
- I seek out situations where it is likely that I will have to think in depth about something.
- I enjoy learning about subjects that are unfamiliar to me.
- I find it fascinating to learn new information.

Which of these statements ring true for you? Which feel like a stretch? If you had lots of Strongly Agrees, you're a natural explorer; if you had lots of Strongly Disagrees, try focusing on the one statement that feels most palatable to you and starting your exploration inroads there. It turns out that there are different curiosity types[7] and these different types have different passionate interests, expertise, and habits.

The take-home message here is that exploration doesn't look the same for all people. If you find yourself not feeling contemplative enough or adventurous enough, try letting yourself off the hook. Stop comparing what your curiosity looks like to someone else's—you may find the genuine exploration of your inner spiritual terrain to be as catalyzing as someone else finds a multi-week outdoor trek to be. There isn't any one right way to explore. What matters most is how curious you are in the domains that are most compelling to you. The more of a life explorer that you challenge yourself to be, in whatever way feels true to you, the more likely it is that the muse of inspiration will dance across your threshold, gracing you with lots of fodder for fast fuel.

One note of awareness: As you amp up your explorer's mindset, don't be surprised if you find yourself experiencing some fear and anxiety. Any time we change our current status quo in favor of growth, it's likely that the fears that were keeping us from taking action before are going to rear their ugly heads. According to psychologist Abraham Maslow, understanding our fears—really knowing them—is one of our most effective ways to reduce our anxiety around them.[8] In fact, people who are willing to embrace their fears of change and become habitual explorers tend to have higher levels of "stress tolerance," a state that is highly correlated with important dimensions of well-being (including happiness, meaning in life, satisfaction of the needs of mastery, autonomy, relatedness, and positive emotions).[9] So if you feel yourself starting to get triggered with old anxiety, you might first take a deep breath and give yourself time to get to know the fear and where it is coming from in you. (You might even try revisiting one of the seven-step clutter clearing processes from the previous chapters to help you zero-in on what's going on "below the waterline" for you.) Then, trust that you will get better and better at becoming a curious explorer and that each time you make the effort, you'll become more stress-tolerant (therefore also enhancing your well-being . . . not a bad side-effect). There is no doubt that shedding your defenses and challenging yourself outside your comfort zone can be incredibly stress-inducing. It will also be growth-promoting, I promise. Don't underestimate how capable you are and how inspiring it will be as you give yourself the opportunity to gather more and more of your own "fast fuel."

Belle had felt as though she had been drifting for a long time. One of four kids in her sibling group, she was the only one who could not seem to find her "thing." She tried her hand at real estate—buying and flipping houses in the neighborhoods near her, but she found herself getting bored. She loved the outdoors and tried being a ski instructor, but found it was too hard to only have seasonal work. She was intelligent and enjoyed learning, so she thought about law school but didn't score well on the LSATs and decided it probably wasn't a fit. Frustrated with feeling like she was stalling out at every turn, she asked if she could go work at a ranch that her family had recently purchased. It took her no time at all to recognize that she was built for the hard, outdoor labor of running a ranch. Belle loved working with the animals and tending to the land. She got curious about the practices for sustainable agriculture and soon found herself seeking out every resource for learning about regenerative ranching practices. She knew there must be a way to connect healthy animals, a healthy planet, and a healthy business model. While she is still deep in the learning curve, Belle has found a commitment to a vision that is bigger than herself and to which she will happily put in long days of learning and hard work. It was Belle's willingness to step out of her comfort zone and try something entirely novel that sparked her interest and lit the fire that burns in her now.

Igniting Your Fire—Your Unique Spark

Which brings us to the last ingredient you need to start your own fire. You need a spark. Every one of us has a spark inside of us—a unique catalyst that is the alignment of our experiences, talents, priorities, and purpose. There is no one right way to ignite your fire—there are as many ways to live purposeful, productive, value-creating lives as people living them. Next we're going to look at two of the most common ways rising gen ignite positive sparks—through impact work and impact giving.

But first, I want to be clear. Just because you have been born into a unique situation and have access to financial resources doesn't mean you must find your way to impact work or learn how to be a modern-day philanthropist. There are many paths to thriving and to creating a life of meaning and value. The way you define this for yourself is up to *you*. As Peter Buffet describes in his book, a fundamentally important part of the journey is your own individual development. In fact, I'll underscore that point and assert that individual well-being is an autotelic pursuit. That means it has its own intrinsic value. It is an end-goal in itself. It needs no other justification or end. So if focusing on finding your individual voice and your individual journey to a meaningful life is where you're at on your path of growth right now, that's perfect.

If you're feeling charged up and inspired, however, to create impact for a certain community or in a field or issue you care about—perhaps locally or on a national or even global scale—these next two sections are for you.

★ ★ ★ ★ ★

"In some ways, suffering ceases to be suffering at the moment it finds a meaning."
—Viktor Frankl, *Man's Search for Meaning*

★ ★ ★ ★ ★

Kindle Your Spark: Impact Work

In Chapter 8 we unpacked the concepts of work and contribution and identified how family wealth can accelerate the formation of Contribution Clutter. We explored how, as humans, we're wired to produce, how contributing is fundamentally important to our well-being and our experience that our lives and our existence matter. But work can be even more than this in one's life. Work itself can become a pathway for transcending from merely doing—heeding our hard-wired drive to produce—to actually creating lives of impact. And the first pathway toward this transcendence is called impact work.

In their book, *The New Reason to Work: How to Build a Career That Will Change the World*, Roshan Paul and Ilaina Rabbat describe how the reasons for our work—and therefore the meaning of work—has changed over time.[10] For our early ancestors, work was about securing basic human needs: food, shelter, childcare, warmth. This basic function of work changed as the Industrial Revolution and the rise of daily mass communication allowed people to not only earn income for their labors, but also for one's work to become a greater source of identity and self-worth as it became more tightly connected to recognition, power, and status. And, still, work most often remained transactional—you provide a service or product and get paid for your efforts. This transactional nature of work is still true for many people today—even some of the highest-paid executive leaders in big companies are likely to admit, in their most honest moments, that their work is more transactional than transformational. Yet, now more than ever, people are waking up to the idea that there are much more heart-centered and intrinsically motivating *reasons* to work.

With more ways to earn income than ever before, people are feeling more agency in selecting what they want to do. Both Millennials and Gen Z, for example, predominantly believe that jobs should be less transactional and more transformational. One study revealed that both generational cohorts indicate they wouldn't hesitate to leave a job if they disagreed with a company's values, politics, or business practices.[11] What they're feeling drawn to are jobs that align with their values, are less transactional, and more impactful.

Impact work is defined as jobs where "you use the *majority* of your time and effort with the primary intention to improve the human and/or planetary condition, instead of just your own or your organization's bottom line. It is where social impact is not a possible side-benefit, but in fact, the core purpose of the job, where your day is organized around moving towards impact."[12] Roshan and Rabbat go on to highlight that impact work can be possible regardless of what job you hold or what sector you work in. The differentiator is whether the primary goal of the work is solely maximizing profit or to solve a social problem or enhance human or planetary well-being. Which, by the way, doesn't mean the business can't also be financially successful. If an enterprise is going to have staying power, ultimately, it *has* to have positive cash flow. There are many successful (read: profitable) impact businesses. The difference between an impact-focused business and a profit-focused business is that the decisions you make, what you create, and how you create it are different when you're optimizing around impact versus optimizing around exploiting a market opportunity. It fundamentally changes the business decision-making filters that are used.

Rob Gary is the youngest child of Sam Gary, Denver oilman and someone who was a social entrepreneur long before the term was in vogue.

(Again, when I use the first and last name of a rising gen in this chapter, I'm not referring to a client whose identity I'm protecting but rather a public figure and the person's real name.) Sam believed that business and community did not exist separate from each other and that a business's success was only a veneer unless the community it existed in was also thriving.[13] According to Rob, his dad was known for saying, "You can't have a thriving business and a failing community," and equally known for his call to action to fellow business leaders to solve social problems with the same imagination and energy they use to finance a factory or make a deal.[14] Rob internalized this message, eventually founding several impact businesses collectively known as HayCamp Companies. Rob explains the philosophy that underscores all of the HayCamp businesses this way:

> *Business can be done in a way that one person wins and then every time you want to go do more business, you have to find someone else to do it with. Or it can be done in a way that everyone wins—you just have to figure out how the collective fits together to successfully solve the problem. Then, the next time, you build from whatever you learned last time and with whomever you learned it with. You find you just create a continual positive feedback loop of more business and more impact. People are quick to go to "either/or" when they think about business—it either has to be good for people or good for profits—but really, a good impact business is just a good business. The difference between the two is that with impact business, we're taking more into consideration than just the financials.[15]*

Rob goes on to explain why he was drawn to impact work over any other type of work (or not working at all):

> *Not only was it intrinsic to how my dad thought about business, but working to create value has been important to me on my own path. As someone who grew up with wealth, there were a lot of patterns I created and beliefs I held about myself that weren't helpful or healthy. Today, the fact that I can invest in ideas and create companies that are value-producing influences how I feel about myself. I don't want to live off of someone else's success or generosity. You can't control the money, but you can keep it from controlling you. Do I have to work? No. In fact, I'd probably be wealthier if I didn't [laughs]. So then it's about creating value—for me, my team, my community, my family, the ranch animals, the planet. All of it. To me it's not worth getting involved in if it's just transactional.[16]*

In the past, most impact-type work existed in the realm of foundations, nonprofits, and nongovernmental organizations. However, today, as social entrepreneurism continues to rise and even traditional for-profit organizations see the value of the triple-bottom line (people, planet, *and* profits), there are more possibilities for creating or working in an impact job than ever before.

Finally, in a happy synergy—or, as Peter Buffet would say, an "enrichment loop"—it turns out that people who orient themselves toward impact work not only have higher job satisfaction, they also have greater physical and mental health and report higher *life* satisfaction.[17] In this paradigm, what is good for others can also be good for you! Purpose, challenge, and growth. We are definitely starting to collect the themes that consistently show up on the pathway to thriving.

Now let's turn our attention to another pathway for igniting your spark: impact giving.

Kindle Your Spark: Impact Giving

As unprecedented global challenges highlight significant limitations of governmental and other traditional institutions, many rising gen are waking up and realizing that *each of us* have the power to affect positive change. Thank goodness. Because, in short, the world needs you.

It is no accident that you have arrived on the scene during what's been identified as the Great Wealth Transfer.[18] As members of the Baby Boomer generation come to the end of their lives, tens of trillions of dollars are pegged to be transferred out of their estates and given to their families and philanthropic causes in the coming decades. The implications for you, as an engaged and awake rising gen, as well as the potential ramifications for society as a whole are immense. According to Sharna Goldseker and Michael Moody's research, conducted for their book, *Generation Impact: How the Next Gen Donors are Revolutionizing Giving*, ". . . if current trends in wealth and giving continue, these rising major donors will be the most significant philanthropists ever."[19]

You have an impressive legacy to refer to both historically and contemporarily. American philanthropy has a long history of successfully addressing seemingly intractable social problems around the globe as well as close to home. Consider for a moment these two historical examples of businessmen-turned-philanthropists—John D. Rockefeller, Sr. and Andrew Carnegie. Both men were business titans who built their fortunes during the American Industrial Revolution and both created significant social change as a result of their philanthropic efforts. Rockefeller supported many causes; early in its history, the Rockefeller Foundation focused on education (including Spelman Seminary, later Spelman College, for African American women) and medical research (supporting the development of a meningitis vaccine in 1908, for example, and a campaign to treat hookworm that started in the United States and then spread overseas).[20] With similar breadth of focus, in the early 1900s Andrew Carnegie donated more than $50 million to build more than 2,800 public libraries in the United States and Great Britain. In 1910 he founded the Carnegie Endowment for Peace to support the efforts of international peace.[21] These Gilded Age philanthropists paved the way for private dollars to make a difference, a legacy of change that continues today as illustrated in initiatives like the Giving Pledge—a pledge made by some of the wealthiest people in the world to give away the majority of their wealth to charitable causes.[22] These are shining examples of the power of concentrated wealth to create social change. Today a new generation of donors is stepping up to redefine philanthropy once again. Maybe this even includes you.

Take, for example, Justin Rockefeller, a fifth-generation member of the well-known family and a direct descendent of John D. Rockefeller, founder of the Standard Oil Company. As mentioned previously, John D. was a noteworthy philanthropist—as were (and are) many of his decedents. Building on this significant family legacy of giving, Justin has connected his experience with impact work (his work for a company called Addepar, a software company that makes complex portfolios easier to understand, a critical step in allowing investors to align their values with their investments) to his ideas around impact giving. In Goldseker and Moody's *Generation Impact*, this modern-day Rockefeller sheds light on some of the questions that deepened his commitment to giving and creating impact: "'What does my tool belt look like, and how do I maximize it for social change?' If my tools include credibility with an influential network, a surname that opens doors, time, energy, motivation, relevant experience, limited personal capital, and working at a company that has best-in-class technology, then how could I use these tools for change in deeper ways?"[23] He goes on to explain that initiatives like the Giving Pledge are helpful because they provide financial input, but there is also a need for measurable outcomes—the ability to measure impact created through the dollars invested in a cause. This is the heart of impact investing. Along with his friend, Josh Cohen, he co-founded The ImPact, a nonprofit network of family enterprises (family offices, foundations, and businesses) committed to impact investing, the purpose of which is to "improve the probability and pace of solving social problems by increasing the flow of capital to investments that generate measurable social impact."[24] This is a hallmark of rising gen donors—they are finding ways to not only use their financial capital to create change, but they are also actively tapping into their intellectual capital, social capital, and human capital.[25] And they are not waiting until they retire to a "life of philanthropic leisure"[26] to jump in and become catalysts for change.

★ ★ ★ ★ ★

As philanthropists, we are nothing more than conduits of power.
—Liz Simons and Mark Heising's *Giving Pledge Letter*

★ ★ ★ ★ ★

Justin Rockefeller stands among a tribe of rising gen who are looking to make an impact through their giving, social agents of change like Liz Simons and her husband Mark Heising. Liz is the daughter of billionaire hedge fund manager, mathematician, and founder of Renaissance Technologies, James Simons. Liz and Mark have their own private foundation where they focus on investing in work that impacts climate change, advancing scientific research, early childhood education, and human rights. In 2016 they were among an increasing number of rising gen who have signed the Giving Pledge.[27] Liz and Mark's daughter, Caitlin Heising, is also notable as she charts her own impressive path in the space of impact giving. Caitlin sits on the board of her family's foundation and has become a role model for other rising gen who emerging onto the philanthropic stage and are interested in making a significant difference. When asked what the greatest asset of rising gen donors are, Caitlin shared her perspective:

This is a wide generalization, but I see next generation donors giving with less ego involved than the traditional philanthropist. They often have a humble disposition and prioritize impact and justice over social recognition and personal causes or institutions.

As more next gen donors come onto the scene, I believe their approach will lead to more funding in areas like social justice and climate than we've seen in the past.[28]

Another noteworthy player in the space of impact giving is Nicholas Berggruen, who took a $250,000 trust and, through his investing, grew his initial trust capital into billions of dollars. In 2010 he founded the Berggruen Institute, an independent think tank that, at a time in our history when our foundational systems such as capitalism and democracy are in flux, focuses on reshaping political and social institutions.[29] The nonpartisan institute is addressing some of the most complex challenges we face as a global community. In addition to his financial support of and work with the Berggruen Institute, Nicholas has also signed the Giving Pledge and intends to give the majority of his wealth away through his charitable trust.[30]

These are just a couple of examples—historically and contemporarily—of the power of concentrated wealth to create social change. Each of these people and their organizations have had significant impact in their communities and in the world due to their vision and commitment, along with their willingness to put their money behind their ideals. Rockefeller and Carnegie hail from the Gilded Age, until now considered America's greatest eras of giving, and today philanthropic observers are starting to postulate that we're heading into a new age of giving that will exceed in size and impact even that of the Gilded Age.[31] This is the era of giving and transformation in which you have the opportunity to participate.

It's No Easy Street . . . But It's Worth It

If all of this sounds like a lot of work, you're right. It *is* work. There are times that you are going to feel dog tired and at your wits end as you stretch into learning, try out new ideas, ask big questions, and push the envelope of possibility. As Peter Buffet writes, "Writing a check is easy. But trying to give something back to the world, as a function of one's own energy and convictions and unique set of abilities, is tough. It calls for exactly the same kind of commitment that ambitious and hardworking people usually reserve for their day jobs. But giving back is just as important as taking in. Why should it call for anything less than the same level of effort and determination?"[32]

Thankfully, for as much capacity as you have to create impact, there are also many personal rewards for the effort you invest. According to 2015 research on the drivers of job satisfaction conducted by the Happiness Research Institute, a sense of purpose and striving for a goal—fully embracing the true and deep challenge of something meaningful—was highly correlated to happiness.[33] It's not surprising that challenge and happiness are connected. Psychologist Mihaly Csikszentmihalyi's findings underscores this interconnection in his work on Flow Theory, where he defines the conditions that exist when people most consistently report experiencing a "flow state." When in this state of flow—where people describe a feeling of time disappearing and the process of the work becoming its own reward—it is the presence of both a high level of skill *and* a high level of challenge that produce the much sought-after optimal state.[34] Think of it this way: In a flow state, you're at the limits of what you can do but still able and in control. If the challenge far exceeds your skill, you're likely to feel frustrated and disengage. If your skill far outpaces the challenge, you'll get bored and turn your attention elsewhere. It is finding the match between endeavors that have you stretching and experiencing challenge *and still* able to meet those challenges where you'll find the optimal experience of flow. But once you experience it, it's so compelling that you'll be hooked and looking for ways to stretch, grow, and challenge yourself so you can experience it again.

Igniting Your Spark: A Path to Becoming Who You Are

The path to self-actualization—to becoming wholly and truly who you are and bringing all of you to engage the world—is not a straight line and there is no one route for getting there. As Abraham Maslow, the psychologist who dedicated his life to trying to understand self-actualized people, says, "There seems to be no intrinsic reason why everyone shouldn't be this way [self-actualizing]. Apparently, every baby has possibilities for self-actualizing, but most of them get it knocked out of them. . . . I think of the self-actualizing man not as an ordinary man with something added, but rather as the ordinary man with nothing taken away."[35] You don't need a special magic or a Midas touch. You don't need an elusive "success gene" or to be any different than you are today. You only need to be fully *you*.

You can start by simply asking yourself the following questions:

- What about me have I—or others—overlooked or undervalued?
- What strengths do I have from my unique life experiences that would equip me to create meaningful change?
- What tools do I have in my tool belt that would support me to use my strengths to magnify my impact?
- What cause or social issue persistently knocks on the door of my heart? What do I see in the world that is calling to me—that is begging me to sit up and pay attention?

Remember from Chapter 8 that Maslow also said that "self-actualizing people are, without one single exception, involved in a cause outside their own skin, in something outside of themselves."[36] Is now your time to lean in and think more deeply about the impact you want your life, work, and resources to have? You don't have to wait until your sitting on your family's foundation board or have a foundation of your own. You can start with small steps today. If there is an issue or cause you care about, invest time in learning more about it and begin by making a small gift of your own. You can get your feet wet by volunteering at a civic, nonprofit, or social organization and give of your time while you learn more about how these kinds of organizations work and what they need to be successful. You can start with baby steps. Getting started is what matters.

You may have gained some insight on this topic while you were doing some of your clutter clearing work earlier in this book. Try looking back at your responses and "mining" your reflections for an idea that ignites you. Or try some of the "getting engaged" tips from Caitlin Heising, the high-capacity donor from earlier in this chapter:

For me, it was helpful to find like-minded communities with peers who I could learn from and alongside. I networked, had lots of coffees, and joined learning and co-giving groups like the Philanthropy Workshop, Maverick Collective, Solidaire, and Human Rights Watch's San Francisco Committee. Finding your people helps you test ideas, find impactful giving opportunities, and grow into your giving with support. It can also help you build the confidence and experience to challenge traditional giving paradigms.[37]

If Caitlin's advice resonates with you and you're seeking inspiration from even more rising gen donors, Goldseker and Moody's *Generation Impact*[38] is brimming with stories from rising gens who are creating significant impact in their communities and in the world. Finally, the new Updated and Expanded version of *Generation Impact* includes several practical guides for engaging in the ideas highlighted in the book, including one focused on eight best practices and corresponding implementation tips for rising gen families that can help you get started.

Research tells us that there are 10 common characteristics of self-actualizing people: truth seeking, acceptance, purpose, authenticity, continued freshness of appreciation, peak experiences, humanitarianism, good moral intuition, creative spirit, and equanimity.[39] (You can even take a free, 10-minute self-actualization assessment at www.selfactualizationtests.com; you'll find out in which characteristics you are strong and in which you could use growth.) As you continue to evolve and develop—taking the spark that is burning in you and turning it outward to ignite change that impacts others—you will also continue on a path of your own growth. Soon you'll find you have even more to offer than you knew. That's the power of the enrichment loop.

12

The Missing Chapter in Your Parenting Book

Caleb and Kristina are the parents of two young kids. Kristina's father is a successful entrepreneur in biotech and has built the family net worth to more than $100 million. Through her trust, Kristina has access to $20 million dollars. Kristina's father began having financial success when she was quite young, so she was raised going to private school, riding horses competitively, and living a life that was relatively untethered to financial boundaries (though her mother was a grounding force, committed to having her kids learn to work and know the value of a dollar). Caleb was raised with a penny-pinching father and a strong work ethic. Caleb has built a thriving business in real estate development and is finding his own financial success. Knowing that there are separate trusts that Kristina's father set up for his grandkids (in addition to what will eventually be passed down from Caleb and Kristina), the young couple have started to worry about the impact of wealth in their kids' lives and wonder how they can parent well and prepare their kids for this future.

Caleb and Kristina are ahead of the curve in terms of thinking about these topics while their kids are still toddlers. I meet very few people who have the advantage of starting this intentional work of parenting within an environment of affluence when their kids are little, either because it doesn't occur to them or, more often, because at the time that their kids are little, they haven't yet created significant financial success, so it is just not part of their thinking. If you have little kids and you've got this book in your hands—good for you! You've got a head start. However, it's not necessary to begin when your kids are "littles" to help them find their path to thriving. Even if your rising gen is now a grown adult, there's plenty you can learn and do as a parent (or even grandparent) to support them. Wherever you're at today is the place to start.

Parenting—The Role That Never Ends

Because of your journey through this book, and even more importantly, due to your lived experience, you'll likely agree that despite all the security and opportunities that growing up with wealth can offer, it can also generate some hidden tripwires and notable clutter. Tripwires that need to be sighted and dismantled. And clutter that, when not openly explored and cleared out, can impact the ultimate well-being of rising generation family members. Hopefully you've learned a lot about where those tripwires and that clutter comes from and, also, how you can support the rising gen that you love to clear these—or, better yet, to help them to not let these form in the first place. And now your turn has come. As the parent of a rising gen, this chapter is for you.

We've already explored what a rising gen needs in order to build their own fire of thriving, generating enough intrinsic fuel to sustain that fire for the course of their lifetime. We called these sustaining character traits and skills "the big logs": Growth Mindset, Grit, Mastery-Orientation, Close Positive Relationships, and Foundational Character Strengths. Now, we'll look at your significant role—as an engaged, aware, and invested parent, grandparent, or guardian—in supporting the long-term success of the rising gen you love and some specific things you can do to be a positive force in their growth. As a parent, I know that it often feels like you're flying on a trapeze without a net. While I can't take away all of the angst about "doing it right," I can give you some clear guidance on what you can do to be most helpful. This chapter is written to give you tangible and actionable ideas to integrate into your interactions with your loved one *today*. So whether you're the parent of little ones or big ones, you probably already know that you're in a role that never ends. The good news is that also means you have a lot of opportunity to continue to love, support, and encourage your rising gen to develop these lifetime success skills.

The Land of Wealth

We previously laid the framework for what it is about wealth that can actually make parenting *more* challenging. Again, there is no contention that money makes life easier. However, research also indicates that more money only increases emotional well-being to a point, after which, more money can become a stressor in itself.[1] As was highlighted in Chapter 4, one of those stressors is the question of how to address parenting in the context of the inverted-U (Figure 4.1).

The inverted-U, the concept that there is no such thing as an unmitigated good,[2] means that some aspects of parenting are harder when you have excess financial resources. For instance, you have to be even more intentional in the messaging you give your children. Claiming that your family values financial stewardship but not insisting that your kids to learn about money or how to build and live within a budget sends a mixed message. Telling your young adult children that you want them to "make it on their own" but then supplying them with enough inherited income that they never have to do the hard work of crafting their own path is not only de-motivating, it sends a confusing message too. Another way surplus wealth makes parenting harder is that because external financial circumstances aren't going to force you to make prioritized decisions about what you will and won't support of your children's interests and activities, you have to get extremely clear on what *values* you prioritize in their lives and want to encourage in them—and then make decisions that are in alignment with that philosophy. Like the examples from Chapter 4 illustrated, it's much harder to tell your children, "No, we're not going to do that because it doesn't align with how we want to raise you" than it is to say, "No, we're not going to do that because we can't afford to."

But learning to parent intentionally is worth it. Remember, helplessness isn't learned; it's the default state. It is *control* over our choices and responses to circumstances that is learned.[3] Early life adversity, in appropriate doses, can inoculate the rising gen you love to later life helplessness. There is great value to children learning to work through struggle and to tolerate frustration; to discovering that their own efforts can result in rewards; and to proving to themselves that they can try something new, sometimes falter or fail, and still survive.

If it feels strange to have to be so intentional in how you're parenting in this blessed financial position you find yourself in, remember that 80% of American wealth is new wealth—it has not been inherited from a previous generation.[4] Most of you are attempting to do something that has not been role modeled by your own parents and which was not role modeled by theirs either. Family wealth consultant and psychologist James Grubman refers to this situation as the parents being "immigrants" to the land of wealth, a land to which their children are natives.[5] And like immigrants to a new country, there is a whole host of new customs and skills one has to build in order to be successful.

As with the actions that your children can take to become thriving adults, so, too, can you support them on the path with intentional parenting that focuses on developing a Growth Mindset, cultivates Grit, encourages a Mastery-Orientation, helps them to engage in Close Positive Relationships, and supports them to grow their innate Foundational Character Strengths. This chapter outlines the practical and relevant applications of these "big logs" and is written for you, the brave and engaged parents, grandparents, and guardians who are committed to learning how to parent well in this new land.

Parenting for a Growth Mindset

As we explored a couple chapters ago, significant research indicates that cultivating a Growth Mindset—the belief that skills and traits are learnable with effort—leads to both short-term achievement and long-term success.[6] And my own research has found this to be especially true for rising gens. Growth-minded people tend to value learning over looking smart, they value effort over ease, and they tend to overcome setbacks more easily than their fix-mindset counterparts. According to Carol Dweck, the researcher most well known for her work on Growth Mindset, learning to praise effort rather than outcome can be one of the most effective ways to encourage a Growth Mindset.[7] It's a built parenting skill, and it can be tough in the moment to tap into, but it's possible to bolster your Growth-Mindset-growing approach with some intentional awareness.

This morning I was listening to my husband helping my youngest daughter with fractions. In a scene that most parents can relate to, I could hear the tensions rising as my daughter wasn't understanding him and he was working hard to try to find new ways of explaining the concept. I could hear my daughter start to cry, and I was about to break in and suggest that it might be a good time for them to take a break, when I heard my husband make a smart pivot in his approach. He took a deep breath, calmed his voice, and said, "Clara, this is what learning feels like. No one is born understanding fractions—we all have to put in effort to learn them. You may not get it today, but as you keep at it, it'll make sense, and then no one can take that understanding away from you. Learning is work, and it is work for all of us. Figuring out that you can be uncomfortable—and even unhappy at times—when you're learning something new is part of becoming a learner. Why don't we take a break and commit to coming back to this later, okay?" I smiled as I celebrated his Growth-Mindset-promoting approach, knowing that our daughter got a little deposit in her Growth Mindset bank with that interaction.

To support growth-minded kids, rather than adopting a style of praising intelligence, skill, or a specific outcome, which can harm motivation and performance, try acknowledging the tenacity or concentration that you witnessed. While it is easy to praise good grades, a more nuanced approach that'll put the focus on the process rather than the outcome would be to say, "Ted, you clearly worked hard this semester and your grades show that. I was particularly impressed with how you put in so much effort and extra time when you got stuck with calculus. Your commitment to learning is enjoyable to see, and I'm proud of you." Teach your children to love challenges, enjoy effort, be curious about mistakes, and to continually be seeking new strategies for solving problems. As parents, instead of seeing your role as the person to praise your child's every success, embrace the idea that they are developing people and your role is to be committed to that development.[8]

Parenting Pro Tip: **Focus on *effort* over *outcome*.** Praise the process of learning, struggle, and growth that you see in your children's efforts. Celebrate the times you watch them toil and still stick with it. And don't discount the power of the role modeling you provide—share stories from your own life of times you struggled and what you learned from that process.

Parenting for Grit

As we defined in Chapter 10, Grit is passion and perseverance in pursuit of a long-term goal.[9] Similar to Growth Mindset, Grit has been linked to long-term success and achievement. Like all human traits, Grit has components that are influenced by both genes and environment,[10] so while some people are born grittier than others, we all have the ability to increase our Grit. Angela Duckworth, the superstar psychologist who has been the driving force behind our collective understanding of the importance of Grit, says that one of the most important ways parents can increase the Grit in their children is to be gritty themselves. Role modeling the passion and perseverance it takes to pursue a long-term goal will show your children what Grit looks like and what it can yield. Duckworth also suggests that a particular parenting style—one she calls "wise parenting"—is most encouraging of gritter kids. Wise parenting is an approach where you thread the needle between being both supportive *and* demanding. It is a "child-centric" style where you are supportive of your children's needs and interests, but don't always assume that they are the best judge of what to prioritize, when to give up, and how hard to work. The following graphic is an adaptation of Duckworth's map of parenting styles:[11]

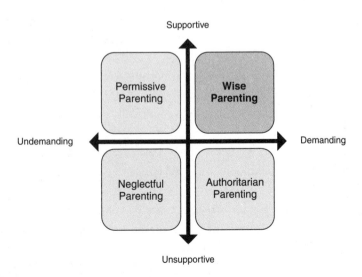

Figure 12.1

This kind of wise parenting showed up in the exemplar rising gen interviews I conducted, where one interviewee recalled a story from her teenage years:

> *When my dad was sick with cancer, my grandpa took me aside and let me know I wasn't cutting it. He told me he knew I was more capable than I was showing, and he expected more from me. Then he told me he wanted to go out to breakfast every Saturday and we'd talk about my week. I knew he expected more from me than I was delivering at that point, but I also felt his love and support. It made all the difference.*

You can see in this example how the combination of both high-expectations *and* support creates an environment where this rising gen knew she was loved, but she also knew she needed to up her game.

Duckworth asserts that wise parenting will help your children develop the Grit they need to succeed because "parents in this quadrant are accurate judges of the psychological needs of their children. They appreciate that children need love, limits, and latitude to reach their full potential. Their authority is based on knowledge and wisdom, rather than power."[12]

Parenting Pro Tip: **First of all, be gritty yourself**—challenge yourself to stick with worthwhile pursuits even when they're hard. And if you already are gritty in your daily life, be sure to share the stories of this with your kids. Making transparent what you grapple with each day is a powerful form of role modeling. Secondly, work to find your own brand of wise parenting where you're balancing holding a high bar for your kids while also providing them with the encouragement and support to lean into their potential.

Parenting for Mastery-Orientation

As was highlighted earlier in this book, Mastery-Orientation is closely linked to the development of both Growth Mindset and Grit, so you'll see many of the same parenting themes in this section as you've just read (which means as long as you're employing at least *some* of these you're likely getting more impact for your effort than you even know!).

Mastery-Orientation can be taught to children, even very early in life. Parents and primary caregivers are big drivers of whether this approach is adopted early in a child's development.[13] Parents of Mastery-Oriented children seem to be both sensitive and responsive to their kids' abilities and requests for help and maintain a positive affect and focus on the learning rather than outcome. Similar to the process of supporting both Growth Mindset and Grit, when faced with a challenge, the parents of Mastery-Oriented children focus on the process and the learning rather than the cause of the failure or the outcome.[14] This can be particularly salient for children raised by people who have been able to turn their ideas and hard work into significant financial wealth. These children often have the feeling that it will be nearly impossible to measure up, inherently focusing on the outcome (financial success) rather than the process (hard work, commitment, self-expression, vision, and values).

My own mother was a natural when it came to parenting for Mastery-Orientation. School always came easy to me. I loved getting straight A's, and it wasn't very hard for me to do so. Then when I was in the seventh grade, I got placed in the advanced math class where I struggled. I worked hard all semester, but I just didn't get it. After the first semester I received my report card, and I saw that I'd earned my first C in school. When I got home with my grades in hand I was in tears. I gave the report card to my mom and waited to hear how she would respond. She looked through my grades and with a bright smile exclaimed, "We're going out for ice cream!" Confused, I replied, "We are? Why?" Inspired by her natural mom-wisdom, she said, "Look at you—you got a C, and you've actually survived. I think it's time to celebrate." We went out for ice cream and with the dried tear stains still on my cheeks, we talked about what this experience had taught me regarding hard work, how it felt to not be at the top of my class, and what support I needed to be more successful the next semester. Everything my mom did that day was right out of the playbook of raising Mastery-Oriented kids. I'm so grateful for her wise and inspired approach.

Parenting Pro Tip: **Support your children to focus on the process and their learning,** and teach them to embrace failure as a part of their growth. Additionally, learning to speak about success in broader terms than just financial success can create a bigger space in which your children can define their own successes.

Parenting to Encourage Close Positive Relationships

The parents I talk to during the course of my work often say that their wealth can have an isolating effect. They may outwardly look like everything has finally fallen into place in their lives and they have it all, but they don't often have close friends with whom they can share their experiences and concerns without sounding insensitive to the daily challenges in their friends' lives. Relationship research shows that it is just as important to have people to help you celebrate when things go right as it is to have people to support you when things go wrong,[15] and that is an experience that is just as important for your kid as it is for you. It is likely that your rising generation children feel the same confusion and isolation about their own friendships that you may sometimes feel about yours.

This is another of those places where your role modeling can be invaluable. Being able to note where you feel comfortable or uncomfortable in your friendships, and then being able to invite conversations with your kids about their experiences, can help both of you feel less isolated and gain more clarity in how to discern true friends.

As you've read in many of the rising gen stories in this book, it is common for these heirs to feel like they can't fully be themselves in all contexts of their lives, and yet it is impossible to form authentic friendships or romantic relationships without bringing one's true self to the table. One of the obstacles to authenticity for many rising gen is the feeling that they are liked more for what they have (or what their last name is) than for who they are. One thing you can do is keep your eyes out for times when you see ongoing power imbalances in friendships. This may show up as your teenager always being the one to drive because they have the nicest car, or the kids only ever hanging out at your house because it has the nicest things. While as a parent these situations might make you feel good because it feels like you have more control or like the blessings that you've bestowed on your kids are appreciated, this lack of parity in your kids' friendships can sow seeds of doubt in your rising gen's mind about whether their friends are *really* their friends, or just friends of circumstance.

Parenting Pro Tip: **Be conscious of imbalances in power dynamics in friendships,** even when your kids are young. One way to do this is to be intentional about play dates. When setting up play dates for your younger children, don't defer to always hosting the play date at your house just because you have more toys or fun things to do—it creates a power imbalance in friendships that is hard to overcome. As your kids get older and can engage in more nuanced conversations, find ways to talk to your kids—even your adult kids—about your experiences with friends and romantic relationships, identifying when and how you were able to discern between genuine friendships and circumstantial ones. Be curious about their experiences and give them the space in your conversation with them to explore their own friendships—both the authentic ones and the circumstantial ones. In doing so, you'll support them to trust their instincts regarding how they feel when they spend time with different friends, which will help them discern between genuine friends and those who are hanging out because your kids offer cool things to do and have the nicest "stuff."

Parenting to Enhance Foundational Character Strengths

The field of character strengths is so deep and rich that we could write a whole book about parenting to cultivate Foundational Character Strengths. In fact, psychologist Lea Waters has. In Waters' book, *The Strength Switch: How the New Science of Strength-based Parenting Can Help Your Child and Your Teen Flourish*, she writes, ". . . in my professional opinion, our society has a case of 'right intention—wrong direction.' We mistakenly believe that the way to make our kids optimistic and resilient is to weed out all their weaknesses. Strength-based science shows the opposite is true. It tells us to turn the bulk of our attention to expanding their strengths rather than reducing their weaknesses."[16]

Back in Chapter 10 we explored the VIA Character Strengths Assessment and its categorization of the 24 culturally agnostic character strengths that form the backbone of human thriving. While this isn't the only way to think about and define character strengths, it's a useful one when parenting because (1) it gives us a common language of strengths to refer to and (2) it was originally developed as an assessment tool for youth. So unlike many traditional personality and skills assessments on the market, it has validated assessments for both youth (13–17 years old) and adults, making it a wonderful tool for supporting the human capital of the whole family.

Like the other big logs we've identified in this chapter, flipping the "strengths switch" in your parenting requires awareness and intentionality. In her book, *Daring Greatly*, Brene Brown tells a story where writer Toni Morrison, in an interview with Oprah Winfrey, talks about the messages a child gets about him or herself from the look on our faces when they enter the room: "Ms. Morrison explained that it's interesting to watch what happens when a child walks into a room. She asked, 'Does your face light up?' She explained, 'When my children were little, I looked at them to see if they had buckled their trousers or if their hair was combed or if their socks were up . . . . You think your affection and your deep love is on display because you're caring for them. It's not. When they see you, they see the critical face. *What's wrong now?*' Her advice was simple, but paradigm shifting for me," writes Brown, "She said, 'Let your face speak what's in your heart. When they walk in the room my face says I'm glad to see them. It's just as small as that, you see?'"[17]

I don't know about you, but I find that I can relate to what Toni Morrison describes more than I'd like to admit. When I'm thinking about my daughters I can so easily tap into the love and admiration I have for the people they are and the people they are becoming. Then, in the bustling chaos of daily life, I often observe that the words coming out of my mouth are more demanding and critiquing than supportive and encouraging. That instead of focusing on the strengths they each naturally show, I am more inclined to focus on how they are doing something differently than I would. How often do our words—and the looks on our faces—communicate how truly and deeply we appreciate and admire our children? Could we take one simple step toward shifting to a strength-focused paradigm by slowing down, seeing how they shine, and reflecting that back to them in our words of support and encouragement?

A final note on the value of strengths-based parenting: New research is showing that, while character strengths can always be grown with intentional effort, our innate character strengths (often known as Signature Strengths) are relatively stable across time.[18] As a parent, I think this is helpful and reassuring to know. Because, as any parent of teens can attest, the teen years can be a tumultuous time as your child goes through the necessary developmental work to eventually break free and become their own, individuated adult. Using Foundational Character Strengths as a tool for affirming the goodness you see in your kids can help to remind them (especially during those rough teen years) of who they are and what lies at their strong and capable cores. We, too, as parents can experience anxiety over our kids in their teen years. As you watch your child change before your eyes, possibly even challenging your perceptions of who he or she is, you'll be glad to know that some things can be counted on.

Parenting Pro Tip: **Consciously integrate strengths-based parenting into your daily interactions.** First, have the whole family take the free, validated VIA Character Strengths Assessment at www.viacharacter.org. Then begin to integrate emphasis on Character Strengths into your everyday parenting. It's simplest to start with each child's Signature Strengths and build from there. This can be as easy as strength-spotting (which is the act of intentionally noticing and calling out when someone is at their best) when you see your kids—or your spouse or partner—using a strength. And like all of these big logs, role modeling is powerful. Be willing to actively grow your own strengths and talk about your process of self-growth— what's working and what's challenging you—with your kids. It doesn't have to be formal—it can be as easy as naturally flowing mentions in dinnertime conversation or leveraging the times when your kids are captive in the car with you. (See Appendix A for more resources on Character Strengths and strengths-based parenting.)

More Tools for Sustaining Your Family's Fire

This chapter's focus has been to help you—the parents, grandparents, and guardians of the rising generation—to gain some tangible and actionable ideas on how you can support the growth and development of the "big logs"—the character traits and skills—that will help your beloved rising gen to thrive. But remember, you not only have these tools in your parenting tool belt, but you also have the helpful methods that we explored in Chapter 4:

- Making decisions grounded in values, not circumstances
- Positive role modeling
- Intentional family culture

Use these tools as well to support your rising gen and to help create a "family fire" of thriving for your whole clan.

Bonus Parenting Pro Tip: **Put your hands in your pockets.** As a last bonus, I want to share one more go-to strategy. I'm calling this one "put your hands in your pockets." This technique comes from my husband's lineage of boot-strapping Midwest farmers. It's a very effective but often underused parenting technique where, if you want your kids to learn something, don't do it for them; put your hands in your pockets and allow them to do it for themselves. Wealth creators are incredibly capable people who are often fast to solve problems. Unfortunately, this high capacity doesn't help your kids develop skills themselves. In fact, it often sends the message that you don't believe your children have what it takes problem-solve and take action on their own. By putting our hands in our pockets (while still being engaged and observing) and letting our children struggle to solve their problems, we give them space to develop and strengthen their own Growth Mindsets, Grit, Mastery-Orientation, Close Positive Relationships, and Foundational Character Strengths. This one might be the easiest of all for you. Or it might be the hardest. Either way, it is remarkably effective.

★ ★ ★ ★ ★

All together, these intentional, supportive "tools" become a positive virtuous cycle where each component is additive to the others. They start to become the storyline to the narrative that all family members can connect to, the basis for the collective understanding of "who we are" as a family, where there is room for both individual growth *and* healthy family connectivity, where expectations for individual self-actualization are high, and the love and support to help each person achieve their potential is equally as robust.

13

The Role of the Trusted Advisor

Recently I was on a call with a group of female advisors from all different advisory disciplines—wealth management, family dynamics, rising gen coaching, trusts and estate law, and philanthropic advising. We were talking about the dance we do with client families between meeting them where they're at and inviting them into new ideas and possibilities. How, as an advisor, it can take a lot of courage to challenge a client to try on a new perspective or change a narrative that is not serving them or their family. Collectively we talked about the need to let go of fear-based narratives and the power of a more purposeful, strengths-focused client approach. And yet, for so long our client families have heard that wealth is difficult to transition between generations, that it's a corrosive force in families, and that it's likely to ruin their kids. We wondered how we even start to chip away at that belief system that was keeping so many of our client families stuck with fear and worry.

Your Influence Is Greater Than You Think

If the Land of Wealth consists of immigrants (the wealth creating generation) and natives (the wealth inheriting generation),[1] there is a third participant in this land—the trusted advisor. The advisor, more often than not, is a "commuter" to the Land of Wealth.[2] Certainly, many advisors who work in the family wealth landscape have personal stories of family wealth themselves, which are often the catalyst for their chosen field of work. But there are also many who do not. For many of you, you picked your profession and now find yourself working with and serving families who have a very different lived experience than your own. This is complex terrain, for sure. Your role in navigating it is even more important than you may think.

While not a part of the inner circle the way that family and friends often are, as a trusted advisor (regardless of whether you are a financial advisor, trustee, attorney, family enterprise consultant, family dynamics consultant, counselor, coach, or some other key professional), you can be one of the most influential guides to your rising gen client. As a professional, you understand the behaviors and technicalities that often trip up your clients, but you may not always feel comfortable supporting the rising generation as they navigate this unique psychological landscape. This chapter will give you the insight and tools to confidently—and effectively—come alongside your younger clients and become both a thinking partner and a gentle guide.

Wealth 3.0 Is Dawning

As you consider the influence you have, and how you can use that influence in growth-promoting and life-enhancing ways, I think it is helpful to understand that the landscape in which you're operating is shifting. As a collection of related advisory fields, an important paradigm shift is currently taking place in our midst, moving us toward what we're calling "Wealth 3.0."[3] To fully understand this shift, let's first gain some perspective by taking a look at where we've come from.

The multi-disciplinary family wealth and family enterprise advising field of today has evolved significantly from where we were 40 years ago. In an article published by *Trusts & Estates* magazine in February 2022,[4] James Grubman, Dennis Jaffe, and I explored the roots of our industry and invited readers into the next turn of our field—Wealth 3.0.

Prior to 1980, in an era we might consider "Wealth 1.0," the focus was a family's money, not the family itself.[5] Published material about wealth and the wealthy were generally the stories of dynastic families (such as the Carnegies, Rockefellers, Vanderbilts, and the Mellons), which were more of a peek into the lives of the rich and famous than useful information to aid in the advising of affluent families. Families generally had one primary advisor, and that person's charge was to protect and increase a family's wealth. Period. The dynamics, psychology, and wellness of families were irrelevant, circumvented, or ignored.

The next era of the advisory field—what we might term "Wealth 2.0"—began to emerge in the 1980s. In this era, the voices of the wealthy themselves increased our understanding of the commonalities—and challenges—of being wealthy. Wealth 2.0 broadened our collective awareness that there could be capitals within a family that went beyond just the financial capital, including human, social, and intellectual capital.[6] In fact, in this era it was first asserted that these other forms of capital might, in reality, be *more important* than financial capital to a family's well-being and success through multiple generations.[7] Jay Hughes, the influential wealth advisor whose work we've discussed previously, was the first person I ever heard suggest that the most generative use of financial capital might be in its role in supporting the growth of the nonfinancial capitals. It is an idea that is common today but was paradigm-shifting when I first heard him say it. And for the first time, families and their advisors began to acknowledge family dynamics and the psychology of wealth as relevant.

Unfortunately, Wealth 2.0 also introduced a narrative that stoked families' deepest fears: Their money would ruin their children's lives, and their wealth would likely be lost. I think it is unlikely that anyone in our field at the time intended to propagate fear. Humans have an innate negativity bias, and I hypothesize that as we first began openly talking about the impact of wealth in families, that negativity bias influenced what we observed and what we spoke about and wrote about. Our collective field was still new, and we were all trying to understand it. However, these fear-based narratives have persisted, despite the fact that they are rooted in outdated statistics and poorly designed research (which we'll touch on more later in this chapter).

Once again—and thankfully—there is a shift happening in our field: the emergence of "Wealth 3.0." This new **Wealth 3.0** era, based in advances in the studies of cognitive and behavioral science and rooted in research-based fields such as positive psychology and organizational development, focuses advisors and families on strengths, purpose, and collaboration. Said another way, it advocates for motivating through positive, empowering means rather than through fear and for providing guidance for advisors grounded in rigorous science and data. Wealth 3.0 imparts a new mindset and a broader set of tools for wealth-owning and enterprising families. This era also invites our field to professionalize through the creation of a common foundational curriculum, credentialing, and the development of a common code of ethics. And while the focus of this chapter isn't to unpack the need for the professionalization of our collective and integrated advisory fields, it is an important part of the sea change we are in the midst of and, therefore, worth noting.

Becoming a Wealth 3.0 Advisor

Making this shift will require both a change in mindset as well as how you engage with clients. What can you get started on today to enhance your Wealth 3.0 advisory skills? It's a combination of self-awareness, ceasing to do some things, and starting to do others. If you have this book in your hands, it means you're ready for this.

As Humans, Our Thinking Is Flawed—Learn to Spot Bias

The first step on your pathway to becoming a Wealth 3.0 advisor, capable of meeting your rising gen clients where they are at and giving them safe spaces in which to grow, is to recognize that you are inherently biased. It's not just you. As humans, we all are. Cognitive psychology has given us a peek into the systematically flawed decision-making to which we are all susceptible, helping us to understand that we likely have more confidence in human judgment than we should.[8] These systematic flaws (which evolved in humans to help us take in and assimilate massive amounts of information around us quickly) create biases (which are basically filters in our cognition), and these biases influence our behavior.

Try this test. Following is a fact pattern for a standard, run of the mill, rising generation family member. When you read these facts, what is your assessment of the person?

- Twenty-two-year-old male
- Graduated college, currently not employed
- Living at home, but wants to find his own place
- Has formed some ideas of what industries he is interested in, but doesn't know how to get started
- Didn't have a job in high school or college, so doesn't have a work history to leverage, but also doesn't want to "start at the bottom"
- Acts confident, but has bravado that suggests an underlying lack of self-confidence

What is the first thing you think of when you read this?

A) The die is cast and this guy is going to be a noncontributor in life, just like most next gen I see in my client families.

B) This is developmentally appropriate behavior. He is not getting traction yet, but with some clutter clearing and some appropriate environmental motivation (i.e., it might be time for his parents to tell him to move out and begin supporting his own life expenses), he'll get there.

C) His behavior is probably due to the common bad parenting of the rich.

Whatever quick-judge assessment you made based on this fact pattern is likely colored by your own experiences. What were you doing when you were 22 years old? How many families have you observed where the emerging adults really struggled to gain traction in their lives? How often do you see salacious accounts in the media about bad-behaving heirs? How often have you read in industry books and articles that wealth ruins kids, that it is hard to maintain wealth through generational transfers, and that most families are destined to dissipate their wealth within a handful of generations?

Every one of these personal data points you have colors your perception of this rising gen's story and his likelihood of taking the driver's seat in his own life. If at 22, you were fresh out of college and working 80 hours a week as a newbie consultant in one of the big firms, that would impact what you think of this rising gen. If you're reading articles that highlight the changing trends in the timing for when young adults are launching,[9] you might have a different perception about this 22 year old. If you yourself were raised in a wealthy family where some of your siblings or cousins may have hesitated to dive into adulthood, but now the majority of your family peers are quietly going about living their lives, being contributors, and finding their own way to thriving, you will see this rising gen through a different lens. Every one of your life experiences and what you expose yourself to will become part of the filter for the information you take in—and influence how you translate that information—regarding this young man and his chances to create a successful life for himself.

In a recent family meeting, I watched an advisor pull an expert Wealth 3.0 move with a rising gen family member. The matriarch of the family had asked all of her adult grandchildren to go around the table and share what they were doing. This grandma had a strong presence, and no one dared cross or disappoint her. As each went in turn, talking about graduate school, their career progression, or their recent experiences with motherhood, I watched one of the rising gen family members get more and more nervous. She had struggled in college and ended up leaving her chosen school and was taking a break while she figured herself out. I knew she was having a hard time, and in a family of high achievers, she already felt like she wasn't "cutting it." When it got to be her turn, her face turned red and she mumbled toward the table that she was volunteering at a local animal clinic. The room was quiet as everyone tried to determine how the matriarch would react. Her brow furrowed, but before she could comment, one of the family's advisors spoke up and said, "I think that's great, Beverly. You've loved animals for as long as I've known you, and I'm betting you're learning a lot by working in the clinic. I actually find some of our best new hires in the firm are following a less traditional path these days—taking some time off school to explore different options before they finish their degrees." Beverly's face lit up. It was the first time in a long time that she felt seen as doing something valuable in her family. In this case, the advisor was the difference-maker because he chose to see Beverly through a lens of strengths and highlight what was useful in her current life choices rather than focusing on how she wasn't following the family's traditional playbook. In that moment, he helped all her family members to do the same.

Daniel Kahneman has won the Nobel Prize in Economics and has dedicated his professional life to studying and understanding human decision-making. In his book, *Thinking Fast and Slow,*[10] he discusses the cognitive biases that influence our decision-making. While our perceptions and decision-making as advisors (and humans) are likely subject to many different biases, the one I think it is highly useful to watch out for is confirmation bias. Confirmation bias is "the seeking or interpreting of evidence in ways that are partial to existing beliefs, expectations, or a hypothesis in hand."[11] This basically means that we seek to confirm what we already believe. So, if we think that wealthy families are going to fail, we are more likely to prioritize information that confirms our belief and deprioritize information that disconfirms our belief. If we believe that money ruins kids, we will quickly latch on to the stories where we assume that to be true and ignore the many stories of rising gen who are living lives of meaning, contribution, and impact.

To counteract our hidden cognitive biases—including confirmation bias and others—we become aware of our own blind spots. Especially when it comes to money, wealth, and the wealthy. Let's face it—culturally and historically, as a society, we've got a conflicted relationship with both money and wealth and that conflicted relationship fuels the biases we bring to our work. Start by going back to the money-related exercises in Chapter 5, including the seven-step clutter clearing process. While not every one of those questions is going to fit for you in your role as an advisor, a great many of them will. And if you take them on honestly and from your heart, I guarantee you'll gain some useful new insight. Being more aware of your own relationship to money and wealth will only enhance your ability to meet your rising clients where they are at and, even more importantly, to see them for who they really are.

So while we can't escape having cognitive biases, the more awareness we bring to our own thinking, the more we can mitigate their damaging effects on our perception and, ultimately, on our behaviors. Understanding our cognitive biases will impact the advice we give—or don't give—to our client families.

Advising Pro Tip: **Pay attention to your thinking and the conclusions you jump to** when you observe or interact with the rising gen in your client families. How well do you know that rising gen—the person sitting in front of you—and how much have you filled in beliefs about who you *think* they are? Try having a conversation and learning a little more about the person. You are likely to find someone who has a lot to give and is yearning to figure out how to give it. Also, seek out articles, podcasts, and other information that continue to give a broad spectrum of stories about the impact of wealth in families. Finally, actively look for and notice those rising gen in your client base or environment who are productive, responsible, and self-aware. The more each one of us can broaden our perspective to take in the whole picture, the more effective we will be at meeting our client families where they are at.

Stop Fueling Fear

The second important step on your pathway to becoming a Wealth 3.0 advisor—able to meet and gently guide both your client families and the rising generation within them—is to stop insinuating that they are going to fail. The messages that were staples of Wealth 2.0 are not the path to a brighter, more purposeful, more collaborative future in Wealth 3.0.

And they're also not the truth.

★ ★ ★ ★ ★

"Wealth 2.0 has become a drumbeat of fear-based, unnecessarily pessimistic messages that perpetuate stereotypes about wealth and the wealthy."

—Grubman, Jaffe, and Keffeler *Trusts & Estates*, February 2022

★ ★ ★ ★ ★

As a collection of advisory fields, for years we've been telling families that failure is almost like gravity and that they are more likely to fail then to succeed. We tell them that "based on the research," 70% of families will fail at transitioning wealth. We prophesize that "based on the research," they are likely to lose their financial resources and their family relationships will be strained. We tell them that most family wealth is dissipated, and most family enterprises have failed by the third generation. Believe me, early in my career I started more presentations than I can count with a doomsday message based on some Wealth 2.0 "truism" about family wealth failures. I bet you have too.

The problem is, historically, we haven't *had* good research on the outcomes of wealthy families. As an industry, we are still in our toddlerhood of creating well-designed and well-executed research that explores the outcomes of affluent and enterprising families. In the recent article, "There is No '70% Rule': Improving Outcome Research in Family Wealth Advising," Grubman systematically debunks the trifecta of family wealth and family enterprise failure "rules" that we have collectively been touting as facts for decades.[12] In this meticulously researched article, he addresses the three most common "truisms" that have been perpetuated throughout the Wealth 2.0 era:

- "Shirtsleeves to shirtsleeves in three generations."
- Thirty percent of family enterprises survive through the second generation, 13% into the third generation, and 3% into the fourth.
- Seventy prcent of families will fail to transfer their wealth from the first generation to the second.

While many of us has likely repeated one—if not all three—of these for years, Grubman's article deconstructs the shaky foundation of each, leaving no question that it is time to retire this broken triangle.

Grubman summarizes that our often-repeated prophecy of "shirtsleeves to shirtsleeves in three generations" is basically an antiquities adage—a phrase that has been repeated so often we now accept it as truth but has little empirical validity.[13] It was likely originally intended as a helpful motivator for families to actively engage in conversations about wealth and its impact, but it has turned from a "carrot" inviting conversation to a "stick" instilling fear. While we each may anecdotally be able to identify families who have risen and fallen in three generations, that doesn't make it a law of family wealth cycles. Additionally, how "true" it *is* or *isn't* is less important than the question of how *helpful* it is. I can't tell you how many rising gen family members, upon hearing me share this adage, have nervously laughed and said, "Well, I guess there's not much I can do then."

Grubman goes on to illustrate how the original "30-13-3" failure rule in family business was based on John Ward's 1987[14] study of family enterprises and, although groundbreaking at the time, has ultimately been found to have methodical weaknesses and has never been replicated.[15] Newer research is showing that when we follow the family—not the business—there is a much higher transgenerational success rate.[16] "Individual businesses rise and fall like any other, but the founding business family often endures successfully across multiple generations as it diversifies into other industries and spawns new ventures."[17] This is a very different message for a rising gen to hear than that each succeeding generation is less likely than the one before them to effectively navigate family enterprise transitions.

Finally, Grubman tackles the third "truism" in the trifecta by looking more closely at the roots of the "70% Rule." This rule was an outgrowth of the work that Roy Williams and Vic Preisser published in their book, *Preparing Heirs*.[18] Grubman rigorously traces back all citations and source material for this statistic and concludes that there is no "there" there.[19] It turns out that the statistic we've all been citing as a fact isn't actually a statistic (or a fact). What *is* the failure rate (or, more compellingly, the success rate) for affluent families from one generation to the next? We don't actually know that information yet. Again, what a liberating gift we can give our rising gen clients by *not* telling them that they have only a 30% chance of successfully integrating and passing on the resources their parents or grandparents created.

★ ★ ★ ★ ★

"Ultimately, we know deeply that the other side of every fear is a freedom."
—Marilyn Ferguson

★ ★ ★ ★ ★

With the broken triangle of truisms now debunked, we are fully ready to enter a new era with our clients. Let's stop using fear as a motivator. Let's stop stoking their natural fears with false stats. It doesn't serve them, and it puts an immense mantle of pressure on their rising gen, who feel destined to fail. It is reasonable that families are fearful about the future, but our mistake is in validating their fears by naming failure as the most common outcome.[20] Fears are normal, *but they are not outcomes*.[21] Instead, we can help them to recognize the tripwires that are present in the landscape of affluence, identify the capacity they have within their family members—and especially in their rising generation—and use that capacity to navigate family wealth well.

Finally, as you are considering how to pivot from a fear-based approach to a strengths-and-capacity-based approach in your client practices, pay close attention to the resources that are emerging from our own colleagues. Books like Sharna Goldseker and Michael Moody's *Generation Impact*, Dennis Jaffe's *Borrowed from Your Grandchildren*, Coventry Edwards-Pitt's

Raised Healthy, Wealthy, and Wise, Jamie Weiner's *The Quest for Legitimacy*, Hartley Goldstone, Jay Hughes, and Keith Whitaker's *Family Trusts*, and Keith Whitaker and Tom McCullough's *Wealth of Wisdom: Top Practices for Wealthy Family and Their Advisors*. Books like these illustrate that the shift in our industry is already at play. These are just a few of the more Wealth 3.0-focused works that have emerged in our field in the last decade—and more are on their way. These books are written specifically for you, an advisor seeking to find a more empowered and empowering way of engaging with your client families and the rising generation within those families. It's an exciting time to be doing our work.

Advising Pro Tip: **Be transparent rather than citing old, fear-based "rules" of failure that fuel a negative narrative** where there is little room for family to succeed—especially the rising generation. Instead, you can say, "Honestly, we don't know. Some families do not navigate affluence skillfully. And lots of families do. We don't actually have statistics on the success rate yet, but we do have some research-based foundational practices that we know help families integrate wealth well." Expose the rising gen in the families you're working with to role models of their peers who are engaged, courageous, and making a difference. Offer them this book, if it may help. And see Appendix A for other books that can assist in providing a new, positive narrative to inspire your rising gen clients.

Start Focusing on Strengths and Capacity

The next tool in your toolkit for becoming a Wealth 3.0-oriented advisor is shifting to a focus on strengths and capacity. Every one of the ideas outlined in Chapter 12, "The Missing Chapter in Your Parenting Book," is one you could adapt and use directly with rising gen clients or use as supportive material when the parents or grandparents of those rising gen are seeking encouragement and advice. Remember, the goal is to help the rising gen in your client families gather the "big logs" for sustaining their own unique fire and definition of success—Growth Mindset, Grit, Mastery-Orientation, Close Positive Relationships, and Foundational Character Strengths. It truly does take an engaged community to support each of us to thrive, and having a common toolset and language around these big logs increases their "stickiness" and the likelihood of being masterfully adopted by your rising gen clients.

In addition, don't hesitate to borrow from other fields that are even more advanced in purposeful and positive researched-based practices, fields such as positive psychology, organizational development, and leadership coaching. Following are a sampling of the useful techniques and models from these fields that may be adapted to your advisory practice:

- **Appreciative Inquiry:** A strengths-based, positive approach to leadership and organizational change.[22]

- **Motivational Interviewing:** An evidenced-based approach to clarifying one's ambivalence to change and supporting them to find the appropriate intrinsic motivation for positive behavior change.[23]

- **Family-Centered Positive Psychology:** An approach, including tools and interventions, designed to support families based on the recognition of the inherent strength and assets in a family system, rather than its deficits.[24]

- **VIA Character Strengths and Virtues:** A framework of 24 culturally agnostic strengths and six overarching virtues that can be used to facilitate human growth and thriving.[25]

- **Job Crafting:** An evidenced-based, visual, and interactive method for redesigning one's job based on values, passions, and strengths.[26]

- **High-Quality Connections:** An intentional way for interacting with others that demonstrates they matter and builds trust, connection, and relational capital.[27]

- **Peak-End Theory:** A cognitive bias that impacts how we remember experiences. Rather than remembering the totality of the experience, this bias emphasizes our memory of what we experience at the "peak" (the highest emotional point) and the "end" (where an experience completes).[28] A valuable cognitive bias we can use to our advantage when intentionally designing compelling and enjoyable family meetings and experiences.

The simple act of deliberately choosing your questions when communicating with your clients makes all the difference. An easy example of this is instead of asking the common question, "What keeps you up at night?" you can instead ask, "What strengths do you see in your family (or children) that will help you meet adversity in the future?" Where we focus our attention impacts the questions we ask, the information we gather, and the narrative that our clients hear in their own stories. We can ask questions that continue to focus them on their fears, or we can use the wisdom from models like Appreciative Inquiry, for instance, which guides us to ask questions that illuminate strength and possibility.[29]

We have the tools—both emerging in our collective advisory fields as well as outside of our industry—and our job is to challenge ourselves to change "how we've always done things." Start considering what outdated practices you are ready to leave behind and what new ideas are you ready to lean into yourself—and invite your clients to lean in as well.

A final note about Wealth 3.0 and a strength-focused approach to client work: A strengths-based approach isn't about putting a yellow smiley face on everything and pasting over the challenges and difficulties that families and rising gen face as they work to integrate wealth into their lives well. It's not about being positive and grinning while fundamentally important aspects of family dynamics—like communication, the expression of love, and the creation of clear agreements—are being ignored. The tripwires of affluence and accumulation of inner and outer clutter are real things. In order to address them, we need to see and acknowledge them. What this is instead is a call to action. As trusted advisors we have important and influential roles in the client families we serve. We can either validate our clients' fears and help them circle the wagons, in doing so, creating an even smaller place for rising gen to find their footing, or we can hear the fears of our clients and help them to see how strong and resourceful they are to face those fears and challenges. Confirmation bias informs us that we will seek information that confirms our beliefs. Let's help our client families—and especially the rising gen in those families—to create a new set of beliefs about what is possible for them. Then let's help them build the capacity to get there.

Becoming the Bellows to Their Fires

I remember when I was a kid, back when it was much more common to make an actual fire rather than flip a switch in a gas fireplace, my uncle kept a "bellows" at the edge of his hearth. (I thought this was very funny because his last name also happened to be "Bellows.") A bellows is a device that has a big leather bag attached to a moving, pivoting frame. You expand the frame to "inhale" air and contract it to push air out the other side. It can be used to provide extra oxygen to a fire, keeping it lit or helping it grow bigger. Sometimes I think the greatest service we can provide to our rising gen clients is to be the bellows to their sparks. We can provide a safe space to explore, feel foolish, ask questions, and flounder around for a bit. While Wealth 2.0 advising would inadvertently starve a rising gen's passion and possibility of the oxygen needed for growth, we can instead be the bellows that fans the early flames. And when the time is right, we can reflect back to them what we see in them that is bright, true, and strong. In doing so, we help them to remember they have what it takes to "become." We can provide that little extra oxygen just when they need it. Ultimately, they have to find their own way and clear enough of their own clutter so the oxygen moves freely about them, but as advisors we can be the bellows at critical times—just when they might need a little extra support to help their spark ignite.

Conclusion: Beyond the Myth of the Silver Spoon

We are here. At the end of one journey . . . but the beginning of another. I hope by now we have fully debunked for you the Myth of Silver Spoon—that misconception and cultural bias that says the next generation within significantly wealthy families don't or shouldn't have problems in their lives. The myth that says that being raised amidst wealth magically makes difficulties go away—makes the birds sing, the sun shine, and life is easy by default and full of happiness. The false narrative that says children and grandchildren of successful wealth creators should also find a way to create a financial windfall themselves or else they're "failures"—and that being "rich" is the most salient aspect of their identity. That destructively claims those with gifted wealth are somehow less deserving of what they have, less worthy of authentic friendships and love, and less capable of contributing meaningfully to society. And that the *more* money one's family has, the *more* all this holds true.

I hope we have finally—fully—trashed and kicked to the curb this myth, along with its hidden tripwires and the clutter it can cause in your head, heart, and life.

The reality is you are *so much more* than your wealth, your future holds so much more, and I hope this book has been a vehicle for transformation, freedom, and flourishing.

Let's pause now for a moment. Inhale, exhale. Appreciate yourself and what it takes to have even contemplated the questions that have been posed in these pages. Consider the courage it takes to hold yourself with compassion and, simultaneously, hold yourself accountable to the life you really want to live. To be willing to reflect on your life and choices and the forces "below the waterline," which may have been steering your decisions and actions for years . . . and then to be decisive about what you keep and what you let go. And to recognize that you have a spark in you that is precious, unique, and worth tending to.

★ ★ ★ ★ ★

Joseph Campbell's myth of the Hero's Journey[1] captures the story arc of human transformation. In it, the individual sets out on a quest, is met with many challenges along the way, finds some helpers at just the right times, has some decisive losses and victories, and returns back to the place they started, the same person, but transformed. You are your own hero. Throughout this journey together, we've identified how to clear out the various types clutter—money, identity, relationship, and contribution—that inherited wealth can generate (with a proven 7-step clutter clearing process); we've named the big logs of slow burning fuel (Growth Mindset, Grit, Mastery-Orientation, Close Positive Relationships, and Foundational Character Strengths) necessary to support long-term success; we've discussed viable sources for fast-burning fuel (your ideas, dreams, and inspiration); and we've explored some of the pathways—impact work and impact giving—to ignite your spark and set you on a path to not only self-fulfillment, but to creating a positive ripple to others as well.

You know you've won the "birth lottery." That doesn't mean you're not allowed to struggle, question, and sometimes fall. By bringing often hidden challenges out into the open air, we can put a voice to them and turn what can be a debilitating self-narrative into fuel for your own fire. From this new, clutter-free place, you can experience the freedom of your own identity and the power of your own ideas. It's a win-win. You gain a happy and meaningful life and we—your family, friends, and society at large—gain the benefits of your contributions.

So now it is time to move beyond the Myth of the Silver Spoon. You are on the path—and it is likely going to be a lifetime expedition. Pack up your gear and don't forget everything you'll need to light and tend to your own fire. Now more than ever, we could use the hearts and brains of engaged and thoughtful rising gen. Just like you. And if you need a little inspiration, remember the stories in this book—people like Cassie, Lindsay, Trent and Dani, Kamal, and Beau, to name a few. While these are not their real names, each one of these is a real story. There are lots of rising gen out there who are just like you—who care enough to do the deep work of finding their place and their voice. And it's working. They are clearing their clutter, finding their sparks, and tending their fires. You can, too.

To the parents, grandparents, and guardians of the rising generation, as I continue to work in this field, I am gratified to see how much you care. Many of you are "immigrants to the land of wealth," and the challenges that the rising gen in your life are facing may seem like a surprise to you. I'm glad you're here and grateful that you'll work to learn how you can best support them to finding their own path to lifetime success.

To my fellow colleagues, I am grateful to you as well. You have a significant role in guiding your client families and the rising gen in those families. To acknowledge their fears, but not feed them. To support them with ideas and resources that can help them find their footing and gain traction in their lives. To be the bellows to their sparks. We have some big work ahead of us as we continue to chart the course into a new Wealth 3.0 paradigm. As we turn the corner (and persist in turning our own thinking inside out), we will face questions about the professionalization of our collective advisory fields, the design and execution of solid research to support our work with families, and how we can collaborate across our disciplines to continue to provide a cohesive net of support for our client families. They are counting on us.

* * * * *

And now the invitation. The invitation is for you, brave and curious rising gen, to actively and fully participate in your life and in the world that awaits your contribution. The journaling, reflection, and discussion you've begun puts you squarely on the path to discovering your right relationship with money and wealth, uncovering the core of who you are, finding relationships where you feel genuinely seen and celebrated, and exploring how you can create impact through your contribution. As you go further with this, you will be increasingly liberated to consciously and joyfully determine what matters most to you. You may one day even want to begin sharing your story with others.

I am confident that you have a uniquely inspired life to live. The wealth creator who came before you in your family had the Midas touch for generating great wealth; you most certainly can have the touch for creating great good. I'll meet you out there on that path.

A

Resources to Support Rising Gen, Their Parents, and Their Advisors

- **21/64 Money Messages Tool** (and other interactive tools to support multigenerational conversations)—Website: https://2164.net/tools/

- **Character Strengths—Assessment, Books, and Other Tools**
  - VIA Character Strengths Assessment (a free, open-access resource): www.viacharacter.org
  - *Character Strengths Interventions: A Field Guide for Practitioners* (Niemiec, 2017)
  - *The Power of Character Strengths: Appreciate and Ignite Your Positive Personality* (Niemiec & McGrath, 2019)
  - *The Strength Switch: How the New Science of Strength-based Parenting Can Help Your Child and Teen Flourish* (Waters, 2017)
  - Character Strengths Intervention Cards (a card deck with all 24-character strengths) (Steeneveld & van den Berg, 2020)
  - Character Lab (https://characterlab.org): Angela Duckworth's weekly blog for parents and teachers on building character in the children that they love

- **Books to Inspire the Rising Generation**
  - *Generation Impact: How Next Gen Donors Are Revolutionizing Giving* (Goldseker & Moody, 2021)
  - *A New Reason to Work: How to Build a Career That Will Change the World* (Roshan & Rabbat, 2021)
  - *Grit: The Power of Passion and Perseverance* (Duckworth, 2016)
  - *Mindset: The New Psychology of Success* (Dweck, 2008)
  - *Flourish: A Visionary New Understanding of Happiness and Well-being* (Seligman, 2012)
  - *The Quest for Legitimacy: How Children of Prominent Families Discover Their Unique Place in the World* (Weiner, 2022)
  - *Raised Healthy, Wealthy, and Wise: Lessons from Grounded Inheritors and How They Got That Way* (Edwards-Pitt, 2014)

- **Books for Relationships and Families**
  - *Positivity: Top-Notch Research Reveals the 3:1 Ratio That Will Change Your Life* (Fredrickson, 2009)
  - *Happy Together: Using the Science of Positive Psychology to Build Love That Lasts* (Pawelski & Pawelski, 2018)
  - *Seven Principles for Making Marriages Work* (Gottman, 2015)

- **Books to Support Parents and Advisors**
  - *Borrowed from Your Grandchildren: The Evolution of 100-year Family Enterprises* (Jaffe, 2020)
  - *Wealth of Wisdom: Top Practice for Wealthy Families and Their Advisors* (McCullough & Whitaker, 2022)
  - *Strangers in Paradise: How Families Adapt to Wealth Across Generations* (Grubman, 2013)
  - *The Cycle of the Gift: Family Wealth and Wisdom* (Hughes, Massenzio, & Whitaker, 2013)
  - *Family Trusts: A Guide for Beneficiaries, Trustees, Trust Protectors, and Trust Creators* (Goldstone, Hughes, & Whitaker, 2016)

B

In Their Own Words—Advice from the Rising Gen to the Rising Gen

(Based on interviews conducted in 2018)

"I think curiosity has a lot to do with it. Just to be able to figure out what are all the other things in the world that could be of interest and that resonate with that person. I don't know I think parents in family create really specific environments. My sense is that regardless of different parenting techniques or different family environments is that the environment inherently is very narrow. You're creating a very specific context. I think the goal would be figure out in that environment what you want to assume. Don't over assume. This is why it connects back to what I love about your other example of the other person you talked to about gender. So many people in the world assume that they're straight or assume that they're anything. Once that assumption gets broken, regardless, even if you end up in the same place that journey was really valuable. I think the experience for someone who's coming into their own adulthood and identity is about having a lot of things pinging off of that person in a way that's like, 'React to this. React to this' in a way that starts to shape. At that age you are really malleable. You're not shaped by things that you're not touched by."

208   In Their Own Words—Advice from the Rising Gen to the Rising Gen

"To me it's develop the ability to understand money. I call it financial literacy or self-sufficiency. Whatever age you are, learn how to deal with money. Learn how to budget, learn how to save, learn how to feel comfortable not overextending yourself, learn the ability to feel like if you needed to be on your own and take care of yourself at whatever point, that you could do that, and I think the worst thing that I see, the anxiety that comes with money and wondering if I could do it on my own, and that attachment to the inheritance, and the trust, and the family house, put yourself in a position where you are able to succeed. So, develop a budget, develop an ability to control your spending in a way that you have targets as far as what you're saving and that you develop discipline around money. Start focusing on credit scores, and managing credit effectively, and getting a part-time job, and being able to generate income. That might be 5 hours a week, it might be 10 hours a week, but saving that, knowing how much you're spending, figuring out all your sources and uses [for money], and having a goal for how much you're putting away in the bank each month, and [then] putting that away [and saving it]. That feeling of discipline will last your entire life. And [on the] opposite [side], if you feel reckless and out of control, and [have] an anxiety around money and questioning your ability to make smart decisions, that'll follow you your whole life."

"Oh, boy. The first thing that comes to mind is to get away, gain some sort of perspective. Go someplace where people don't care who you are so that you can start to figure out who you actually are. You get a say in who you are. No one ever really told me that. I thought I was just carrying the torch. And also, you don't need to have all the answers. I spent my whole life thinking if I had the answers, then I'm good. But to figure out what the right questions are [is more important] or just figure out any questions [that you're actually asking yourself]. Start somewhere."

"My advice to them would be nothing feels as good as personal accomplishment, and those personal accomplishments are usually based on a lot of personal work which no one will ever see, and it's all behind the scenes. You don't have to disown your family. In fact, you should always seek to use whatever resources are available to you, but you need to know that you're driving your own creation. This work will also let you feel less guilty about any uneven gifts that you receive through that affiliation with your family. It's a [psychological] thing, and thinking about [being] stuck and unstuck, I have personally had waves of times when I wasn't producing or wasn't working on things that felt like they were resulting in something. When you go back to getting something that you produce, you do it, you work with a team and you do it well or whatever. That high, that elation about how that went, I definitely have felt those waves. And sometimes it's just you're doing all the prep in the background and

you just have to do that. Part of it is, being an introvert, I sometimes would choose to do my own thing and not work with other people or to do things in private as opposed to doing things that were more public, and doing something in public and/or with a group where you can reach a milestone of accomplishment . . . whether you are recognized for it, or it's a pausing place [for you], it feels really good."

"I think this kind of new engaged commitment that I have for myself about doing things that are mutually nourishing. I think that also applies in every kind of walk of life. Do the thing that you're passionate about. Do that thing that you're excited about. That same psychotic woman [I referred to earlier] also said to me, 'There's a reason they call it work, bitch.' And that was also helpful. Yeah, it's not gonna be great every moment of your life, but if you can find the things that nourish you that you feel excited about, and the people and the relationships. And if you focus more about how you can be a contribution to the world instead of competition and comparing and what you're not, I just find that that makes for so much more happiness. And really to look at what you are good at, as opposed to trying to make yourself something else."

"Have a goal for your personal self, your business self and really let people know that you have this goal. Don't hide it because if you just have this goal and it's a private goal, no one is going to support you and they're just going to put that stereotype of 'oh you're just the next generation's wealth, you're a trust fund baby.' And let them know that you do have drive and that you are someone that wants to make your own name. If you tell people that you're driven or show people that you're driven and you tell them that you want to do something, they're more likely to support you than if you just keep it to yourself and hope that one day it will happen because they're just going pretty much put you in the category of 'she's just a trust baby or she's just going to get whatever she wants from her mom and dad.' And also to know it's okay to fail. It's okay to say, I changed my mind I don't really want to do this."

"I do think some element of self-exploration is important and to have that as a sort of intentional project that you undertake, but I also think limiting that and just getting out in life, getting out of your comfort zone and working, getting a job and a real career and pay your rent, pay for your car insurance, I think is important, just going out and doing that and try to build, even if you come back to say a family business or you come back and manage the wealth, I just feel like that people that have gone their own path and built their own career, even if they have wealth, are able to create an identity on their own and I think there's much [good that happens] from that. And experimenting with different ideas in life is good too, but it can suck you

more into the wealth. When you go out and experiment and you become an artist or get on the Peace Corps or do all these different things, if you don't build confidence that you can do it on your own, those things can almost suck you more into the wealth. I think that that is a tricky balance because I think that can be very beneficial to go have life adventures, but you can't get stuck doing just that. Having that freedom, planning out who you are, but I also think that sort of pulls you further into the wealth trap and doesn't allow you to build your own career, build your own identity and just have that pattern of success. I do think that success is a pattern. People that are successful tend to . . . success tends to breed success."

"My advice to any rising gen would be to make yourself proud. There is so much to be said for how often we're trying to make other people proud, and there is something to be said for setting small goals, learning every day, and making it all mean something to you. How you create a wealthy/rich life that has nothing to do with money. This is how you make the path to feeling good about yourself, and then the money is just a tool."

"I think what I would say is find something that you're interested in. Don't get hung up on the fact that it's [something you have to] do for the rest of your life. But, find something that you're interested in, and then just kind of dive in and go after it. Get involved, and go out and make connections, and meet people, and just kind of commit yourself to what it is that you're interested in and just go after it. Then, after a period of time, you may find that it's not something that you're interested in anymore. You can shift to something else, or you may find that that's what you ultimately want to do and live, for the rest of your life or career. But, that's been a recurring theme in my life is I was really blessed to get exposed to the concepts of money and investing, and personal finance, and all of that at a really early age, having started investing in stocks at 6 years old, and buying my first piece of commercial real estate when I was 16, an taking an active part of my stock portfolio. Moving that forward to when I was in college, I was interested in real estate, and was interested in private equity, and mergers and acquisitions. I joined industry associations, and I was going to meetings, and joining committees, and going to events, and meeting people, and fast forward to today, and that's paid a lot of dividends in terms of gaining a lot of knowledge and expertise in certain areas, and developing a really robust network around me. So, I think that's kind of what I would suggest . . . find what you're interested in and dive in.

C

Research
Methodology

Note: This appendix is a summary of the methodology that guided the research conducted with exemplar rising gen family members in the spring of 2018. Many of the quotes presented in this book are from those research interviews. If you are interested in seeing the full results and data explication from those interviews, please contact Kristin Keffeler at kristin@illumination360.com or download the complete thesis from the University of Pennsylvania Scholarly Commons website: https://repository.upenn.edu/mapp_capstone/142/.

Introduction to Methodology

This research project was primarily a qualitative observational study based on semi-structured interviews. These interviews were conducted with rising generation exemplars—defined as those who illustrate the upper-end of development of a particular characteristic, or set of characteristics, in a population[1]—in this case, in ultra-high net worth (UHNW) families. The research study also contained one quantitative component, the PERMA Meter, which was used as a validation of interviewee well-being.

211

Research Design Rationale

Qualitative research provides a form of data that offers contextual richness and a depth of reflective and relational information that many other research methods aren't able to capture.[2] In particular, semi-structured interviews are a useful qualitative method when two key elements are present: (1) the research question necessitates enough structure to address specific dimensions present in the subject's lived experience and (2) when the data being gathered would also benefit from study participants having enough flexibility to share information that may bring new meaning to the topics being studied.[3] The semi-structured interview questions are informed by theory, and the interviewing process allows for valuable flexibility. Through the unfolding narrative of the participants, this flexibility creates a nuanced understanding of the often unnoticed, and sometimes highly complex, common phenomena present in the stories of the interviewees.

Another important factor of this project's research design is that it is based on the exemplar methodology. The exemplar methodology is used to study the individuals who exhibit a highly developed version of the characteristic traits that are illustrative of a paragon within that population,[4] which helps us to understand more about the upper end of development within the population of study. In the case of this study, I was hoping to understand if, and how often, wealth inheritors experience the feelings of helplessness that can be prevalent among children in UHNW families and what inner traits or outer experiences—specifically those studied within the field of positive psychology—helped them to move past the limiting and paralyzing experience of this helplessness into a life of autonomy, contribution, and engagement.

Finally, while the majority of data gathered for this project were qualitative and based on semi-structured interviews, one quantitative component was used as a validation measure of participant well-being. As interview candidates for this research were either nominated to be interviewed by a professional within my network, or they self-nominated having met the established exemplar criteria (see *Implementation of Research Design* section next), it felt important to have a quantitative assessment that would validate the nominator's perception that the interviewee did, indeed, experience a high level of well-being. PERMA is an acronym that stands for the five components of well-being, as defined by Seligman[5]: Positive emotion, Engagement, Relationships, Meaning, and Accomplishment. The quantitative measure that was administered was the PERMA Meter, a widely used and validated five-question measure of well-being, as defined by PERMA. So in addition to the perception of the nominator, the PERMA Meter provided quantitative data for each individual interviewee, serving to validate their well-being through this self-reported assessment.

Implementation of Research Design

To use the exemplar methodology, it is necessary to define the criteria participants need to exhibit in order to qualify for the research project. One method used to define exemplar criteria is to rely on the relevant literature in concert with consulting experts in the field of study.[6] I created an initial list of potential exemplar criteria based on the key texts addressing the attributes of thriving rising generation family members. I then sent that list to four established experts within the UHNW advisory field and requested their feedback. Based on these two methodologies, I defined the inclusion criteria for this study. For this study, exemplars demonstrate the following:

- Mutually satisfying/positive relationships
  - Is able to show up authentically in relationships in their lives
  - Feels seen and appreciated in close relationships for skills and unique gifts they bring to the relationship
- Solid sense of self ("Knows Thyself")
  - Understands their talents/skills/gifts
  - Does not identify solely as someone with wealth or solely in relationship to the wealth creator or family name
- Personal agency
  - Feels that they are in control over their own lives
  - Demonstrates individual decision-making, even when it doesn't align with family decision-making
  - Able to dream their own dream
  - Ability to create impact or contribute in meaningful ways
- Grit
  - Demonstrates passion and perseverance toward a long-term goal(s)
  - Able to work hard and tolerate frustration
  - Shows a "stick-to-itiveness"

The study design, along with these exemplar criteria, was summarized and sent to all study candidates along with an emailed invitation. Through this recruitment process, I was seeking an interviewee cohort of 10–12 individuals between the ages of 21 and 65.

In accordance with best practices for research involving human subjects, I submitted this research design to the institutional review board of the University of Pennsylvania and received approval to proceed. As a part of ensuring an ethical research project, I requested all participants to sign an informed consent prior to participating in the interview.

The interview guide was developed based on the literature review of the key constructs being studied—helplessness; growth mindset; grit; mastery-orientation, mastery experience(s), and learned mastery; and positive relationships—and refined with the guidance of my Capstone Advisory Board. The interview guide was sent to participants the day before our interview. You can see the interview guide in the full research report (https://repository.upenn.edu/mapp_capstone/142/).

The interview format was based on the semi-structured methodology—it was guided by the questions in the interview guide but allowed enough flexibility for participants to share relevant stories and insights. Interviews were 1-hour long and were recorded so they could be transcribed.

The PERMA Meter was sent via email immediately following the interview and interviewees were asked to respond with the completed assessment as quickly as possible.

Finally, the qualitative data contained within the interview transcripts were categorized by relevant themes, a process called coding. A software program called NVivo (www.qsrinternational.com) was used to code and organize all of the interview data. NVivo is a qualitative research tool that is designed to support researchers to organize their data so it is easier to ascertain important themes and trends.

While there are different approaches to determining the useful information buried within qualitative data, the approach I used was the phenomenological approach. Phenomenology uses the lived experience of small groups of individuals, captured via narrative, to understand the concepts of the phenomena that they have in common.[7] One of the key elements of the phenomenological approach is that it allows the researcher to reduce individual experiences within an area of study and distill those differences to a universal essence. Using this approach, it is possible to achieve research saturation with as few as two to 10 participants, all of whom participate in an extensive interview. Additionally, because this method focuses on distilling the interviews down to their core themes while keeping in mind the context of the whole, the process of working with this qualitative data is referred to as an explication rather than as an analysis.[8]

In order to code the data from the interviews, each concept—helplessness, grit, growth mindset, mastery experience, and positive relationships—was considered as its own phenomena. The coding process for each was iterative in that, as more detailed information about each concept emerged (e.g., stories illustrating that growth mindset was encouraged by parents or other trusted adult, or a story of an experience where a growth mindset was valuable), each phenomena was coded with more specific units of meaning. These more specific units of meaning were subcategories of the parent phenomena category. A full list of the coding categories can be found in the complete findings (https://repository.upenn.edu/mapp_capstone/142/). Ultimately, these units of meaning were clustered together in order to create a composite understanding of each phenomena. During the coding process, it was noted where themes began to emerge that did not align with the original hypothesis and where themes began to emerge that did align with the original hypothesis.

Summary of Results

The results of the exemplar interviews indicate that there are indeed common experiences among the rising generation family members who have successfully navigated the potential pitfalls of unearned wealth to create lives of individual identity, personal satisfaction, autonomy, and engagement. The working hypothesis that has formed the framework for this inquiry is as follows:

Helplessness → Learned Mastery = Growth Mindset + Grit + Mastery – orientation / Experience(s) + Positive Relationships

The goal of this study was to help identify the phenomena—the internal mindsets and external support—most consistent in the lives of exemplars that differentiate the rising generation from the next generation of inheritors.

Description of Sample

The 12-person sample of rising generation exemplars consisted of eight women and four men. The age range for the sample was 32–65 years old. The sample consisted of six participants who identified as second generation (G2); two who identified as third generation (G3); two who identified as fourth generation (G4), one of whom self-described as a G4/G5; and two who identified as fifth generation (G5), one of whom self-described as G5/G6. It is not uncommon for next generation family members to identify as two different generations, such as G5/G6. In affluent families, when the initial wealth creator has a son or daughter who grows the family wealth significantly larger (usually through the creation or expansion of a business), it is common for the family to recognize their generational relationship to both the original wealth creator and also the person who increased the wealth. Finally, seven of the participants self-reported that they did not have any control over their inherited assets; two self-reported that they had total control over their inherited assets; and three self-reported that they had "some" control over their inherited assets (see *Figure 1* for full demographic data of sample).

Participant #	Gender	Age	Which Generation in Relation to Wealth Creator?	Control Inherited Assets?
1	F	32	G2	No
2	M	42	G3	Some
3	F	34	G5/G6	No
4	M	48	G4/G5	No
5	F	51	G2	Some
6	F	30	G2	No
7	F	51	G2	No
8	F	37	G2	No
9	M	48	G4	Some

Participant #	Gender	Age	Which Generation in Relation to Wealth Creator?	Control Inherited Assets?
10	M	34	G3	Yes
11	F	65	G5	Yes
12	F	44	G2	No
TOTALS	F = 8 M = 4	Range: 32–65	G2 = 6 G3 = 2 G4 = 1 G4/G5 = 1 G5 = 1 G5/G6 = 1	No = 7 Yes = 2 Some = 3

Figure 1   Demographic data of exemplar sample

Coding: Discerning the Essence of the Experience

The goal of my qualitative analysis was to discern the essence of the common experiences, and any notable outliers, of the interviewed exemplars. When using the phenomenological approach to data explication, it is important to identify the phenomena that are being explored.[9] The overall question being explored for this cohort of interviewees was whether certain psychological factors were present to enable thriving in the presence of unearned wealth. However, it was each of the constructs—helplessness, growth mindset, grit, mastery-orientation/experience(s)/learned mastery, and positive relationships—that served as the individual phenomena of inquiry for the study. By understanding the universal essence present in each of the individual phenomena (i.e. the constructs), I would hopefully be able to construct a more detailed understanding of what experiences support rising generation family members to thrive.

The goal of phenomenology is to reduce individual experiences within a common phenomenon into a universal essence of the experience[10]—a "grasp of the very nature of the thing."[11] It is a methodology that attempts to extract the very essence of the common experience. Based on the data coding and sorting steps, the outcome is to create a composite description—or a gestalt[12]—that captures what the population of study experienced and how they experienced it.[13] To that end, each of the study constructs, as well as emergent themes from the research interviews, are presented in a descriptive paragraph, including representative quotes from the interviews. Any outliers to the universal crux of the experience were also noted. The interview consisted of four context-setting questions, six phenomenon-related questions, a question on the advice the interviewee would give a younger next generation individual, and three demographic questions. You can find the full data explication in the complete research findings at https://repository.upenn.edu/mapp_capstone/142/.

PERMA Meter: Validation of Thriving

Finally, the PERMA Meter is a quantitative component that was used as a validation measure of participant well-being. Interview candidates for this research were either nominated to be interviewed by a professional within my network, or they self-nominated having met the established exemplar criteria (see previous section). The intention was to complement these nominations with a quantitative assessment that would validate the nominator's perception that the interviewee did, indeed, experience a high level of well-being. The PERMA Meter includes questions addressing the five key components that compose overall well-being: Positive emotion, Engagement, Relationships, Meaning, and Accomplishment.[14]

On the whole, interviewees scored average (a score of three) or above-average (a score of four or five) in all components measured with the PERMA Meter, though it is not necessary to score above average in all five PERMA measures in order for one to be considered thriving. Results from this measure are presented in *Figure 2* and confirm that the individuals nominated for this study have self-reported well-being scores that indicate that they are, indeed, thriving in their lives.

	P	E	R	M	A	Mean
Interviewee 1	3	4	4	4	4	3.8
Interviewee 2	5	4	5	5	5	4.8
Interviewee 3	4	4	4	4	4	4.0
Interviewee 4	4	5	5	4	4	4.4
Interviewee 5	5	4	5	4	4	4.4
Interviewee 6	4	5	5	4	5	4.6
Interviewee 7	4	4	4	5	4	4.2
Interviewee 8	4	3	5	4	4	4.0
Interviewee 9	4	3	4	4	4	3.8
Interviewee 10	4	4	4	4	4	4.0
Interviewee 11	4	4	4	4	4	4.0
Interviewee 12	5	4	5	4	4	4.4

Figure 2   PERMA Meter scores for interviewees

Summary of Insights from Data

It was interesting to uncover that while many next generation family members express behaviors of helplessness, these exemplars did not have such experiences on their path to thriving. So while the original hypothesis was that thriving rising generation family members must have overcome helplessness in order to experience flourishing in their lives, in fact, helplessness wasn't a significant part of their experiences. However, there was consistency of the presence of the other constructs—growth mindset, grit, mastery experiences, and positive relationships. While these do not comprise the definitive list of skills and traits a rising generation family member needs to thrive, the research points to the fact that these four constructs are likely an important part of the equation.

To read the full data explication, learn more about the limitations of this research, or read about suggested future areas of study, please read the complete research findings at: https://repository.upenn.edu/mapp_capstone/142/ **or contact Kristin Keffeler at kristin@illumination360.com for the full report.**

Notes

Introduction

1. Hughes, J. Personal Communication, October 2019.
2. Havens, J., & Schervish, P. (2014). *A golden age of philanthropy still beckons: National wealth transfer and potential for philanthropy technical report* [Unpublished manuscript]. Center on Wealth and Philanthropy, Boston College.

Chapter 1

1. World Wealth Report 2020
2. WealthX World Ultra Wealth Report 2017
3. Hughes, J. E., Massenzio, S. E., & Whitaker, K. (2014). *The voice of the rising generation: Family wealth and wisdom.* Hoboken, NJ: Wiley.
4. Cote, J. (2000). *Arrested adulthood: The changing nature of maturity and identity.* New York: New York University Press.
5. Haimowitz, K. & Dweck, C. S. (2016). What predicts children's fixed and growth intelligence mindsets? Not their parents' views of intelligence, but their parents views of failure. *Psychological Science, 27,* 859–869.
6. Duckworth, A., Peterson, C., Matthews, M. D., & Kelly, D. R. (2007). Grit: Perseverance and passion for long-term goals. *Journal of Personality and Social Psychology, 92*(6), 1087–1101.
7. Diener, C. I., & Dweck, C. S. (1980). An analysis of learned helplessness: The process of success. *Journal of Personality and Social Psychology, 39,* 940–952.

8. Gable, S. G., & Gosnell, C. L. (2011). The positive side of close relationships. In K. M. Sheldon, T. B. Kashdan, & M. F. Steger (Eds.), *Designing positive psychology: Taking stock and moving forward* (pp. 265–279), New York: Oxford University Press.
9. Peterson, C., & Seligman, M. E. P. (2004). *Character strengths and virtues: A handbook and classification.* New York: Oxford University Press.

Chapter 2

1. Not his real name; this story is a compilation of several family stories, written as an illustrative narrative.
2. Hughes, J. E., Massenzio, S. E., & Whitaker, K. (2014). *The voice of the rising generation: Family wealth and wisdom.* Hoboken, NJ: Wiley.
3. Jaffe, D., & Grubman, J. (2007). Acquirers' and inheritors' dilemma: Discovering life purpose and building personal identity in the presence of wealth. *The Journal of Wealth Management.* Fall 2007.
4. Willis, T. (2005). *Navigating the dark side of wealth: A life guide for inheritors.* Portland, OR: New Concord Press, p. 4.
5. Jaffe, D., & Grubman, J. (2007). Acquirers' and inheritors' dilemma: Discovering life purpose and building personal identity in the presence of wealth. *The Journal of Wealth Management.* Fall 2007.
6. Shoenberg, E. (n.d.). *When too much is not enough: Inherited wealth and the psychological meaning of money.* Unpublished manuscript, Department of Psychology, Columbia University, New York, NY.
7. Gardner, J., & Oswald, A. (2001). *Does money buy happiness? A longitudinal study using data on windfalls.* Royal Economic Society.

Chapter 3

1. Furnham, A., & Argyle, M. (1998). *The psychology of money.* New York: Routledge, p. 2.

Chapter 4

1. Kahneman, D., & Deaton, A. (2010). High income improves evaluation of life but not emotional well-being. *Proceedings of the National Academy of Sciences, 107*(38), 16489–16493.

2. Grant, A., & Schwartz, B. (2011). Too much of a good thing: The Challenge and opportunity of the inverted U. *Perspectives on Psychological Science 6*(10), 61–76.
3. Grubman, J. (2013). *Strangers in paradise: How families adapt to wealth across generations*. Author.
4. Erikson, E. (1959, 1980). *Identity and the life cycle*. New York: Norton.
5. Hughes, J. E., Massenzio, S. E., & Whitaker, K. (2014). *The voice of the rising generation: Family wealth and wisdom*. Hoboken, NJ: Wiley.
6. Bandura, A., Ross, D., & Ross, S. A. (1961). Transmission of aggression through imitation of aggressive models. *The Journal of Abnormal and Social Psychology, 63*(3), 575–582.
7. Everything Psychology. (2012, August 28). Bandura's bobo doll experiment. https://www.youtube.com/watch?v=dmBqwWlJg8U
8. Lewin, K. (1936, 2014). *Principles of topological psychology*. Munshi Press.

Chapter 5

1. Money Messages©2018 21/64, Inc. You can purchase this tool online at https://2164.net/tools/.
2. Gallo, E., & Gallo, J. (2011). *Emerging adulthood and the results-oriented trust environment*. Gallo Consulting white paper.
   Gallo, E., & Gallo, J. (2005). *The financially intelligent parent: 8 steps to raising successful, generous, responsible children*. New York: New American Library.
   Gallo, E., & Gallo, J. (2002). *Silver spoon kids: How successful parents raise responsible children*. New York, Contemporary Books.
   Godfrey, J. (2003). *Raising financially fit kids*. Berkeley, CA: Ten Speed Press.
   Morris, R., & Pearl, J. (2010). *Kids, wealth and consequences: Ensuring a responsible financial future for the next generation*. New York: Bloomberg Press.

Chapter 6

1. Erikson, E. (1964, 1986, 1993). *Childhood and society*. New York: W.W. Norton.
2. Cote, J. (2000). *Arrested adulthood: The changing nature of maturity and identity*. New York: New York University Press.
3. Jay, M. (2012). *The defining decade: Why your twenties matter—And how to make the most of them now*. New York: Twelve (Hatchet Book Group), p. 7.

4. Pro Football Hall of Fame. (n.d.). Wikipedia. https://en.wikipedia.org /wiki/Pro_Football_Hall_of_Fame
5. Estimated probability of competing in professional athletics. (2020). NCAA. https://www.ncaa.org/sports/2015/3/6/estimated-probability -of-competing-in-professional-athletics.aspx
6. Players. (n.d.). Pro Football Hall of Fame. https://www.profootballhof. com/players/
7. Football's father and sons. (n.d.). Pro Football Hall of fame. https:// www.profootballhof.com/footballs-fathers-and-sons/
8. Jaffe, D., & Grubman, J. (2007). Acquirers' and inheritors' dilemma: Discovering life purpose and building personal identity in the presence of wealth. *The Journal of Wealth Management*. Fall 2007.
9. Goldbart, S., Jaffe, D. T., & J. DeFuria. (2004). Money, meaning and identity: Coming to terms with being wealthy. In T. Kasser & A. Kanner (Eds.), *Psychology and the consumer culture*. Washington, DC: American Psychological Association.
10. Schervish, P., Coutsoukis, P., & Lewis, E. (1994). *The gospels of wealth*. Westport, CT: Praeger Publishers.

Chapter 7

1. Brown, B. (2021). *Atlas of the heart: Mapping meaningful connection and the language of human experience*. New York: Random House.
2. Brown, B. (2021). *Atlas of the heart: Mapping meaningful connection and the language of human experience*. New York: Random House, p. 158.
3. Brown, B. (2021). *Atlas of the heart: Mapping meaningful connection and the language of human experience*. New York: Random House, p. 158.
4. Dutton, J., & Heaphy, E. D. (2003). The power of high-quality connections. In K. S. Cameron, J. E. Dutton, & R. E. Quinn (Eds.), *Positive organizational scholarship* (pp. 263–279). San Francisco: Berrett-Koehler Publishers, p. 264.
5. Dutton, J. (2003). *Energize your workplace: How to create and sustain high-quality connections at work*. Hoboken, NJ: Wiley.
6. Fredrickson, B. L. (2013). *Love 2.0: Finding happiness and health in moments of connection*. New York: Plume.
7. Gable, S. G., & Gosnell, C. L. (2011). The positive side of close relationships. In K. M. Sheldon, T. B. Kashdan, & M. F. Steger (Eds.), *Designing positive psychology: Taking stock and moving forward* (pp. 265–279), New York: Oxford University Press.

Chapter 8

1. *Work.* (n.d.). Cambridge Dictionary. https://dictionary.cambridge.org/us/dictionary/english/work

2. Gardner, H. Csikszentmihalyi, M., & Damon, W. (2001). *Good work: When excellence and ethics meet.* New York: Basic Books.

3. Maslow, A. (1971). *The farther reaches of human nature.* New York: Penguin Publishing.
   Kaufman, S. B. (2020). *Transcend: The new science of self-actualization.* New York: Tarcher Perigree, p. 149.

4. Brooks, A. (2020). How to build a life: The three equations for a happy life, even during a pandemic. *The Atlantic,* April 9, 2020.

5. Lykken, D., & Tellegen, A. (1996). Happiness is a stochastic phenomenon. *Psychological Science,* 7(3).

6. Brooks, A. (2020). How to build a life: The three equations for a happy life, even during a pandemic. *The Atlantic,* April 9, 2020.

7. Brooks, A. (2020). How to build a life: The three equations for a happy life, even during a pandemic. *The Atlantic,* April 9, 2020.

8. Shenk, J. W. (2009). What makes us happy? *The Atlantic,* June 2009.

9. Jay, M. (2012). *The defining decade: Why your twenties matter—and how to make the most of them now.* New York: Twelve (Hatchet Book Group).

10. Hughes, J. E., Massenzio, S. E., & Whitaker, K. (2014). *The voice of the rising generation: Family wealth and wisdom.* Hoboken, NJ: Wiley, p. 65.

11. Brooks, A. (2022). *From strength to strength: Finding success, happiness, and deep purpose in the second half of life.* New York, NY: Penguin Books.

12. Jay, M. (2012). *The defining decade: Why your twenties matter—and how to make the most of them now.* New York, NY: Twelve (Hatchet Book Group).

13. Hughes, J. E., Massenzio, S. E., & Whitaker, K. (2014). *The voice of the rising generation: Family wealth and wisdom.* Hoboken, NJ: Wiley. p. 72.

Chapter 9

1. Peterson, C. (2006). *A primer in positive psychology.* New York: Oxford University Press.

2. Seligman, M. E. P. (1999). The president's address. *American Psychologist,* 53, 559–562.

3. Seligman, M. E. P. (2011). *Flourish: A visionary new understanding of happiness and well-being.* New York: Atria.

4. Csikszentmihalyi, M. (1990.) *Flow: The psychology of optimal experience.* New York: HarperCollins Publishing.

5. Boring, E. G. (1950). *A history of experimental psychology* (2nd ed.). New York: Appleton-Century-Crofts.

6. Dahlsgaard, K., Peterson, C., & Seligman, M. E. P. (2005). Shared virtue: The convergence of valued human strengths across culture and history. *Review of General Psychology.*

7. Seligman, M. E. P., & Csikszentmihalyi, M. (2000). Positive psychology: An introduction. *American Psychologist, 55,* 5–14.

8. Seligman, M.E.P., & Csikszentmihalyi, M. (2000). Positive psychology: An introduction. *American Psychologist, 55,* 5–14.

9. American Psychiatric Association. (2013). *Diagnostic and statistical manual of mental disorders* (5th ed.). Washington, DC: Author.

10. World Health Organization. (2022). *International classification of diseases and related health problems* (11th ed.). Geneva, Switzerland: Author.

11. *World health organization definition of health.* (n.d.). Retrieved on July 1, 2018, from www.who.int/kobe_centre/about/faq/en/. As listed in the Preamble to the Constitution of the World Health Organization as adopted by the International Health Conference, New York, June 19–22, 1946; signed on July 22, 1946 by the representatives of 61 States (Official Records of the World Health Organization, no. 2, p. 100) and entered into force on April 7, 1948.

12. Seligman, M.E.P, & Csikszentmihalyi, M. (2000). Positive psychology: An introduction. *American Psychologist, 55,* 5–14.

13. Peterson, C. & Seligman, M. E. P. (2004). *Character strengths and virtues: A handbook and classification.* New York: Oxford University Press.

14. Easterbrook, G. (2001, March 5). I'm OK, you're OK. *The New Republic,* p. 23.

Chapter 10

1. Seligman, M. E. P. (1990, 1998). *Learned optimism: How to change your mind and your life.* New York: Pocket Books.

2. Seligman, M. E. P. (2011). *Flourish: A visionary new understanding of happiness and well-being.* New York: Atria, p. 83.

3. Seligman, M. E. P. (2011). *Flourish: A visionary new understanding of happiness and well-being.* New York: Atria.

4. Seligman, M. E. P., & Maier, S. (1967). Failure to escape traumatic shock. *Journal of Experimental Psychology, 74,* 1–9.

5. Seligman, M. E. P., & Maier, S. (2016). Learned helplessness at fifty: Insights from neuroscience. *Psychological Review, 123,* 349–367.
6. Haimowitz, K., & Dweck, C. S. (2016). What predicts children's fixed and growth intelligence mindsets? Not their parents' views of intelligence, but their parents views of failure. *Psychological Science, 27,* 859–869.
7. Dweck, C. (2006). *Mindset: The new psychology of success.* New York: Random House.
8. Dweck, C. (2006). *Mindset: The new psychology of success.* New York: Random House.
9. Accessed at https://sparqtools.org/mobility-measure/growth-mindset-scale/ April 19, 2022.
10. Duckworth, A., Peterson, C., Matthews, M. D., & Kelly, D. R. (2007). Grit: Perseverance and passion for long-term goals. *Journal of Personality and Social Psychology, 92*(6), 1087–1101.
11. Duckworth, A. (2016). *Grit: The power of passion and perseverance.* New York: Simon & Schuster.
12. Duckworth, A. (2016). *Grit: The power of passion and perseverance.* New York: Simon & Schuster.
13. Diener, C. I., & Dweck, C. S. (1980). An analysis of learned helplessness: The process of success. *Journal of Personality and Social Psychology, 39,* 940–952
14. Bandura, A. (1977). Self-efficacy: Toward a unifying theory of behavioral change. *Psychological Review, 84,* 191–215.
15. Bandura, A. (1977). Self-efficacy: Toward a unifying theory of behavioral change. *Psychological Review, 84,* 191–215.
16. Bandura, A. (1982). Self-efficacy mechanism in human agency. *American Psychologist, 37,* 122–147.
17. Gable, S. G., & Gosnell, C. L. (2011). The positive side of close relationships. In K. M. Sheldon, T. B. Kashdan, & M. F. Steger (Eds.), *Designing positive psychology: Taking stock and moving forward* (pp. 265–279), New York, NY: Oxford University Press.
18. Gable, S. L., Gonzaga, G. C., & Strachman, A. (2006). Will you be there for me when things go right? Supportive responses to positive event disclosure. *Journal of Personality and Social Psychology, 91*(5), 904–917.
19. Peterson, C., Beermann, U., & Park, N., (2007). Strengths of character, orientations to happiness, and life satisfaction. *The Journal of Positive Psychology, 2*(3): 149–156.
20. Kashdan, T., Blalock, D., Young, K., & Machell, K. (2017). Personality strengths in romantic relationships: Measuring perceptions of benefits and costs and their impact on personal and relational well-being. *Psychological Assessment, 30*(2).

21. Hone, L., Jarden, A., Schofield, G., & Duncan, S. (2014). Measuring flourishing: The impact of operational definitions on the prevalence of high levels of wellbeing. *International Journal of Wellbeing*, *4*(1): 62–90.
22. Harzer, C., & Ruch, W. (2015). The relationships of character strengths with coping, work-related stress, and job satisfaction. *Frontiers in Psychology*, *6*(165).
23. *Bring your strengths to life & live more fully*. (n.d.). VIA Institute on Character. www.viacharacter.org
24. Peterson, C., & Seligman, M. E. P. (2004). *Character strengths and virtues: A handbook and classification*. New York: Oxford University Press.

Chapter 11

1. Buffet, P. (2002). *Life is what you make it: Find your own path to fulfillment*. New York: Random House, p. 224–225.
2. Buffet, P. (2002). *Life is what you make it: Find your own path to fulfillment*. New York: Random House, p. 225.
3. Buffet, P. (2002). *Life is what you make it: Find your own path to fulfillment*. New York: Random House, p. 244.
4. Kashdan, T. B., & Silva, P. J. (2011). Curiosity and interest: The benefits of thriving on novelty and challenge. In S. J. Lopez & R. Snyder (Eds.), *The Oxford handbook of positive psychology* (pp. 367–374).
5. Liu, L., et al. (2021). Understanding the onset of hot streaks across artistic, cultural, and scientific careers. *Nature Communications, 12*, 5392.
6. Kashdan, T. B. et al. (2018). The five-dimensional curiosity scale: Capturing the bandwidth of curiosity and identifying four unique subgroups of curious people. *Journal of Research in Personality, 73*, 130–149.
7. We won't get into it here, but you can take a quiz and learn more about the various types on researcher Todd Kasdan's website at https://toddkashdan.com/curiosity/.
8. Maslow, A. (1962). Toward a psychology of being. Floyd, VA: Sublime Books, p. 76.
9. Kashdan, T. B., & Silva, P. J. (2011). Curiosity and interest: The benefits of thriving on novelty and challenge. In S. J. Lopez & R. Snyder (Eds.), *The Oxford handbook of positive psychology* (pp. 367–374).
10. Roshan, P., & Rabbat, I. (2021). *The new reason to work: How to build a career that will change the world*. Lioncrest Publishing.

11. *The Deloitte Global Millennial Survey 2019.* (2019). Deloitte. https://www2.deloitte.com/us/en/insights/topics/talent/deloitte-millennial-survey-2019.html

12. Roshan, P., & Rabbat, I. (2021). *The new reason to work: How to build a career that will change the world.* Lioncrest Publishing, p. 10.

13. https://garycommunity.org, accessed April 25, 2022.

14. Rob Gary, personal communication, May 18, 2022.

15. Rob Gary, personal communication, May 18, 2022.

16. Rob Gary, personal communication, May 18, 2022.

17. Wrzensniewski, A., McCaulty, C., Rozin, P., & Schwartz, B. (1997). Jobs, careers, and callings: People's relations to their work. *Journal of Research in Personality, 31*(1), 23–27; Peterson, C., Park, N., Hall, N., & Seligman, M. (2009). Zest and work. *Journal of Organizational Behavior, 30*(2), 161–172.

18. Havens, J. & Schervish, P. (2014). *A golden age of philanthropy still beckons: National wealth transfer and potential for philanthropy technical report* [Unpublished manuscript]. Center on Wealth and Philanthropy, Boston College.

19. Goldseker, S., & Moody, M. (2017, 2021). *Generation impact: How next gen donors are revolutionizing giving.* Updated and Expanded Edition. Hoboken, NJ: John Wiley & Sons, p. 3.

20. Telgen, D. (2012). *The gilded age.* Detroit, MI: Omnigraphics, Inc.

21. Telgen, D. (2012). *The gilded age.* Detroit, MI: Omnigraphics, Inc.

22. www.givingpledge.org, accessed April 26, 2022.

23. Goldseker, S., & Michael Moody, M. (2017, 2021). *Generation impact: How next gen donors are revolutionizing giving.* Updated and Expanded Edition. Hoboken, NJ: John Wiley & Sons, p. 81.

24. Goldseker, S., & Moody, M. (2017, 2021). *Generation impact: How next gen donors are revolutionizing giving.* Updated and Expanded Edition. Hoboken, NJ: John Wiley & Sons, p. 81.

25. Collier, C. (2012). *Wealth in families* (3rd ed.). Harvard Press.

26. Goldseker, S., & Moody, M. (2017, 2021). *Generation impact: How next gen donors are revolutionizing giving.* Updated and Expanded Edition. Hoboken, NJ: John Wiley & Sons, p. 3.

27. https://www.hsfoundation.org/mark-heising-liz-simons-join-giving-pledge/, accessed April 26, 2022.

28. Caitlin Heising, personal communication, May 18, 2022.

29. https://www.berggruen.org/about/, accessed at April 26, 2022.

30. https://givingpledge.org/pledger?pledgerId=166, accessed April 27, 2022.

31. Goldseker, S., & Moody, M. (2017, 2021). *Generation impact: How next gen donors are revolutionizing giving*. Updated and Expanded Edition. Hoboken, NJ: John Wiley & Sons.
32. Buffet, P. (2002). *Life is what you make it: Find your own path to fulfillment*. New York: Random House, p. 232.
33. *Job Satisfaction Index 2015: What Drives Job Satisfaction?* (2015). Happiness Research Institute. https://www.happinessresearchinstitute.com /publications
34. Csikszentmihalyi, M. (1990). *Flow: The psychology of optimal experience*. New York: HarperCollins Publishing.
35. Lowry, R. (1973). *A. H. Maslow: An intellectual portrait*. Monterey, CA: Brooks/Cole Publishing, p. 91.
36. Maslow, A. (1971). *The farther reaches of human nature*. New York: Penguin Publishing; Kaufman, S. B. (2020). *Transcend: The new science of self-actualization*. New York: Tarcher Perigree, p. 149.
37. Heising, C. Personal Communication, May 18, 2022.
38. Goldseker, S., & Moody, M. (2017, 2021). *Generation impact: How next gen donors are revolutionizing giving*. Updated and Expanded Edition. Hoboken, NJ: John Wiley & Sons.
39. Kaufman, S. B. (2020). *Transcend: The new science of self-actualization*. New York: Tarcher Perigree, p. 89.

Chapter 12

1. Kahneman, D., & Deaton, A. (2010). High income improves evaluation of life but not emotional well-being. *Proceedings of the National Academy of Sciences, 107*(38), 16489–16493.
2. Grant, A., & Schwartz, B. (2011). Too much of a good thing: The challenge and opportunity of the inverted U. *Perspectives on Psychological Science, 6*(10), 61–76.
3. Seligman, M. E. P., & Maier, S. (2016). Learned helplessness at fifty: Insights from neuroscience. *Psychological Review, 123*, 349–367.
4. Grubman, J. (2013). *Strangers in paradise: How families adapt to wealth across generations*. Author.
5. Grubman, J. (2013). *Strangers in paradise: How families adapt to wealth across generations*. Author.
6. Dweck, C. (2010). Even geniuses work hard. *Educational Leadership, 68*(1), 16–20.

7. Dweck, C. (2006). *Mindset: The new psychology of success.* New York: Random House.

8. Dweck, C. (2006). *Mindset: The new psychology of success.* New York: Random House.

9. Duckworth, A., Peterson, C., Matthews, M. D., & Kelly, D. R. (2007). Grit: Perseverance and passion for long-term goals. *Journal of Personality and Social Psychology, 92*(6), 1087–1101.

10. Duckworth, A. (2016). Grit: The power of passion and perseverance. New York: Simon & Schuster.

11. Duckworth, A. (2016). *Grit: The power of passion and perseverance.* New York: Simon & Schuster, p. 316.

12. Duckworth, A. (2016). *Grit: The power of passion and perseverance.* New York: Simon & Schuster, p. 315.

13. Hokoda, A., & Fincham, F. (1995). Origins of children's helpless and mastery achievement patterns in the family. *Journal of Educational Psychology, 87,* 375–385.

14. Diener, C. I., & Dweck, C. S. (1978). An analysis of learned helplessness: Continuous changes in performance, strategy, and achievement cognitions following failure. *Journal of Personality and Social Psychology, 36*(5), 451–462.

15. Gable, S. L., Gonzaga, G. C., & Strachman, A. (2006). Will you be there for me when things go right? Supportive responses to positive event disclosure. *Journal of Personality and Social Psychology, 91*(5), 904–917.

16. Waters, L. (2017). *The strength switch: How the new science of strength-based parenting can help your child and your teen flourish.* New York: Avery Publishing, p. 7.

17. Brown, B. (2012). *Daring greatly: How the courage to be vulnerable transforms the way we live, love, parent and lead.* New York: Penguin Group, p. 223.

18. Gander, F., Hofmann, J., Proyer, R. T., & Ruch, W. (2020). Character strengths—Stability, change, and relationships with well-being changes. *Applied Research Quality Life, 15,* 349–367.

Chapter 13

1. Grubman, J. (2013). *Strangers in paradise: How families adapt to wealth across generations.* Author.

2. James Grubman, personal communication, May 2022.

3. Grubman, J. (2019). PPI Rendezvous Keynote Address. Denver, CO.

4. Grubman, J., Jaffe, D., & Keffeler, K. (2022, February). Wealth 3.0: From Fear to engagement for families and advisors. *Trusts & Estates*.
5. Elements of the following history of the field are derived from Grubman, Jaffe, & Keffeler, 2022, *Trusts & Estates*.
6. Collier, C. (2012). *Wealth in families* (3rd ed.). Harvard Press.
7. Hughes, J. (2004). *Family wealth: Keeping it in the family*. New York: Bloomberg.
8. Kahneman, D. (2011). *Thinking fast and slow*. New York: Farrar, Straus, and Giroux Publishing.
9. Arnett, J. (2015). *Emerging adulthood: The winding road from the late teens through the early twenties*. New York: Oxford University Press.
10. Kahneman, D. (2011). *Thinking fast and slow*. New York: Farrar, Straus, and Giroux Publishing.
11. Nickerson, R. S. (1998). Confirmation bias: A ubiquitous phenomenon in many guises. *Review of General Psychology, 2*(2): 175.
12. Grubman, J. (2022, June). There is no "70% rule": Improving outcome research in family wealth advising, *International Family Offices Journal*, pp. 33–38.
13. Grubman, J. (2022, June). There is no "70% rule": Improving outcome research in family wealth advising, *International Family Offices Journal*, pp. 33–38.
14. Ward, J. L. (1987). *Keeping the family business healthy: How to plan for continuing growth, profitability, and family leadership*. San Francisco: Jossey-Bass
15. Grubman, J. (2022, June). There is no "70% rule": Improving outcome research in family wealth advising. *International Family Offices Journal,* p. 33-38.
16. Zellweger, T. M., Nason, R. S., & Nordqvist, M. (2011). From longevity of firms to transgenerational entrepreneurship of families: Introducing family entrepreneurial orientation, *Family Business Review, 20*(10): 1–20.
17. Grubman, J., Jaffe, D., & Keffeler, K. (2022, February). Wealth 3.0: From fear to engagement for families and advisors. *Trusts & Estates*, p. 20.
18. Williams, R., & Preisser, V. (2003). *Preparing heirs: Five steps to a successful transition of family wealth and values*. Brandon, OR: Robert Reed Publishers.
19. Grubman, J. (2022, June). There is no "70% rule": Improving outcome research in family wealth advising. *International Family Offices Journal,* p. 33-38.
20. Grubman, J., Jaffe, D., & Keffeler, K. (2022, February). Wealth 3.0: From fear to engagement for families and advisors. *Trusts & Estates*.
21. James Grubman, personal communication, 2021.

22. Cooperrider, D., Whitney, D., & Stavros, J. (2008). *The appreciative inquiry handbook* (2nd ed.). Brunswick, OH and Oakland, CA: Crown Custom Publishing and Berrett-Koehler Publishers.
23. Miller, W., & Rollnick, S. (2002). *Motivational interviewing: Preparing people for change* (2nd ed.). New York: Guilford Press.
24. Sheridan. S. & Burt, J. (2009). Family centered positive psychology. In S. J. Lopez & C. R. Snyder (Eds.), *The Oxford handbook of positive psychology* (2nd ed.), New York: Oxford University Press.
25. Niemiec, R. M. (2018). *Character strengths interventions: A field guide for practitioners*. Boston, MA: Hogrefe.
26. University of Michigan Center for Positive Organizations, https://positiveorgs.bus.umich.edu/cpo-tools/job-crafting-exercise/.
27. Dutton, J. (2003). *Energize your workplace: How to create and sustain high-quality connections at work*. Hoboken, NJ: Wiley.
28. https://positivepsychology.com/what-is-peak-end-theory/, accessed May 18, 2022.
29. Cooperrider, D., Whitney, D., & Stavros, J. (2008). *The appreciative inquiry handbook* (2nd ed.). Brunswick, OH and Oakland, CA: Crown Custom Publishing and Berrett-Koehler Publishers.

Appendix C: Research Methodology

1. Bronk, K. C., King, P. E., & Matsuba, M. K. (2013). An introduction to exemplar research: A definition, rationale, and conceptual issues. In M. K. Matsuba, P. E. King, & K. C. Bronk (Eds.), *Exemplar methods and research: Strategies for investigation. New directions for child and adolescent development, 142,* 1–12.
2. Yin, R. (2016). *Qualitative research from start to finish* (2nd ed.). New York: Guilford Press.
3. Galletta, A. (2013). *Mastering the semi-structured interview and beyond: From research design to analysis and publication*. New York: New York University Press.
4. Bronk, K. C., King, P. E., & Matsuba, M. K. (2013). An introduction to exemplar research: A definition, rationale, and conceptual issues. In M. K. Matsuba, P. E. King, & K. C. Bronk (Eds.), *Exemplar methods and research: Strategies for investigation. New directions for child and adolescent development, 142,* 1–12.
5. Seligman, M. E. P. (2011). *Flourish: A visionary new understanding of happiness and well-being*. New York: Atria.

6. Bronk, K. C., King, P. E., & Matsuba, M. K. (2013). An introduction to exemplar research: A definition, rationale, and conceptual issues. In M. K. Matsuba, P. E. King, & K. C. Bronk (Eds.), *Exemplar methods and research: Strategies for investigation. New directions for child and adolescent development, 142,* 1–12.

7. Creswell, J. W. (2007). *Qualitative inquiry and research design: Choosing among five approaches* (2nd ed.). Thousand Oaks, CA: Sage Publishing.

8. Groenewald, T. (2004). A phenomenological research design illustrated. *International Journal of Qualitative Methods, 3*(1), article 4. http://www .ualberta.ca/~iiqm/backissues/3_1/pdf/groenewald.pdf

9. Creswell, J. W. (2007). *Qualitative inquiry and research design: Choosing among five approaches* (2nd ed.) Thousand Oaks, CA: Sage Publishing.

10. Creswell, J. W. (2007). *Qualitative inquiry and research design: Choosing among five approaches* (2nd ed.) Thousand Oaks, CA: Sage Publishing.

11. van Manen, M. (1990). *Researching lived experience: Human science for an action sensitive pedagogy.* London, Ontario, Canada: The University of Western Ontario, p. 177.

12. Groenewald, T. (2004). A phenomenological research design illustrated. *International Journal of Qualitative Methods, 3*(1), article 4. http://www .ualberta.ca/~iiqm/backissues/3_1/pdf/groenewald.pdf

13. Creswell, J. W. (2007). *Qualitative inquiry and research design: Choosing among five approaches* (2nd ed.) Thousand Oaks, CA: Sage Publishing.

14. Seligman, M. E. P. (2011). *Flourish: A visionary new understanding of happiness and well-being.* New York: Atria.

Conclusion: Beyond the Myth of the Silver Spoon

1. Campbell, J. (2008). *The Hero with a Thousand Faces.* Novato, CA: New World Library.

Index